ABOUT YOUR DICTIONARY

Where a letter should be doubled when changing the form as in beg, begging, this is also given.

The small figures at the beginning of the words as in ¹saw, ²saw, ³saw show that each similar word has a separate use of meaning, and the most usual is given first. When a word has two main meanings that are the same part of speech, again the most usual appears first.

The Ladybird Dictionary is based on
definitions from Longman Dictionaries and
was published by arrangement with
Pearson Education Ltd. The publishers
wish to thank Heather Gay BSc PhD
for her considerable help in the preparation
of the first edition, and Della Summers
for the second edition.

Published by Ladybird Books Ltd
A Penguin Company
Penguin Books Ltd., 80 Strand, London WC2R 0RL, UK
Penguin Books Australia Ltd., Camberwell, Victoria, Australia
Penguin Books (NZ) Ltd., Private Bag 102902, NSMC, Auckland, New Zealand

1 3 5 7 9 10 8 6 4 2

ILLUSTRATIONS © LADYBIRD BOOKS LTD MCMXCVII
THIS EDITION © LADYBIRD MMIV

Printed in China

LADYBIRD
POCKET
DICTIONARY

Aa

a (also **an** before a vowel sound)
1 one; **2** each; every: *five times* ***a*** *day*

abbreviation *noun* a shortened form of a word

ability *noun* power and skill

able *adjective* having the power, skill, knowledge, time, etc, needed to do something

about *adverb, preposition*
1 concerning; of; **2** a little more or less; almost, nearly; **3** here and/or there

above *adverb, preposition* **1** in or to a higher place; higher than; **2** greater or more than

abroad *adverb* to or in another country: *living* ***abroad***

absent *adjective* not present; away; **absence** *noun*

absolutely *adverb* totally; to the maximum amount

accept *verb* **1** to take or receive something; **2** to agree to; **acceptable** *adjective*

accident *noun* something, especially something unpleasant or damaging, that happens by chance; **accidental** *adjective*; **accidentally** *adverb*

accurate *adjective* the exact amount; **accurately** *adverb*

ache (*say* ayk) *verb* to have a continuous pain; **ache** *noun*

¹**acid** *noun* a chemical substance that burns

²**acid** also **acidic** *adjective* having a bitter or sour taste like that of lemons

acorn *noun* the nut of the oak tree

acquaintance *noun* a person you have met but do not know well

acre *noun* a measure of land equal to 4840 square yards or 4047 square metres

acrobat *noun* a person skilled in walking on ropes or wires, balancing, walking on hands, etc, especially at a circus; **acrobatic** *adjective*; **acrobatically** *adverb*

tightrope walker

across *adverb, preposition* **1** from one side to the other; **2** to, at, or on the opposite side

¹**act** *verb* **1** to play the part of somebody in a play or film; **2** to behave as if playing a part; to pretend; **3** to behave in a certain way: *to* ***act*** *bravely*

²**act** *noun* **1** something done: *an* ***act*** *of cruelty*; **2** a law; **3** one of the main parts into which a play is divided

action *noun* **1** movement using force or power for some purpose; **2** something done; **3** **out of action** not working properly

active *adjective* always doing things; **actively** *adverb*

activity *noun* **1** the condition of a lot of action; **2** something that is done, especially for interest

actor (*feminine* **actress**) *noun* a person who acts in a play or film

actual *adjective* real and clear; **actually** *adverb*

add *verb* **1** to put a number, etc with another number; **2** to say something extra; **addition** *noun*; **additional** *adjective*

address *noun* the number of the building, name of the street and town, etc, where a person lives or works

adjective *noun* a word that describes something

admire *verb* to think of with pleasure and respect; to have a good opinion of something or somebody; **admiration** *noun*

admit *verb* (**admitted**) **1** to allow somebody to enter; to let in; **2** to confess; **admission** *noun*

adult *noun* **1** a fully grown person, especially a person over eighteen; **2** a fully grown animal or bird; **adult** *adjective*

advantage *noun* something that may help you to be successful or to get something you want; **advantageous** *adjective*

adventure *noun* an exciting and often dangerous journey, activity, etc; **adventurous** *adjective*

adverb *noun* a word that tells you how, when, or where something is done

advertise *verb* to make something known to a lot of people; **advertisement** *noun*

advice *noun* a suggestion from one person to another on how that other should act

advise *verb* to tell somebody what you think he or she should do

¹**aerial** *noun* a wire, rod, etc, that receives or sends out radio waves

satellite
TV dish
aerial

²**aerial** *adjective* from or in the air: *an* **aerial** *view*

aerobic *adjective* exericse which helps the heart and lungs **aerobics** *noun*

aerosol *noun* a small container used to spray liquid, such as paint

afford *verb* to have enough money to be able to buy or pay for something

afraid *adjective* **1** full of fear; **2** sorry for something that has happened or is likely to happen: *I'm* **afraid** *I've broken your pen*

after *preposition* following in time, place, or order; later than; behind

afternoon *noun* the part of the day between midday and evening

afterwards *adverb* later; after that

again *adverb* **1** once more: *Please say that* **again**; **2** **now and again** sometimes, but not very often

a

against *preposition* **1** on an opposite side to; **2** next to; touching

age *noun* **1** the period of time a person has lived or a thing has existed; **2** a period of time in history: *the Middle Ages*; **3 ages** a long time; **aged** *adjective*

ago *adjective* back in time from now; in the past

agree *verb* to have the same thoughts, opinions, or feelings as somebody else; **agreement** *noun*

ahead *adverb, adjective* **1** in front; into a forward position; **2** in or into the future

aim *verb* **1** to point or direct something at an object, especially with the intention of hitting it; **2** to intend to do something; **aim** *noun*

¹**air** *noun* **1** the mixture of gases that surrounds the Earth and that we breathe; **2** an appearance or feeling: *an air of excitement*; **3** a tune; !! **heir**

²**air** *verb* **1** to make clothes, sheets, beds, etc, warm or dry; **2** to make a room fresh by letting in air; !! **heir**

aircraft *noun* a flying vehicle, such as a helicopter, plane, or glider

airforce *noun* a group of people who use aircraft for fighting or defence

airport *noun* a place where aircraft can land and take off and that is regularly used by passengers

alarm *noun* **1** something such as a bell or flashing light by which a warning of danger is given; **2** a sudden feeling of fear; **alarm** *verb*

alarm clock *noun* a clock that can be set to make a noise at the time that you want to wake up

alarm clock

album *noun* **1** a book that is used for collecting photographs, stamps, etc; **2** a collection of songs on a CD, etc

alcohol *noun* a substance present in wine, beer, etc, that can make people feel drunk if they have too much of it; drinks containing this liquid; **alcoholic** *adjective*

¹**alert** *adjective* ready to act suddenly

²**alert** *noun* a warning to be ready for danger; **alert** *verb*

alike *adjective, adverb* the same or nearly the same

alive *adjective* having life; living

all *adjective, adverb, pronoun* **1** the complete amount, quantity, or number of; the whole of; **2** completely; **3** everybody or everything

alligator *noun* a large dangerous reptile that is related to and looks like a crocodile

American alligator

alliteration *noun* a feature in poetry where words start with the same letter for effect

allow *verb* to let somebody do or have something

almost *adverb* very nearly

alone *adjective, adverb* **1** without others; **2** only: *He* **alone** *knows the secret*

along *preposition, adverb* **1** in the direction of the length of; following the course of; **2** forward; on

aloud *adverb* **1** in a voice that may be heard; **2** in a loud voice

alphabet *noun* the set of letters used in a language, especially when arranged in order; **alphabetical** *adjective*

already *adverb* by or before a particular time

also *adverb* as well; too

alternative *adjective* something that is offered as a replacement for something else **alternatively** *adverb*

although *conjunction* in spite of the fact that

altogether *adverb* completely; considering all things

aluminium foil *noun* a silver wrapping for cooking

always *adverb* at all times; for ever

am in the morning (short for *ante meridiem*)

amateur *noun* **1** a person who does something, such as acting, painting pictures, or taking part in a sport, for enjoyment and without being paid for doing it; **2** a person who has no skill in doing something; **amateur** *adjective*

amber *noun* **1** a hard yellowish substance used for making ornaments and jewellery; **2** a yellowish colour

ambulance *noun* a motor vehicle for carrying sick or injured people, especially to hospital

among *also* **amongst** *preposition* in the middle of; surrounded by; between

amount *noun* a quantity or number

amp *also* **ampere** *noun* a measure of electric current

amphibian *noun* a creature that can live on land or in water but lays eggs in the water

amplifier *noun* an electronic instrument used in a hearing aid, electric guitar etc, to increase the sound; **amplify** *verb*

amuse *verb* to make somebody laugh or feel cheerful; **amusement** *noun*; **amusing** *adjective*

analyse *verb* **1** to examine something carefully in order to find out what it is made of; **2** to think carefully about the reason for something; **analysis** *noun*

anchor *noun* a heavy metal weight attached to a ship and lowered into the water to keep the ship from moving

ancient (*say* **aynshunt**) *adjective* in, of, or having existed since times long ago

and *conjunction* as well as; too

angel *noun* a messenger from God, who is usually thought of as a person with large wings and dressed in white; **angelic** *adjective*

anger *noun* a fierce feeling that makes you want to hurt or fight somebody; **angrily** *adverb*; **angry** *adjective*

angle *noun* the shape made by two straight lines that meet at a point; the space between these lines

angling *noun* the sport of catching fish with a hook and line; fishing

animal *noun* a living creature that can move itself when it wants to; any living thing that is not a plant

ankle *noun* the thin part of the leg just above the foot

announce *verb* to make something known; to say in public; **announcement** *noun*

annoy *verb* to make somebody a little angry; **annoyance** *noun*

annual *adjective* once a year **annually** *adverb*

another *pronoun*, *adjective* 1 one more of the same sort; 2 a different one

answer *noun* 1 the information that tells you what you want to know when you ask a question; 2 a reply to a greeting, letter, etc; 3 something that is discovered as a result of thinking, using numbers, etc; **answer** *verb*

ant *noun* a small insect that usually lives on the ground in large groups

wood ant

antenna *noun* (*plural* **antennae** *or* **antennas**) 1 either of two long thin parts on the head of an insect, shrimp, etc, that are used for feeling; 2 an aerial

anthology *noun* a collection of short stories or poems

antibiotics *noun* a medicine that makes you feel better by attacking bacteria in your body

anticlockwise *adjective*, *adverb* in the opposite direction to the movement of the hands of a clock; circular movement to the right

antonym *noun* a word with the opposite meaning to another such as hot/cold

anxious (*say* **angshus**) *adjective* 1 worried or fearful; 2 having a strong wish to do something; **anxiety** *noun*; **anxiously** *adverb*

any *adjective*, *pronoun* 1 one, some, or all; a number or amount; 2 no matter which, what, where, how, etc; 3 in any case also at any rate whatever may happen

anybody also **anyone** *pronoun* any person

anything *pronoun* 1 any one thing; something; 2 no matter what

anyway *adverb* whatever else is done; no matter what happens

anywhere *adverb* in, at, or to any place

apart *adverb* **1** separate; away from another or others; **2** to pieces: *to take an engine apart*

ape *noun* a large monkey without a tail or with a very short tail

apologise *verb* to say that you are sorry; **apology** *noun*

apparatus *noun* equipment used in science

appear *verb* **1** to come into sight; **2** to seem; **appearance** *noun*

appetite *noun* a wish for food

applaud *verb* to praise or show that you like something by clapping or cheering; **applause** *noun*

apple *noun* a hard round fruit with a red, green, or yellow skin

appreciate *verb* to like or be grateful for something; **appreciation** *noun*

appropriate *adjective* acceptable in a specific situation **appropriately** *adverb*

approve *verb* to say or think that something is good; **approval** *noun*

approximate *adjective* close to a given point or amount, but not exact **approximately** *adverb*

apricot *noun* a soft juicy yellowish-orange fruit

April *noun* the fourth month of the year

apron *noun* a piece of clothing worn over your other clothes to keep them clean

aquarium *noun* a glass or plastic container for fish; a building containing many of these

aquatic *adjective* something that lives in the water

arch *noun* a top part, often curved, of a door, bridge, etc, that rests on two supports

*a modern arch -
La Grande Arche de la Defense, Paris*

archaeology *noun* the study of the buried remains of ancient times, such as houses, pots, tools, and weapons; **archaeological** *adjective*; **archaeologist** *noun*

area *noun* **1** a particular space, surface, or part of the world; **2** the measure of a surface: *the area of a rectangle*

argue *verb* to disagree in words; to quarrel; **argument** *noun*

arithmetic *noun* the adding, subtracting, multiplying, dividing, etc, of numbers

arm *noun* the part of the body between the shoulder and the hand

armchair *noun* a chair with supporting parts on which you can rest your arms

15th century German armour

armour *noun* a covering of metal worn by fighting men in old times to protect them

arms *noun* weapons; **armed** *adjective*

army *noun* a large number of people trained for fighting

around *adverb, preposition* 1 on all sides; surrounding; 2 in various directions or places

arrange *verb* 1 to put in order; 2 to make plans or prepare for something; **arrangement** *noun*

arrest *verb* to take somebody prisoner; **arrest** *noun*

arrive *verb* 1 to get to a place, especially after a journey; 2 to happen; come; **arrival** *noun*

arrow *noun* 1 a thin straight pointed stick that is shot from a bow; 2 a mark shaped like an arrow which shows you the way

art *noun* the making of beautiful things by drawing, painting, etc; **artist** *noun*

article *noun* 1 a particular or separate thing or object; 2 a piece of writing in a newspaper, magazine, etc

as *conjunction, preposition* 1 used to compare people or things: *He can run **as** fast **as** I can*; 2 for the reason that; because; 3 while, when; 4 like; similar to; in the same way

¹**ash** *noun* the grey powder left after something has burnt

²**ash** *noun* a tall tree with hard wood

ashamed *adjective* feeling shame or guilt

ask *verb* 1 to put a question; 2 to make a request for or to; 3 to invite

asleep *adjective* sleeping

assistant *noun* a helper

asteroid *noun* any of the small bodies that move round the sun mainly in the area between Mars and Jupiter

astrology *noun* the skill of understanding the effects that the stars, planets, etc, are supposed to have on our lives; **astrologer** *noun*

astronaut *noun* a person who travels in a spacecraft

astronomy *noun* the scientific study of the sun, moon, stars, etc; **astronomer** *noun*

at *preposition* 1 used to show where or when; 2 **at all** in any way

athletics *noun* a branch of sport that includes running, jumping, and throwing

atlas *noun* a book of maps

atmosphere *noun* 1 the mixture of gases surrounding a body in space, especially the Earth; 2 the air; **atmospheric** *adjective*

atom *noun* a very small part of a substance; **atomic** *adjective*

a lithium atom

attach *verb* to fix; to fasten; to join; **attachment** *noun*

attack *verb* 1 to be violent towards somebody; to fight, speak, or write against; 2 to harm; **attack** *noun*; **attacker** *noun*

attempt *verb* to make an effort to do something; to try; **attempt** *noun*

attend *verb* 1 to be present at; 2 to listen to or watch carefully; **attendance** *noun*; **attendant** *noun*

attention *noun* the act of fixing the mind on something, especially by watching or listening carefully; **attentive** *adjective*

attic *noun* room at the top of a house, just under the roof

attract *verb* 1 to cause to like, admire, or notice; 2 to draw towards you: *magnets* **attract** *iron*; **attractive** *adjective*

audience *noun* the people listening to or watching a play, speech, show, etc

audio *adjective* concerned with sound

August *noun* the eighth month of the year

aunt also **auntie, aunty** *noun* the sister of your father or mother; the wife of your uncle

aurora *noun* coloured lights in the sky that can be seen at night in the most northern and southern parts of the world

author *noun* a writer

automatic *adjective* able to work without human help

autumn *noun* the season between summer and winter

avenue *noun* 1 a wide street in a town; 2 a road between two rows of trees

average *adjective* 1 being the amount found by adding together several quantities and then dividing by the number of quantities; 2 usual or ordinary; **average** *noun*

avoid *verb* to keep away from somebody or something

awake *adjective* having woken up; not asleep

away *adverb* from this or that place; to, at, or in another place

awful *adjective* very bad; terrible; shocking; **awfully** *adverb*

awkward *adjective* 1 clumsy; 2 not well made for use; difficult to use; **awkwardly** *adverb*; **awkwardness** *noun*

axe *noun* a tool with a heavy metal blade on the end of a long handle, used to cut wood

Bb

baboon *noun* a large monkey

baby *noun* **1** a very young child, especially one who has not learnt to speak; **2** a very young animal or bird

¹**back** *noun* **1** the part of the body of a human or animal down the middle of which runs the spine; **2** the part that is furthest from the front; **3 at the back (of)** behind; **back** *adjective*

²**back** *adverb* **1** towards or at the back; **2** to or at a place or time where something or somebody was before

³**back** *verb* **1** to go or cause to go backwards; **2** to support; **3** to be or make the back of; **4** to bet money on

background *noun* **1** the place behind someone in a photo; space or colour under a drawing or picture; **2** things that happened before that explain an event; **3** someone's family, education, or where he or she comes from

backward *adjective* **1** directed towards the back, the beginning, or the past; **2** behind in development; **backwardness** *noun*

backwards *adverb* **1** away from your front; towards the back; **2** with the back first; **3** with the back where the front should be; back to front

bacon *noun* salted or smoked meat from the back or sides of a pig, often sold in thin slices

bacteria *noun* – *plural* (*singular* **bacterium**) very small living things, some of which cause disease; **bacterial** *adjective*

bad *adjective* (**worse, worst**) **1** not good; **2** serious; severe; **badly** *adverb*; **badness** *noun*

badge *noun* a small sign worn to show what you are or what you do

badger *noun* a grey animal that has a white face with two black stripes and lives underground

badminton *noun* a game like tennis played with a shuttlecock instead of a ball

badminton racket and shuttlecock

bag *noun* a container made of soft material, opening at the top

baggage *noun* the bags, cases, etc, you take with you when you travel

bagpipes *noun* (*always plural*) a musical instrument that is played by blowing air into a bag and through pipes

bake *verb* to cook in an oven; **baker** *noun*

¹**balance** *noun* steadiness

²**balance** *verb* to keep yourself or something else steady, especially in a difficult position

bald *adjective* with little or no hair; **baldness** *noun*

ball *noun* **1** a round object used in games; anything of a round shape; **2** a large party for dancing

ballet (*say* balay) *noun* a form of dancing performed by specially trained dancers whose movements to music tell a story

balloon *noun* **1** a small rubber bag that can be blown up, used as a toy; **2** a large bag of light material filled with hot air or a light gas to make it rise up in the air

hot air balloon

ban *verb* (**banned**) to forbid, especially by law; **ban** *noun*

banana *noun* a long curved fruit with yellow skin

band *noun* **1** a group of musicians; **2** a group of people; **3** a thin flat narrow piece of material for fastening things together: *rubber **band***; **4** an area into which something can be divided, such as a band of radio waves or a range of frequencies

bandage *noun* a long strip of material for winding round a wounded part of the body

bang *noun* **1** a sudden loud noise; **2** a sharp blow; **bang** *verb*

¹**bank** *noun* a place in which money is kept and paid out when you want it: **bank manager, bank note**; **banker** *noun*

²**bank** *noun* **1** land along the side of a river, lake, etc; **2** a heap of earth, sand, snow, etc

¹**bar** *noun* **1** a long piece of wood or metal; **2** a piece of solid material; **3** a group of notes in music, marked off by lines; **4** a place where drinks are sold

²**bar** *verb* (**barred**) **1** to close with a bar; **2** to block

barbecue *noun* a cooker used to cook meat outdoors **barbecue** *verb*

barber *noun* a person who cuts men's hair

bare *adjective* **1** naked; not covered; **2** empty; with nothing in or on it; **bare** *verb*; !! **bear**

barely *adverb* only just; hardly

¹**bark** *noun* the sound made by a dog; **bark** *verb*

²**bark** *noun* the strong outer covering of a tree

barley *noun* a plant grown for food and making drinks, such as beer

barn *noun* a farm building for storing crops

barrel *noun* **1** the part of a gun that is shaped like a tube; **2** a round wooden container, usually for liquids, with curved sides and a flat top and bottom

base *noun* the bottom of anything

b

baseball *noun* a game played with a bat and ball between two teams of nine players each

baseball cap *noun* a hat with a shade at the front but no brim

basement *noun* the rooms in a house below street level

basic *adjective* simple **basically** *adverb*

basin *noun* 1 a shallow container for water; 2 a round container for food

basket *noun* a container made of woven sticks or other such material

basketball *noun* a game in which each team of five players tries to throw a large ball through the other team's basket

bass (*say* base) *noun* the lowest part sung or played in music; **bass** *adjective* !! **base**

bassoon *noun* a musical instrument with a low sound, that is played by blowing

bassoon

¹**bat** *noun* a wooden stick used for hitting a ball in various games; **bat** *verb*; **batsman** *noun*; **batter** *noun*

²**bat** *noun* a flying mammal like a mouse, that is active at night

bath *noun* a large water container in which you can wash your whole body; **bath** *verb*

bathe *verb* 1 to go swimming; 2 to pour water or other liquid over; **bathe** *noun*; **bather** *noun*

bathroom *noun* a room, usually with a bath, where people wash and clean themselves

battery *noun* an object that produces or stores electricity

battle *noun* a fight between enemies; a struggle; **battle** *verb*

bay *noun* a part of the shore which curves inwards

be *verb* (**am, are, is, being, was, were, been, aren't, isn't, wasn't, weren't**) 1 to exist; to live; 2 to become; 3 to belong to the group of; 4 to take place; to occur; 5 to have a particular quality, job, purpose, position, cost, etc; !! **bee**

beach *noun* a shore covered in sand or stones and used for swimming and sunbathing; !! **beech**

bead *noun* a small ball of glass or other material that can be threaded onto a string to make a necklace, etc

beak *noun* the hard horny mouth of a bird

¹**beam** *noun* a large long heavy piece of wood, steel, or concrete, used to support a building

²**beam** *noun* a line of light shining from something bright

³**beam** *verb* 1 to send out light; to shine; 2 to smile brightly and happily

bean *noun* **1** the seed of a climbing plant, often used as food; **2** a seed of some other plants, from which food or drink can be made: **coffee bean**; !! **been**

¹**bear** *noun* a large and heavy animal with thick rough fur; !! **bare**

polar bear

²**bear** *verb* (**bears, bearing, bore, borne**) **1** to carry; to support; **2** to give birth; **3** to suffer; !! **bare**

beard *noun* hair on the face mostly below the mouth; **bearded** *adjective*

¹**beat** *verb* (**beats, beating, beat, beaten** *or* **beat**) **1** to do better than; **2** to move regularly; **3** to hit many times

²**beat** *noun* **1** a repeated hit, stroke, or blow; **2** time in music or poetry

beautiful *adjective* very good looking; very pleasing; **beautifully** *adverb*; **beauty** *noun*

beaver *noun* a fur-covered animal with a broad flat tail, that builds dams across streams

because *conjunction* for the reason that

become *verb* (**becomes, becoming, became, become**) to come to be

bed *noun* **1** an article of furniture to sleep on: **bedroom, bedclothes**; **2** a piece of ground prepared for plants; **3** the bottom of a river, lake, or sea

bee *noun* an insect that makes honey, often lives in groups, and can sting painfully; !! **be**

beech *noun* a tree with a smooth grey trunk, spreading branches, and dark green or copper coloured leaves; !! **beach**

beef *noun* the meat of farm cattle

beer *noun* a drink made from grain

beetle *noun* an insect with hard wing coverings

beetroot *noun* a plant with a large round red root, cooked and eaten as a vegetable

before *preposition, adverb* **1** at an earlier time than; **2** in front of; ahead

beg *verb* (**begged**) to ask for food, money, etc; **beggar** *noun*

begin *verb* (**begins, beginning, began, begun**) to start

behave *verb* to act in a good or bad way; **behaviour** *noun*

behind *preposition, adverb* **1** to or at the back of; where something or somebody was earlier; **2** late

being *noun* a living thing, especially a person

b

17

belief *noun* the feeling that something is true or real; trust; **believable** *adjective*; **believably** *adverb*; **believe** *verb*

bell *noun* a round hollow metal object, which makes a ringing sound when struck

belong *verb* **1** to be your own; **2** to be a part or member of

below *preposition, adverb* in or at a lower place than; underneath

belt *noun* a piece of cloth or leather worn round the waist

bench *noun* a long seat for two or more people

bend *verb* **(bends, bending, bent)** to force something into or out of a curve or angle; **bend** *noun*

beneath *preposition* in or at a lower position than; below

bet *verb* **(bets, betting, bet** *or* **betted)** to risk money on the result of a future event; **bet** *noun*

between *preposition* **1** in the space or at the time separating; **2** as a connection of; **3** with a part for each of

beyond *preposition, adverb* **1** on or to the further side of; **2** later than; **3** out of reach of; much more than

Bible *noun* the holy book of the Christians, consisting of the *Old Testament* and the *New Testament*; **biblical** *adjective*

bibliography *noun* a list of books used for reference

bicycle also **cycle** or **bike** *noun* a two-wheeled vehicle which you pedal with your feet; **bicyclist** *noun*

tandem - a bicycle for two people

berry *noun* a small soft fruit; !! **bury**

beside *preposition* at or close to the side of

besides *adverb, preposition* as well; also

best *noun* **1** something that is the most good; **2** your greatest, highest, or finest effort, state, or performance

big *adjective* **(bigger)** large in size, weight, importance, etc

big bang theory *noun* the idea that everything in the universe began with the explosion of a single piece of material so that the pieces of it are still flying apart

bill *noun* **1** a list of things bought and their price; **2** a plan for a new law

bin *noun* a large wide container with a lid for bread, flour, etc, or for waste

an archbishop is in charge of other bishops

binary (*say* **bye-nary)** *adjective* using the numbers 0 and 1 only, as computers do

bingo *noun* a game played by covering numbered squares on a card

binoculars *noun (plural)* a pair of special glasses used for looking at objects in the distance

biology *noun* the scientific study of living things; **biological** *adjective*; **biologically** *adverb*; **biologist** *noun*

birch *noun* a tree with smooth wood and thin branches

bird *noun* a creature with wings and feathers that lays eggs

birth *noun* the act or time of being born; !! **berth**

birthday *noun* the date on which you were born

biscuit *noun* any of many types of flat thin dry cake

bishop *noun* a priest in charge of other priests

¹bit *noun* **1** a small piece, quantity, or amount; **2** the smallest piece of information that can be held on a computer

²bit *noun* **1** a metal bar put in the mouth of a horse as part of a bridle and used for controlling its movements; **2** a part of a tool for making holes

bitch *noun* a female dog

¹bite *verb* **(bites, biting, bit, bitten)** to cut or wound with the teeth; !! **byte**

²bite *noun* **1** an act of biting **2** a piece bitten off; **3** a wound made by biting; !! **byte**

b

bitter *adjective* 1 having a sharp, sour taste; 2 very cold; 3 causing anger, pain, or sadness; **bitterly** *adverb*; **bitterness** *noun*

black *noun* 1 the colour of coal; the darkest colour; 2 a person with dark-coloured skin; **black** *adjective*; **blackness** *noun*

black hole *noun* a part of outer space containing a star whose gravity is so strong that not even light can escape from it

blade *noun* 1 the flat cutting part of a knife, sword, or other cutting tool; 2 a long flat leaf of grass

blame *verb* to say that somebody is the cause of something bad; **blame** *noun*

blanket *noun* a thick warm cloth made of wool, used as a cover on a bed

blazer *noun* a jacket, sometimes with the badge of a school, club, etc, on it

bleach *verb* to make something white; **bleach** *noun*

bleed *verb* (**bleeds, bleeding, bled**) to lose blood

¹**blend** *verb* to mix two or more things together so that they appear as one

²**blend** *noun* in learning to read, two letters next to each other, read at the same time

bless *verb* 1 to ask God's favour for something; 2 to make holy; **blessing** *noun*

¹**blind** *adjective* unable to see; **blind** *verb*; **blindly** *adverb*; **blindness** *noun*

²**blind** *noun* a covering for a window, made of cloth or other material

blink *verb* to shut and open the eyes quickly; **blink** *noun*

¹**block** *noun* 1 a large piece of wood, stone, etc; 2 a large building divided into separate flats or offices; 3 a building or group of buildings between two streets; 4 something that gets in the way

²**block** *verb* to prevent movement

blond (*feminine* **blonde**) *adjective* with light-coloured hair and fair skin

blood *noun* red liquid that carries oxygen to all parts of the body and is pumped round by the heart; **bloody** *adjective*

blossom *noun* the flowers of a flowering tree or bush

apple blossom

blouse *noun* a loose piece of clothing for women, reaching from the neck to the waist

¹**blow** *verb* (**blows, blowing, blew, blown**) 1 to move by a current of air; 2 to send air out quickly from your mouth or nose; 3 to force air into or through something; 4 **blow up** to break by exploding

²**blow** *noun* **1** a hard hit with the hand, a weapon, etc; **2** a shock

blue *noun* the colour of the clear sky on a fine day; **blue** *adjective*; **blueness** *noun*; **bluish** *adjective*; !! **blew**

blunt *adjective* **1** not sharp; **2** rough and plain, without trying to be polite or kind; **bluntness** *noun*; **bluntly** *adverb*

blurb *noun* writing on the back of a book

blush *verb* to become red in the face because you feel shy

¹**board** *noun* **1** a thin flat piece of cut wood; **2** a stiff flat surface used for a special purpose: **chessboard, dartboard, noticeboard**; **3** a group of people with a special job, like running a company; **4** the cost of meals; **5 on board** or **aboard** in or on a ship or public vehicle

²**board** *verb* **1** to go on board a ship or public vehicle; **2** to cover with wooden boards; **3** to get or supply meals and somewhere to live for payment; **boarder** *noun*

boast *verb* to praise yourself; **boaster** *noun*; **boastful** *adjective*

boat *noun* a small open ship

body *noun* **1** the whole of a person or animal, but not the mind; **2** this without the head or limbs; **3** a dead person or animal; **4** a number of people who do something together; **5** a person: **anybody, nobody, somebody**

bog *noun* area of soft wet ground

¹**boil** *noun* a painful swelling under the skin

²**boil** *verb* **1** to make liquid so hot that it gives off steam; **2** to cook food in boiling water

bold *adjective* daring; brave; without fear; **boldly** *adverb*; **boldness** *noun*

¹**bolt** *noun* **1** a metal bar that slides across to fasten a door or window; **2** a screw with no point

nut and bolt

²**bolt** *verb* **1** to fasten with a bolt; **2** to swallow quickly; **3** to run away suddenly, as if frightened

¹**bomb** *noun* a hollow container filled with materials that will explode

bomb

²**bomb** *verb* to attack with bombs, especially by dropping them from aircraft

21

bone *noun* one of the hard white parts of the body, round which are the flesh and skin; **boneless** *adjective*; **bony** *adjective*

bonfire *noun* a large fire built in the open air

bonnet *noun* **1** a metal lid over the front of a car; **2** a round hat tied under the chin

¹book *noun* a collection of sheets of paper fastened together as a thing to be read, or to be written in: **bookcase, bookmark, book token**

²book *verb* to arrange to have or do something later; **bookable** *adjective*; **booking** *noun*

boot *noun* **1** a shoe of leather, rubber, etc, with a part that covers the ankle; **2** a space at the back of a car for luggage

riding boots

border *noun* **1** an edge; **2** the dividing line between two countries; !! **boarder**

¹bore *verb* to make somebody feel not interested by something dull; **boredom** *noun*; **boring** *adjective*

²bore *noun* a person or thing that is dull or uninteresting

³bore *verb* to make a round hole or passage in or through something; **borer** *noun*

⁴bore *see* BEAR

born *adjective* **1** given life; **2** at birth; originally; !! **borne**

borrow *verb* to get the use of something that you are going to give back later; **borrower** *noun*; **borrowing** *noun*

botany *noun* the scientific study of plants; **botanist** *noun*

both *pronoun, adjective* the two; this one and the other

bother *verb* to annoy or irritate someone

bottle *noun* a tall round container, usually of glass or plastic, with a narrow neck

bottom *noun* **1** the base on which something stands; the lowest part; **2** the part of the body on which you sit

bough (*say like* **how**) *noun* a branch of a tree; !! **bow**

bounce *verb* **1** to spring back or up again from the ground or something hard; to make something do this; **2** to jump or spring up and down; **bounce** *noun*; **bouncily** *adverb*; **bounciness** *noun*; **bouncy** *adjective*

¹bound *adjective* **1** fastened; **2** certain to; sure to; **3** going towards

²**bound** *verb* to jump or bounce

¹**bow** (*say like* how) *verb* to bend the head or upper part of the body forward to show respect; **bow** *noun*; **bowed** *adjective*; !! **bough**

²**bow** (*say like* go) *noun* **1** a piece of wood held in a curve by a tight string and used for shooting arrows; **2** a knot with loops; **3** a long thin piece of wood with stretched horsehairs fastened along it, used for playing stringed instruments

¹**bowl** *noun* a deep round container for holding liquids, flowers, sugar, etc; **bowlful** *noun*

²**bowl** *verb* **1** to throw the ball towards the batsman in cricket or rounders; **2** to play the games of **bowls** or **bowling**

¹**box** *noun* a container made from wood, cardboard, plastic, or metal, with stiff sides and a lid

²**box** *verb* to fight somebody or hit with the fists; **boxer** *noun*; **boxing** *noun*

boy *noun* a young male person; !! **buoy**

bra *noun* a piece of women's underwear worn to support the breasts

bracelet *noun* a band or ring worn round the wrist or arm as an ornament

bracket *noun* **1** a piece of metal or wood put on a wall to support something; **2** a pair of signs ( ) or [ ] used round a piece of information

¹**brain** *noun* the organ inside the head with which you think and feel

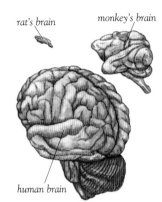

rat's brain

monkey's brain

human brain

²**brain** *verb* (slang) to hit hard on the head

¹**brake** *noun* something for slowing down or stopping a car, bicycle, train, etc; !! **break**

²**brake** *verb* to use brakes; !! **break**

¹**branch** *noun* **1** a stem growing from the trunk of a tree or from another stem; **2** a part of a company, shop, etc

²**branch** *verb* to become divided into two parts

brass *noun* **1** a very hard bright yellow metal; **2** musical instruments made of this metal, such as a trumpet

brave *adjective* having courage and ready to go through danger or pain; **bravely** *adverb*; **bravery** *noun*

bread *noun* a common food made of baked flour

breadth *noun* the distance from side to side; width

23

*a suspension bridge -
Pont de Normandie, France*

¹**break** *verb* **(breaks, breaking broke, broken) 1** to cause to fall to pieces; **2** to fall to pieces; **!! brake**

²**break** *noun* **1** an opening made by breaking or being broken; **2** a pause for rest; **!! brake**

breakfast *noun* the first meal of the day

breast *noun* **1** either of the two parts of a woman's body that produce milk; **2** the upper front part of the body between the neck and the stomach

breath *noun* air taken into and let out of the body; **breathless** *adjective* out of breath

breathe *verb* to take air into the body and let it out; **breathing** *noun*

¹**breed** *verb* **(breeds, breeding, bred) 1** to produce young; **2** to keep animals so that they will produce young ones

²**breed** *noun* a type of animal

brick *noun* a hard piece of baked clay used for building

bridge *noun* something built over a valley, river, etc, so that people can go over it

bridle *noun* leather bands on a horse's head for controlling it

brief *adjective* lasting a short time

bright *adjective* **1** giving out or throwing back light very strongly; **2** having a strong clear colour; **3** clever; quick at learning; **brightly** *adverb*; **brightness** *noun*

bring *verb* **(brings, bringing, brought) 1** to fetch, carry, or take with you; **2** to cause or lead to

broad *adjective* wide; **broadly** *adverb*; **broadness** *noun*

broadcast *verb* to send out by radio or television; **broadcast** *noun*; **broadcaster** *noun*

broken *adjective* **1** in pieces; **2** not working

brooch *noun* an ornament worn on women's clothes, fastened by a pin

broom *noun* a brush with a long handle

24

b

brother *noun* a boy or man with the same parents as another person

brown *noun, adjective* the colour of earth; **brownish** *adjective*

bruise *noun* a mark left on the skin where it has been hit; **bruise** *verb*

¹**brush** *noun* an object for cleaning, smoothing, or painting, made of sticks, stiff hair, nylon, etc: **hairbrush**

²**brush** *verb* to clean or smooth with a brush

¹**bubble** *noun* a hollow ball of liquid containing air or gas; **bubbly** *adjective*

²**bubble** *verb* to make bubbles

bucket *noun* a round open metal or plastic container with a handle, for holding or carrying water, coal, etc

buckle *noun* a fastener for joining the ends of two straps

bud *noun* a flower or leaf before it opens

budgerigar also **budgie** *noun* a small brightly coloured bird often kept in a cage

budgerigar

bug *noun* **1** a small insect; **2** a mistake or fault in a computer program

buggy *noun* a light folding chair with wheels for taking a baby or child out

build *verb* (**builds, building, built**) to make by putting pieces together; **builder** *noun*; **building** *noun*

bulb *noun* **1** a round root of certain plants; **2** the glass part of an electric lamp that gives out light

bull *noun* the male form of cattle and some other animals

bulldozer *noun* a powerful machine used for pushing heavy objects, earth, etc, out of the way

bullet *noun* a type of shot fired from a gun

bully *noun* somebody who likes to hurt or frighten weaker people; **bully** *verb*

¹**bump** *verb* to hit or knock against something

²**bump** *noun* **1** a sudden hit or knock; **2** a raised swelling; **bumpy** *adjective*

bun *noun* a small round sweet cake

bunch *noun* a number of things fastened or growing together

bundle *noun* a number of things tied together

bungalow *noun* a house all on ground level

bunk also **bunk bed** *noun* a bed fixed to the wall (as on a ship); **bunk beds** *noun* two beds one above the other

b

buoy *noun* a floating object fastened to the bed of the sea to show ships where there are rocks; !! **boy**

burger *noun* a piece of meat held in a bun

burglar *noun* a thief who breaks into houses, shops, etc; **burglary** *noun*

¹**burn** *verb* (**burns, burning, burnt** *or* **burned**) **1** to be on fire; **2** to hurt, damage, or destroy by fire

²**burn** *noun* a hurt place produced by burning

burrow *noun* a hole in the ground made by an animal, in which it lives or hides

burst *verb* (**bursts, bursting, burst**) **1** to break suddenly because of the pressure inside; **2** to do something suddenly

bury *verb* **1** to put a dead person into the ground; **2** to hide away; !! **berry**

bus *noun* a large motor vehicle for carrying passengers

bush *noun* a small low tree; **bushy** *adjective*

business *noun* **1** a person's work; **2** trade and the getting of money: **businessman, businesswoman**; **3** an activity, such as a shop, that earns money; **4** a personal or private thing that concerns you; **businesslike** *adjective*

busy *adjective* having a lot to do; **busily** *adverb*

but *conjunction* only; except that

butcher *noun* a person in a shop who sells meat

butter *noun* **1** yellow fat made from milk; **2** a substance like butter: **peanut butter**; **buttery** *adjective*

buttercup *noun* a yellow wild flower

butterfly *noun* an insect with four often beautifully coloured wings

red admiral butterfly

peacock butterfly

button *noun* **1** a small usually round or flat thing fixed to a piece of clothing and passed through a buttonhole to act as a fastener; **2** a knob or object like a button, for starting, stopping, or controlling a machine

buy *verb* (**buys, buying, bought**) to get something by giving money; **buyer** *noun*; !! **by**

buzz *verb* to make a low steady noise, as bees do; **buzz** *noun*; **buzzer** *noun*

by *preposition* **1** near; beside; **2** by way of; through; !! **buy**

byte *noun* an amount of information stored in a computer, equal to eight bits; !! **bite**

Cc

cabbage *noun* a large round vegetable with thick green leaves used as food

cabin *noun* **1** a small room on a ship; **2** a small wooden house

cable *noun* **1** a thick, heavy strong rope, wire, or chain; **2** a set of wires laid under ground and used for carrying electricity, telephone calls, and television programmes: **cable TV**

cactus *noun* (*plural* **cacti** *or* **cactuses**) a prickly plant with thick leaves and stems, that grows in hot dry places

café (*say* **caffay**) *noun* a small restaurant where you can buy drinks and light meals

cage *noun* a box made of wires or bars in which animals or birds may be kept

cake *noun* a food made by mixing and baking flour, eggs and sugar

calculate *verb* to work out by using numbers; **calculation** *noun*; **calculator** *noun*

Scottish medieval cannon - Mons Meg

calendar *noun* a set of tables or sheets of paper showing the days, weeks, and months of the year

calf *noun* (*plural* **calves**) the young of the cow or some other large animals

¹**call** *verb* **1** to name; **2** to shout; to cry out; **3** to make a short visit; **4** to telephone somebody

²**call** *noun* **1** a telephone conversation; **2** a shout; **3** a short visit

calm *adjective* peaceful; quiet; not worried; **calmly** *adverb*; **calmness** *noun*

camel *noun* a large long-necked animal used for riding or carrying goods in desert countries. The *dromedary* has one hump and the *Bactrian* camel has two humps.

camera *noun* an instrument for taking photographs or filming

¹**camp** *noun* a place with tents or huts where people live for a short time or spend their holidays

²**camp** *verb* **1** to make a camp; **2** to sleep in a tent; **camper** *noun*; **camping** *noun*

¹**can** *verb* (**could, cannot, can't**) to know how to; to be able to

²**can** *noun* a tin in which foods are stored

cancel *noun* to stop something happening

candle *noun* a wax stick with a string in the middle which gives light when it burns

cannon *noun* a large and powerful gun

cannot can not

canoe *noun* a long light narrow boat, pointed at both ends, and moved by a paddle; **canoeist** *noun*

cap *noun* **1** a soft flat hat; **2** a covering for the end of a bottle or tube

capital *noun* **1** the chief city of a country, where the government is; **2** a large letter, such as A, B, or C

captain *noun* **1** the leader of a team or group; **2** the person in command of a ship or aircraft; **3** an officer in the armed forces

caption *noun* a short, sometimes funny explanation which accompanies a picture

caravan *noun* **1** a small house on wheels that can be pulled by a car or horse; **2** a group of people travelling together through desert areas

carbohydrates *noun* a type of food energy found in pasta, bread and other food

card *noun* **1** also **playing card** one of a pack of 52 small sheets of stiffened paper marked to show number and suit and used for various games; **2** a piece of stiffened paper, usually with a picture on the front and a message inside, sent to a person on a birthday, at Christmas, etc: a **postcard**

cardboard *noun* a stiff material like thick paper, used for making boxes, book covers, etc; **cardboard city**: where the homeless live

cardigan *noun* a knitted woollen jacket with sleeves

¹**care** *noun* **1** looking after somebody or something; protection; **2** thought; serious attention; **3** something that makes you worried or sad; **careful** *adjective*; **carefully** *adverb*; **careless** *adjective*; **carelessly** *adverb*; **carelessness** *noun*

²**care** *verb* **1** to be worried or concerned about something; to look after somebody; **2** to like; to want

carnivore *noun* a meat eater

carol *noun* a religious song sung especially at Christmas

carpenter *noun* a person who makes and repairs wooden objects; **carpentry** *noun*

carpet *noun* a piece of heavy woven material for covering the floor of a room

carriage *noun* **1** a vehicle with wheels that is pulled by horses; **2** a part of a train in which you sit; **3** the way in which people stand, sit or move

carriage used by HM the Queen - a 1902 state landau

carrot *noun* a long, orange vegetable

carry *verb* to take up somebody or something in your arms, on your back, etc, and move them from one place to another; **carrier** *noun*

cart *noun* a wooden vehicle pulled by an animal and used for carrying goods

cartoon *noun* **1** a funny drawing; **2** a film made by photographing a set of drawings

cartridge *noun* **1** a metal or paper tube containing explosive for use in a gun; **2** a small plastic container that holds ink for use in a cartridge pen

carve *verb* **1** to cut wood or stone in order to make a special shape; **2** to cut meat into pieces or slices; **carver** *noun*

¹**case** *noun* **1** an example of something; a particular occasion; a state or condition; **2** a question to be decided in a court of law; the facts and arguments used on each side

²**case** *noun* a container in which things can be stored or moved; a suitcase or packing case

casserole *noun* vegetables or meat cooked in a dish in the oven

cassette *noun* a small flat plastic case containing tape for use in a tape recorder or cassette recorder

¹**cast** *noun* **1** all the actors and actresses in a play, film, etc; **2** an act of throwing

²**cast** *verb* **1** to make a spell and put it into effect; **2** to throw or drop; to throw off; **3** to make an object by pouring hot metal or plastic into a special shape (a mould)

castle *noun* a large strong building with thick walls and towers

casual *adjective* **1** not planned or arranged; **2** clothing worn when people are not at work or school; **casually** *adverb*

casualty *noun* **1** a person who has had an accident **2** the hospital department where a person goes when they have just had accident

cat *noun* (*young* **kitten**) a small animal with soft fur and sharp teeth and claws, often kept as a pet

catalogue *noun* a list of products that can be bought

¹**catch** *verb* (**catches, catching, caught**) **1** to get in your hand and hold; **2** to run after and take hold of an animal, person, or thing; **3** to get an illness; **catcher** *noun*

²**catch** *noun* **1** something that is caught; **2** a hook or fastener for a door, window, etc

caterpillar *noun* an early stage in the life of a butterfly or moth which is like a small worm with short legs

hawkmoth caterpillar

cathedral *noun* the chief church of a city

cattle *noun* large four-legged animals, especially cows

cauliflower *noun* a vegetable with green leaves around a large white head of flowers

cause *noun* a person, thing, or event that makes something happen; a reason; **cause** *verb*

cave *noun* a deep hollow place in the side of a cliff or hill or under ground

CD *noun* a thin plastic disc used to play recorded music: *a CD player*

CD-ROM *noun* a thin plastic disc used to store computer information and for computer games

ceiling *noun* the inside of the top of a room

celery *noun* a vegetable with greenish white stems used as food

cellar *noun* an underground room used for storing goods; !! **seller**

cello (*say* chello) *noun* a large violin with a deep sound, that is played held between the knees

cello

cellophane *noun* a clear plastic

Celsius *adjective* the scale of temperature in which water freezes at 0° and boils at 100°; compare FAHRENHEIT

cement *noun* a grey powder that becomes like stone when mixed with water and allowed to dry

centimetre *noun* a measure of length equal to 0.01 metres or 0.394 inches

centipede *noun* a creature like an insect, with a long body and many pairs of legs

central heating *noun* a way of heating a building in which heat is produced in one place and is carried by pipes to the other parts of the building

centre *noun* **1** the middle; **2** a place where a lot of people come for a special purpose: **health centre, shopping centre**; **central** *adjective*

century *noun* a period of 100 years

cereal *noun* **1** any kind of grain, such as wheat, oats, and rice; **2** food made from grain, usually eaten at breakfast; !! **serial**

ceremony *noun* a special set of actions used for marking an important event, occasion, or happening

¹**certain** *adjective* sure; **certainly** *adverb*

²**certain** *adjective* some

chain *noun* a length of metal rings joined to one another

chair *noun* a piece of furniture to sit on, which usually has a back, seat, four legs, and sometimes arms: **rocking chair**

chalk *noun* **1** a soft white material formed from the shells of very small sea animals; **2** a piece of this material, white or coloured, used for writing or drawing; **chalky** *adjective*

challenge *verb* **1** to offer to fight or play a game against; **2** to test or question; **challenge** *noun*

chance *noun* **1** an opportunity; a time when something may be done; **2** something that happens without cause; luck; **3** something that may or may not happen; **4** a risk

¹**change** *verb* **1** to make or become different; **2** to give, take, or put something in place of something else; **3** to put on different clothes

²**change** *noun* **1** something that has become different; **2** the money returned when you give too much for something

channel *noun* **1** a narrow piece of water joining two seas; **2** a way along which water can flow; **3** a band of television or radio waves

chant *verb* to repeat the same words again and again; **chant** *noun*

chapel *noun* a small church, or part of a church

character *noun* **1** the qualities and nature of somebody or something; **2** a person in a book, play, etc

¹**charge** *verb* **1** to ask money for; **2** to say that a person has done something wrong; **3** to run or hurry

²**charge** *noun* **1** a price asked for something; **2** a statement that a person has done wrong; **3** a hurried attack; **4 in charge of** responsible for; caring for or looking after

charity *noun* donations given to good causes

chase *verb* to run after; **chase** *noun*

chat *noun* a friendly, informal conversation

cheap *adjective* costing only little money; **cheaply** *adverb*

¹**cheat** *noun* **1** a dishonest person; **2** a trick

²**cheat** *verb* to trick somebody; to do something that is dishonest

¹**check** *verb* to make certain of something; !! **cheque**

²**check** *noun* **1** an act of checking; **2** a pattern of squares; !! **cheque**

cheek *noun* **1** the fleshy part of the face on either side under the eyes; **2** rudeness

cheer *verb* **1** to shout because you are pleased; **2** to make happy; **cheer** *noun*

cheerful *adjective* happy; **cheerfully** *adverb*; **cheerfulness** *noun*

cheese *noun* solid food made from milk

cheetah *noun* a spotted wild animal of the cat family that can run very fast

chef (*say* **shef**) *noun* a head cook in a hotel or restaurant

chemist (*say* **kemist**) *noun* a person who owns or runs a shop where medicines are sold

chemistry *noun* a science that studies substances like gases, liquids, metals, etc; **chemical** *adjective, noun*

cheque *noun* a specially printed order form to a bank to pay money; !! **check**

cherry *noun* a small red round fruit with a seed like a stone; the tree on which this grows

chess *noun* a game for two players, with 16 pieces, or chessmen each, which are moved across a square chessboard with 64 black and white squares

chest *noun* **1** the upper front part of the body; **2** a large strong box

chestnut *noun* **1** a reddish-brown nut; the tree on which this grows; **2** a reddish-brown colour

chew *verb* to crush food with the teeth

chick *noun* the young of a bird, especially a chicken

chicken *noun* a bird kept by people for its eggs and meat

chicken pox *noun* a disease, caught especially by children, causing fever and spots

¹**chief** *noun* a leader; a ruler; the head of a party, group, etc

²**chief** *adjective* the most important; **chiefly** *adverb*

child *noun* (*plural* **children**) a boy or girl; a son or daughter; **childhood** *noun*; **childish, childlike** *adjective*

chimney *noun* a hollow passage for taking away smoke from a fireplace

chimpanzee

chimpanzee *noun* a large ape

chin *noun* the front part of the face below the mouth

china *noun* **1** a hard white substance made by baking fine clay at high temperatures; **2** plates, cups, etc, made from this

chip *noun* **1** a small piece of brick, wood, paint, etc, broken off; **2** a long thin piece of potato cooked in deep fat; **3** a tiny piece of metal or plastic used in computers to store information or make the computer work; **chip** *verb*

microchip, used in computers

chocolate *noun* a sweet or food made from cocoa

choice *noun* the act of choosing; somebody or something chosen

choir (*say* **kwire**) *noun* a group of people who sing together

choke *verb* to have difficulty or stop breathing because of something blocking your throat

choose *verb* (**chooses, choosing, chose, chosen**) to pick out from a number of things or people the one you want

¹**chop** *verb* (**chopping**) to cut with an axe or sharp knife

²**chop** *noun* a slice of meat containing a bone

chorus *noun* **1** a group of singers **2** a verse in a song which is repeated between each of the other verses

Christian *noun* a person who believes in Jesus Christ; **Christianity** *noun*

Christmas also **Christmas Day** *noun* 25th December; the day on which Jesus Christ is said to have been born

chronological *adjective* placed in order according to time or date

church *noun* a building in which Christians meet to pray to God

cinema *noun* a building in which films are shown

circle *noun* **1** a perfectly round, closed, curved line; a ring; **2** a group of people; **circle** *verb*; **circular** *adjective*

circuit (*say* **sir-kit**) *noun* the path of an electric current

circus *noun* a show given by performers and trained animals, often in a large tent

city *noun* a large and important town, often having a cathedral

claim *verb* **1** to ask for something that you say belongs to you; **2** to say that something is true; **claim** *noun*

¹**clap** *verb* (**clapping**) to hit the palms of your hands together loudly when you are pleased by a musical performance, etc

²**clap** *noun* **1** the sound of clapping; **2** a loud noise: *a **clap** of thunder*

clarinet *noun* a musical instrument that you blow

class *noun* **1** a group of people who are taught together or the time during which they are taught: **classroom**; **2** a group of people or things of the same kind

claw *noun* a sharp curved nail on the toe of an animal or bird; **claw** *verb*

cat's claw retracted

cat's claw out

clay *noun* heavy earth, used for making bricks, pots, etc, when baked

¹**clean** *adjective* not dirty; **cleanness** *noun*; **cleanly** *adverb*

²**clean** *verb* to make or become clean; **cleaner** *noun*

¹**clear** *adjective* **1** easy to see through: *clear glass*; **2** easily heard, seen, read, or understood; **3** open; not having anything in the way; **4** bright; sunny and not cloudy; **clearly** *adverb*; **clearness** *noun*

²**clear** *verb* **1** to make or become clear; **2** to take things away

clever *adjective* quick at learning and understanding; **cleverly** *adverb*; **cleverness** *noun*

cliff *noun* a high steep piece of land close to the sea

climb (*say* clime) *verb* to go up, over, or through using the hands and feet; **climb** *noun*; **climber** *noun*

cling *verb* (**clings, clinging, clung**) to hold on tightly

cling film *noun* a clear plastic that you wrap around food to keep it fresh

¹**clip** *noun* a small plastic or metal object for holding things together

²**clip** *verb* **1** to hold with a clip; **2** to cut with scissors or another sharp instrument

clock *noun* an instrument for measuring and showing time

clockwise *adjective, adverb* in the same direction as the movement of the hands of a clock; circular movement to the left

¹**close** (*say like* doze) *verb* to shut

²**close** (*say like* dose) *adjective* near; not far away; **closely** *adverb*; **closeness** *noun*

cloth *noun* **1** material made from wool, cotton, etc, by weaving, and used for making clothes, covers, etc; **2** a piece of this used for a special purpose: **tablecloth, dishcloth**

clothes *noun* the things you wear

clothing *noun* clothes worn together on different parts of the body

cloud *noun* **1** a mass of very small drops of water floating high in the sky; **2** a mass of dust, smoke, etc, which floats in the air; **cloudy** *adjective*

cumulus clouds mean fine weather

clown *noun* a person, especially in the circus, who makes people laugh

club *noun* **1** a group of people who join together for sport, amusement, etc; **2** a heavy wooden stick; **3** a playing card with one or more three-leafed figures printed on it in black

clue *noun* something that helps to find an answer to a question, difficulty, etc

clumsy *adjective* knocking things over; awkward or careless; **clumsily** *adverb*; **clumsiness** *noun*

¹**coach** *noun* **1** a bus used for long-distance travel; **2** a railway carriage; **3** a large four-wheeled vehicle pulled by horses; **4** somebody who trains sports people, students, etc

²**coach** *verb* to train or teach a person or group

coal *noun* a black or dark brown material dug out of the earth, that can be burned to give heat

coarse *adjective* not fine or smooth; rough; **coarsely** *adverb*; **coarseness** *noun*; !! **course**

coast *noun* the land next to the sea

coat *noun* **1** a piece of clothing with long sleeves, worn for warmth; **2** an animal's fur, wool, hair, etc

cobweb *noun* a very fine net of sticky threads made by a spider to catch insects

garden spider's web

cock *noun* a fully grown male bird, especially a chicken

cocoa *noun* **1** a dark brown powder made by crushing the cooked seeds of the cacao tree, used for giving foods and drinks a chocolate flavour; **2** a drink made from hot milk or water mixed with this powder

coconut *noun* a large brown nut with a thick hard shell, white flesh, and a hollow centre filled with a milky juice

cod *noun* a type of large sea fish used for food

code *noun* a way of using words, letters, numbers, etc, to keep messages secret

coffee *noun* **1** a brown powder made by crushing the beans of the coffee tree, used for making drinks or flavouring food; **2** a drink made by adding hot water and/or milk to this powder

coffin *noun* a box in which a dead person is buried

¹**coil** *verb* to wind into a set of rings one above the other

²**coil** *noun* **1** a connected set of rings into which a rope, wire, etc, can be wound; **2** a single one of these rings

coin *noun* a flat round piece of metal, made by a government for use as money

¹**cold** *adjective* having very little heat; not warm; **coldly** *adverb*; **coldness** *noun*

²**cold** *noun* **1** the absence of heat; cold weather; **2** an illness of the nose and/or throat

collar _noun_ **1** the part of a shirt, dress, or coat that stands up or folds down round the neck; **2** a leather or metal band round an animal's neck

collect _verb_ to gather together; **collection** _noun_; **collector** _noun_

college _noun_ a place where people study after they have left school

¹**colour** _noun_ **1** the quality that allows the eyes to see the difference between (for example) a red and a blue flower of the same size and shape; **2** red, blue, green, black, yellow, white, etc; **colourful** _adjective_; **colouring** _noun_; **colourless** _adjective_: without colour

²**colour** _verb_ to put colour into a drawing

column _noun_ **1** a vertical line of numbers or words; **2** a vertical standing block made of stone or other building material, for supporting a building or statue

comb (_say like_ **home**) _noun_ a piece of bone, metal, plastic, etc, with thin teeth, used for tidying the hair; **comb** _verb_

combine _verb_ to put two or more things together

come _verb_ (**comes, coming, came, come**) **1** to move towards the person speaking, or a particular place; **2** to arrive; **3** to happen; **4** to become; **5** **come to** to reach; to add up to something; **6** **come from** to be made by; to be born or live in

comedian (_feminine_ **comedienne**) _noun_ a person who tells jokes, does amusing things, or acts in funny plays and films

comet _noun_ an object in space, with a bright head and a long, burning tail, which moves round the sun

Halley's comet can be seen from Earth about every 76 years

¹**comfort** _noun_ **1** freedom from pain, trouble, etc; **2** help, kindness, etc, given to somebody who is sad, ill, in pain, etc; **comfortable** _adjective_; **comfortably** _adverb_

²**comfort** _verb_ to give comfort to; to cheer up; **comforter** _noun_

comic _noun_ **1** a magazine for children containing stories told in drawings; **2** a person who is amusing; a comedian

comma _noun_ the mark (,) used in writing and printing to separate parts of a sentence

¹**command** _verb_ **1** to order; **2** to be in charge of; **commander** _noun_

²**command** _noun_ **1** an order; **2** power; control

common _adjective_ **1** ordinary; usual; **2** belonging to or shared by two or more people; **3** found or happening often and in many places

communicate *verb* to make known; to pass on or send information

communication *noun* **1** the sending on of a piece of information, news, etc; **2 communications** roads, railways, phones, television, or other ways of sending information, moving goods, or travelling to other places

community *noun* a group of people who live together or near one another and/or who may share the same interests or beliefs

compact disc *noun* a CD or CD-ROM

company *noun* **1** a group of people doing business; a firm; **2** people to be with

compare *verb* to see if things are alike or different; **comparison** *noun*; !! **compere**

bearing compass, used by hikers and mountaineers

compass *noun* an instrument for showing direction, usually with a needle that always points to the north

compensation *noun* a payment of some sort made to someone in retun for damage or wrong-doing

compere *noun* a person who introduces the acts in a show; **compere** *verb*; !! **compare**

competition *noun* a test of strength, skill, etc, to show who is best at something; **compete** *verb*; **competitor** *noun*

complain *verb* to say that you are angry, unhappy, or sad about something; to say that something is not good; **complaint** *noun*

¹**complete** *adjective* whole; with nothing left out; **completeness** *noun*

²**complete** *verb* to make whole or perfect; to finish; **completely** *adverb*; **completion** *noun*

complicated *adjective* difficult to understand or deal with

compliment *noun* something nice said about somebody !! **complement**

comprehension *noun* understanding what you read and hear

computer *noun* an electronic machine that can store information and make calculations at very high speeds

concentrate *verb* to keep all your thoughts, attention, etc, on one thing; **concentration** *noun*

concern *verb* **1** to make unhappy or troubled; to worry; **2** to be about something; **concern** *noun*

concert *noun* music played by a number of singers and/or musicians

concrete *noun* a building material made by mixing sand, small stones, cement, and water

condition *noun* **1** the state that somebody or something is in; **2** something that is said to be necessary or that must happen before something else happens

conductor *noun* **1** a person who controls a group of people playing music; **2** a person who collects fares on a bus or train

cone *noun* a shape or object with a round base and a point at the top: **ice cream cone, fir cone**

confess *verb* to admit a fault or something you have done wrong; **confession** *noun*

confident *adjective* secure, unafraid

conscience *noun* part of your mind that judges whether what you do is good or bad, and makes you feel guilty

conscious *adjective* awake, able to understand what is happening; **consciously** *adverb*; **consciousness** *noun*

consecutive *adjective* one after the other; **consecutively** *adjective*

conservation *noun* saving and protecting trees, the Earth, etc

consider *verb* to think about **considerable** *adjective* fairly large

consist *verb* to be made up of

consonant *noun* any of the letters of the English alphabet, or their sounds, except a, e, i, o, or u; compare VOWEL

constant *adjective* happening all the time; **constantly** *adverb*

constellation *noun* a large group of stars

the Great Bear constellation, sometimes called the Plough

confuse *verb* to mix up in your mind; **confusion** *noun*

conjunction *noun* a word that joins two parts of a sentence

conjuror or **conjurer** *noun* a person who does clever tricks that seem magical, usually by very quick movement of the hands; **conjure** *verb*

connect *verb* to join; **connected** *adjective*; **connection** *noun*

contain *verb* to have inside; to hold; **container** *noun*

content *adjective* satisfied; happy; **contented** *adjective*

contents *noun* what is contained in an object or a book

context *noun* background information which contrbutes to our understanding of a fact or situation

continent *noun* any of the seven main masses of land on the Earth; **continental** *adjective*

continual *adjective* happening often; repeated; **continually** *adverb*

continue *verb* to go on happening or speaking

continuous *adjective* never stopping; **continuously** *adverb*

¹**contract** *verb* to get smaller

²**contract** *noun* a legal agreement between people

contrast *verb* to look at the differences between two things

¹**control** *verb* (**controlled**) **1** to have power over somebody or something; **2** to direct; to guide

²**control** *noun* **1** the ability to control; power; **2** an instrument, knob, switch, etc, for controlling a machine: **volume control**

convenient *adjective* **1** near; easy to get to; **2** easy to use; helpful; **convenience** *noun*; **conveniently** *adverb*

conversation *noun* a discussion; talking with other people

cook *verb* to prepare food for eating by using heat; **cook** *noun*; **cooker** *noun*

cool *adjective* **1** neither warm nor cold; **2** calm; not excited; **cool** *verb*; **coolly** *adverb*; **coolness** *noun*

copper *noun* a soft reddish metal that is easily shaped and allows heat and electricity to pass through it readily

¹**copy** *noun* **1** a thing made to be exactly like another; **2** a single example of a magazine, book, etc

²**copy** *verb* to make or do something exactly the same as something else

cord *noun* a thick string or thin rope

cork *noun* **1** a soft light material that comes from the bark of a particular type of tree; **2** a round piece of this is sometimes used to seal a bottle

corn *noun* the seed of grain plants, such as wheat

corner *noun* **1** the point at which two lines, surfaces, or edges meet; **2** the place where two roads meet

¹**correct** *adjective* right; **correctly** *adverb*; **correctness** *noun*

²**correct** *verb* to make right; to mark the mistakes in; **correction** *noun*

correspond *verb* to answer or report back

corridor *noun* a long narrow part of a building; a passage off which rooms open

¹**cost** *noun* the price you pay when you buy something

²**cost** *verb* (**costs, costing, cost**) to have as a price

costume *noun* the clothes typical of a certain time in history, a country, etc; the clothes worn by an actor or actress

cot *noun* a small bed for a young child

cottage *noun* a small house in the country

cotton *noun* **1** cloth used to make sheets and clothes; **2** the plant grown to make this; **3** **cotton wool** soft white stuff used to put medicine on cuts, etc

couch *noun* a sofa

cough (*say* coff) *verb* to push air out from the throat suddenly, with a rough sharp noise because you are ill; **cough** *noun*

council *noun* a group of people who are chosen to make laws, rules, or decisions or to give advice; **councillor** *noun*; !! **counsel, counsellor**

count *verb* 1 to find out how many there are; 2 to say the numbers in order; 3 to add up; **count** *noun*

counter *noun* 1 a narrow table or flat surface on which goods are shown or at which people in a shop, bank, etc, are served; 2 a small flat object used in playing games

country *noun* 1 an area of land that has its own government; 2 the land outside cities or towns: **countryside**

couple *noun* 1 two things of the same kind; 2 a man and a woman together, especially a husband and wife

courage *noun* the feeling of not being afraid; bravery; **courageous** *adjective*

course *noun* 1 the direction taken by somebody or something; 2 an area of land or water on which a race is held or certain types of sport played; 3 a set of lessons; 4 any of the several parts of a meal; 5 **of course** *adverb* certainly; as everyone knows or must agree; !! **coarse**

court *noun* 1 a place where somebody is questioned about a crime, and where people decide whether or not he or she is guilty; 2 the officials, servants, etc, who attend a king and queen; 3 an open space where games are played: **tennis court**; !! **caught**

cousin *noun* the child of your uncle or aunt

¹**cover** *verb* to place or spread something upon, over, or in front of something else

²**cover** *noun* 1 anything that protects by covering: **bed cover, book cover**; 2 a lid; a top

covering *noun* something that covers or hides

cow *noun* (*male* **bull**, *young* **calf**) the fully grown female form of cattle, elephants, and certain other large animals

coward *noun* a person who avoids danger or pain because he or she has no courage; **cowardly** *adjective*; **cowardice** *noun*; **cowardliness** *noun*

cowboy *noun* a man who rides a horse and looks after cattle in America

CPU *noun* **central processing unit**; the main part of a computer, which deals with the programs and controls other parts

crab *noun* a sea animal with five pairs of legs and a hard shell

fiddler crab

¹**crack** *verb* **1** to break without dividing into separate parts; **2** to make a sudden sharp sound

²**crack** *noun* **1** a thin line or split where something is broken; **2** a loud sharp sound

cracker *noun* **1** a small thin biscuit; **2** a paper toy that bangs when its ends are pulled, used especially at Christmas

cradle *noun* a small rocking bed for a baby

crane *noun* a machine for lifting and moving heavy objects

mobile crane

crash *noun* **1** a sudden loud noise; **2** a violent vehicle accident; **3** a sudden failure of a computer or a computer program; **crash** *verb*

crawl *verb* to move slowly with your body close to the ground, or on your hands and knees

cream *noun* the thick fatty part of milk which rises to the top; **creaminess** *noun*; **creamy** *adjective*

creature *noun* an animal of any kind

credit card *noun* a plastic card that you can use to pay in place of notes and coins

creep *verb* (**creeps, creeping, crept**) to move slowly and quietly

crew *noun* the people working on a ship, plane, etc

¹**cricket** *noun* an outdoor game played with a ball and bat, by two teams of eleven players each; **cricketer** *noun*

²**cricket** *noun* a type of small insect that makes a noise by rubbing its forewings together

crime *noun* something that is wrong and can be punished by law; **criminal** *noun*

¹**crisp** *adjective* **1** hard and dry; easily broken; **2** firm; fresh; **crispy** *adjective*

²**crisp** *noun* a thin piece of potato cooked in hot fat, dried, and sold in packets

criticise *verb* to give a negative opinion

41

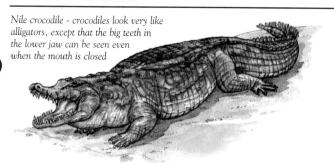

Nile crocodile - crocodiles look very like alligators, except that the big teeth in the lower jaw can be seen even when the mouth is closed

crocodile *noun* a large reptile that lives on land and in lakes and rivers in the hot wet parts of the world

crooked *adjective* not straight; bent; **crookedly** *adverb*; **crookedness** *noun*

crop *noun* 1 a plant or part of a plant such as grain, fruit, or vegetables grown by a farmer; 2 the amount of grain, vegetables, etc, cut and gathered at one time

¹**cross** *noun* 1 a figure or mark formed by one straight line crossing another; anything shaped like x or +; 2 an animal or plant that is a mixture of breeds

²**cross** *verb* 1 to go, pass, or reach over or across; 2 to cause an animal or plant to breed with one of another kind; **crossing** *noun*

³**cross** *adjective* angry; bad-tempered; **crossly** *adverb*

crow *noun* a large shiny black bird with a loud rough cry

crowd *noun* a large number of people gathered together; **crowded** *adjective*

crown *noun* a circle of gold with jewels in it, worn on the head especially by a king or queen

cruel *adjective* liking to hurt other people or animals; unkind; **cruelly** *adverb*; **cruelty** *noun*

crumb *noun* a very small piece of dry food, such as bread or cake

crush *verb* to press heavily; to hurt or damage by doing this

crust *noun* the hard part on the outside of bread or some other things; **crusty** *adjective*

¹**cry** *verb* (**cries, crying, cried**) 1 to produce tears from your eyes; 2 to make loud sounds because of fear, sadness, etc

²**cry** *noun* a loud call; a shout

cub *noun* the young of various types of wild animals, such as the lion, bear, etc

cube *noun* a solid object that has six equal square sides

cuckoo *noun* 1 a grey bird that lays its eggs in other birds' nests; 2 the call of this bird

cucumber *noun* a long green vegetable which is usually eaten raw with cold food

cue *noun* a long straight wooden stick, slightly thicker at one end than the other, used for hitting the ball in snooker, billiards, etc; ‼ **queue**

cup *noun* **1** a small round container, usually with a handle, from which liquids are drunk: **cupful**; **2** a specially shaped bowl, usually made of gold or silver, given as a prize in a competition

cupboard *noun* a piece of furniture with space inside where things may be stored

¹**cure** *verb* to make somebody better when they have been ill; to make a disease, illness, etc, go away

²**cure** *noun* a way of making somebody or something better; a drug or medicine that cures an illness, disease, etc

curious *adjective* **1** wanting to know or learn about things or people; **2** odd; strange; peculiar; **curiosity** *noun*

¹**curl** *verb* to twist into or form a round or curved shape

²**curl** *noun* **1** a roll or round shape; **2** a small piece of twisted hair; **curliness** *noun*; **curly** *adjective*

currant *noun* **1** small dried seedless grape; **2** a small bush or the small fruits in bunches on it; ‼ **current**

current *noun* a flow of water, gas, electricity, etc; ‼ **currant**

curtain *noun* a piece of hanging cloth that can be drawn to cover a window or door or to divide a room

curve *verb* to bend into a smooth round shape; **curve** *noun*

cushion *noun* a bag filled with a soft substance that you put on a chair to make it more comfortable

custard *noun* a thick sweet yellow sauce

customer *noun* a person who buys something

cut *verb* (**cuts, cutting, cut**) to make an opening in, separate, or remove something with a knife, scissors, etc; **cut** *noun*

¹**cycle** *noun* a bicycle or motorcycle

²**cycle** *verb* to bicycle; **cyclist** *noun*

cygnet (*say* signet) *noun* a young swan

cymbals *noun* a musical instrument consisting of a pair of round thin metal plates struck together to make a loud ringing noise; ‼ **symbols**

a pair of cymbals

Dd

dad, daddy *noun* father

daddy-longlegs *noun* a large fly with very long legs

daffodil *noun* a yellow flower that grows in the spring

daily *adjective, adverb* happening or done once every day

dairy *noun* a place where milk, butter, and cheese are made

daisy *noun* a small wild or garden flower, yellow in the centre and white round the edge

daisies

dam *noun* a wall or bank built to keep back water; **dam** *verb*

¹**damage** *noun* harm, especially to things

²**damage** *verb* to cause damage to; to hurt

damp *adjective, noun* slightly wet; not properly dry; **dampness** or **damp** *noun*

¹**dance** *verb* to move to music; **dancer** *noun*

²**dance** *noun* 1 a set of movements performed to music; 2 a party for dancing; 3 a piece of music for dancing

dandelion *noun* a small yellow wild flower

dangerous *adjective* not safe; likely to cause harm or damage; **danger** *noun*; **dangerously** *adverb*

dare *verb* 1 to be brave or rude enough to do or say something; 2 to challenge; **dare** *noun*

dark *adjective* without light; nearly black; **dark** *noun*; **darkness** *noun*

dart *noun* a small pointed arrow thrown at a round board in the game of darts

dash *noun* 1 a sudden quick run; 2 a mark (–) used in writing or printing; **dash** *verb*

data *noun* measurements, facts, and information that can be put into a computer

database *noun* information in a computer, organised so that you can find things quickly

¹**date** *noun* 1 time shown by the number of the day, the month, and the year; 2 an arrangement to meet at a particular time and place especially between a boy and a girl

²**date** *noun* a small brown sweet fruit with a long stone

daughter *noun* a person's female child

dawn *noun* the time of day when light first appears and the sun rises

day *noun* 1 the time when it is light: **daytime, daylight**; 2 twenty-four hours

dead *adjective* 1 no longer alive; 2 unable to feel

deaf *adjective* unable to hear or hear well; **deafness** *noun*

d

deal *verb* (**deals, dealing, dealt**) **1** to give out a share of something; **2 deal with** to do what is necessary with something or somebody; **deal** *noun*; **dealer** *noun*

dear *adjective* **1** much loved; **2** a term used to begin a letter; **3** costing a lot of money; !! **deer**

death *noun* the end of life

decay *verb* to go bad; **decay** *noun*

deceive *verb* to cause somebody to accept as true or good what is false or bad

December *noun* the twelfth and last month of the year

decide *verb* to arrive at an answer or make a choice about something; **decision** *noun*

deciduous *adjective* any tree that loses its leaves in the autumn

¹**decimal** *adjective* having to do with the number ten

²**decimal** *noun* a number like 0.5, 0.375, etc

decipher *verb* to work something out

deck *noun* **1** a floor of a ship or bus; **2** a machine for playing records or tapes: **record deck, tape deck**

decorate *verb* to make something more beautiful or colourful; **decoration** *noun*

deep *adjective* **1** going far down; **2** going a long way in; **3** strong and dark (colour); **4** low (voice); **deeply** *adverb*; **deepness** *noun*; **depth** *noun*

deer *noun* (*plural* **deer**) (*male* **buck**, *female* **doe** *or* **hind**, *young* **fawn**) a large wild animal that eats grass and can run very fast; !! **dear**

definite *adjective* certain

definition *noun* the meaning of a word

degree *noun* **1** a unit for measuring temperature or the size of an angle; **2** a university qualification

delay *verb* **1** to put off until later; **2** to make late; **3** to act slowly; **delay** *noun*

delicacy *noun* something that is good to eat but is rare or costs a lot of money

delicate *adjective* **1** easily harmed or broken; **2** beautiful and pleasing but small and not strong; **delicately** *adverb*

delicious *adjective* nice to smell or taste

delight *verb* to give great pleasure; **delight** *noun*; **delightful** *adjective*

deliver *verb* **1** to send or take something to a particular place; **2** to help somebody to have a baby; **3** to say; to read aloud; **delivery** *noun*

demonstrate *verb* to show or display something

den *noun* **1** the home of a wild animal; **2** a secret place

denim *noun* the material used for making jeans

dentist *also* **dental surgeon** *noun* a person who looks after your teeth

dependant *noun* a person who depends on another; **dependent** *adjective*

fallow deer fawns

45

d

depressed *adjective* when a person is feeling unhappy

describe *verb* to say what something is like; **description** *noun*

¹**desert** (*say dez-ert*) *noun* a large sandy piece of land where there is hardly any rain and very few plants or animals; !! **dessert**

²**desert** (*say de-zert*) *verb* to leave completely; !! **dessert**

deserve *verb* to be worthy of something good, or bad, by doing something good or bad

desk *noun* a table, often with drawers, at which you read, write, etc

dessert (*say de-zert*) *noun* a sweet dish you eat at the end of a meal; !! **desert**

destroy *verb* to ruin or wreck; **destruction** *noun*

detect *verb* to find out or discover; **detection** *noun*; **detector** *noun*

detective *noun* a police officer who finds out about crimes

determined *adjective* having made up your mind to do something; **determination** *noun*

develop *verb* to make or become larger, more active, more complete, etc; to grow; **developer** *noun*; **development** *noun*

devil *noun* **1** an evil spirit or person; **2** **Devil** the most evil spirit; the enemy of God

dew (*say dyoo*) *noun* small drops of water that form on the ground during the night; **dewy** *adjective* !! **due**;

diagonal *adjective* a line that is slanted or at an angle

diagram *noun* a drawing that explains something or shows how its parts are arranged

dialogue *noun* a conversation

diamond *noun* **1** a very hard valuable jewel; **2** a shape with four equal sides that stands on one of its points; **3** a playing card that has these shapes in red

diary *noun* a book with separate spaces for each day of the year, in which you write down things you have done or will do

dictionary *noun* a book that gives the meanings and spelling of words

¹**die** *verb* (**dies, dying, died**) to stop living

²**die** *noun* (*plural* **dice**) a small cube, with a different number of spots from one to six on each side, that is used in many games

different *adjective* not of the same kind; **difference** *noun*; **differently** *adverb*

difficult *adjective* not easy; hard to do, understand, etc; **difficulty** *noun*

dig *verb* (**digs, digging, dug**) **1** to break up and move earth; **2** to make a hole by taking away earth or soil

digger *noun* somebody or something that digs; a tool or machine for digging the earth

digit *noun* **1** any number from nought to nine; **2** a finger or toe; **digital** *adjective*

digraph *noun* two letters that make one sound, such as th, ph

dinner *noun* a main meal, eaten either at midday or in the evening

dinosaur *noun* any of several types of reptiles, some very large, that lived millions of years ago

a recently discovered Chinese dinosaur - a yingshanosaurus

disappoint *verb* to become sad or make somebody sad because what was expected or hoped for did not happen; **disappointed** *adjective*; **disappointing** *adjective*; **disappointment** *noun*

disapprove *verb* to have a bad opinion of somebody or something; **disapproval** *noun*

d

¹**direct** *verb* **1** to tell somebody the way to somewhere; **2** to control or manage; **director** *noun*

²**direct** *adjective* straight towards or straight after or behind; **directly** *adverb*

direction *noun* **1** the course or way in which a person or thing moves; **2 directions** information that tells you where to go or what to do

directory *noun* a list, usually in a book, where you can find out where places or things are

dirt *noun* soil, mud, dust, or anything that is not clean

dirty *adjective* **1** covered with dirt; **2** making you, or your clothes, unclean; **dirtily** *adverb*; **dirtiness** *noun*

disagree *verb* not to agree; **disagreement** *noun*

disappear *verb* to go out of sight; **disappearance** *noun*

disc *noun* **1** round flat thing; **2** a flat piece of plastic on which music or electronic information is stored

disciple *noun* somebody who is faithful to or follows a leader

discipline *noun* good behaviour and the obeying of rules; the training of somebody to behave in this way

disco *noun* a place where people dance to pop music

discover *verb* to find out or find something, especially for the first time; **discoverer** *noun*; **discovery** *noun*

discuss *verb* to talk about a particular subject

disease *noun* an illness; **diseased** *adjective*

dish *noun* **1** a large, flat, and often round plate on which your food is served; **2** prepared food of one kind

dishonest *adjective* not honest; **dishonestly** *adverb*; **dishonesty** *noun*

disk *noun* a computer disc

dislike *verb* not to like; **dislike** *noun*

display *verb* to present or arrange things for show; **display** *noun*

distance *noun* **1** the amount of space between two places; **2 in the distance** far away; **distant** *adjective*

distribute *verb* to give or send out

ditch *noun* a long narrow not very deep channel dug in the ground for water to drain into

dive *verb* **1** to jump head first into water; **2** to move quickly or suddenly; **dive** *noun*

diver *noun* a person who works under water and wears a special diving suit to help him or her to breathe

divide *verb* **1** to separate into smaller parts or groups; to share; **2** to find out how many times one number will go into another; **divisibility** *noun*

division *noun* **1** one of the parts or groups into which something is divided; **2** dividing sums

do *verb* (**does, doing, did, done, doesn't, don't, didn't**) **1** to carry out; to act; **2** to deal with something; **3** to be suitable for something; to be enough; **4 That will do!** That's enough!; **5 How do you do?** a form of words used when introduced to somebody; **6 make do with** to use something even though it may not be perfect or enough

dock *noun* a place where ships are loaded or repaired

doctor *noun* a person whose job is to look after sick people

document *noun* **1** a formal piece of paper such as a driving license, certificate etc; **2** a piece of work on a computer

dog *noun* (*female* **bitch**, *young* **puppy**) a common four-legged animal, kept as a pet or for hunting, working, etc

doll *noun* a toy made to look like a person

scuba diver (scuba stands for self contained underwater breathing apparatus)

d

dolphin *noun* a sea animal that swims in groups and is very intelligent

bottle-nosed dolphin

domestic *adjective* something which relates to the home

donkey *noun* an animal like a horse but smaller, with longer ears and a rough coat

door *noun* **1** a flat surface that opens and closes the entrance to a building, room, or piece of furniture; **2** the opening for a door: **doorway**; **3 answer the door** to go and open the door to see who is there

dot *noun* a small round spot; **dot** *verb*; **dotted** *adjective*

¹**double** *adjective* **1** having two parts; **2** made for two; **double** *adverb*

²**double** *noun* **1** something that is twice as much as another; **2** a person who looks like another; **3 doubles** a game of tennis, badminton, etc, for two pairs of players

³**double** *verb* **1** to multiply a number or amount by two; **2** to fold or bend sharply or tightly over

double bass *noun* a musical instrument with a deep sound, like a very big violin

double-decker *adjective* having two layers or two floors

doubt *verb* not to be sure about something; **doubt** *noun*

dough (*say* doe) *noun* a thick mixture of flour and water used for making bread, cakes, etc; !! **doe**

¹**down** *adverb, preposition, adjective* **1** to or in a lower place or position; **2** along

²**down** *noun* small soft feathers on a bird

downhill *adjective, adverb* towards the bottom of a hill

downstairs *adverb, adjective* on or to a lower floor of a building; **downstairs** *noun*

downwards *adverb* **1** from a higher to a lower place; **2** towards the ground or floor

draft *noun* an outline or rough plan of an idea !! **draught**

drag *verb* (**dragged**) **1** to pull a heavy thing along; **2** to move along slowly; **3** to look for something by pulling a heavy net along the bottom of a lake or river

dragon *noun* an imaginary animal in stories that is said to breathe fire

Welsh heraldic dragon

49

d

¹**drain** *verb* **1** to make a liquid, usually water, flow away; **2** to make or become gradually dry or empty

²**drain** *noun* a pipe, tube, etc, that drains something away

drake *noun* a male duck

mallard drake

draught *noun* air blowing into a room !! **draft**

draughts *noun* a game for two, each with twelve round pieces, on a board of 64 squares

¹**draw** *verb* (**draws, drawing, drew, drawn**) **1** to make pictures with a pencil, pen, etc; **2** to pull; to pull up or out; **3** to move; **4** to attract; **5** to end a game, battle, etc, without either side winning; **6 draw the curtain** to close or open the curtain !! **drawer**

²**draw** *noun* a game, battle, etc, that neither side wins !! **drawer**

drawer *noun* a sliding container, like a box without a top, that fits into a piece of furniture !! **draw**

drawing *noun* a picture done by pencil, pen, etc

¹**dream** *noun* **1** thoughts that you have when you are asleep; **2** something not real that you hope for or imagine

²**dream** *verb* (**dreams, dreaming, dreamed** *or* **dreamt**) to have a dream

¹**dress** *verb* **1** to put clothes on; **2 dress up** to put on special clothes; **3** to clean and cover up a wound

²**dress** *noun* a piece of clothing for a woman or girl that has a top and skirt joined together

drink *verb* (**drinks, drinking, drank, drunk**) to take liquid into the mouth and swallow it; **drink** *noun*

drip *verb* (**dripped**) to fall or let fall in drops; **drip** *noun*

¹**drive** *verb* (**drives, driving, drove, driven**) to make a vehicle or an animal move in the direction you want; **driver** *noun*

²**drive** *noun* **1** a journey in a vehicle; **2** a road to a house: *a* **driveway**

¹**drop** *noun* **1** a small amount of liquid; **2** a small round sweet; **3** a fall in prices, temperature, etc

²**drop** *verb* (**dropped**) **1** to fall suddenly or in drops; **2** to let fall or lower; **3 drop in** to visit

drown *verb* **1** to die by being under water so that you are unable to breathe; **2** to kill by holding under water too long; **3** to make such a loud noise that another sound can no longer be heard

drowsy *adjective* sleepy

drug *noun* a medicine

drum kit

¹**drum** _noun_ **1** a round musical instrument that you play by beating with your hand or a stick; **2** a large container shaped like a drum

²**drum** _verb_ (**drummed**) **1** to beat or play a drum; **2** to make noises like those from a drum; **drummer** _noun_

¹**drunk** _adjective_ having had too much alcohol

²**drunk** _see_ DRINK

¹**dry** _adjective_ **1** not wet; not containing water; **2** thirsty; **3** dull and not interesting; **dryly, drily** _adverb_; **dryness** _noun_

²**dry** _verb_ **1** to make or become dry; **2** to preserve food by removing liquid

¹**duck** _noun_ (male **drake**, young **duckling**) a common water bird with short legs and a short neck

²**duck** _verb_ **1** to lower your head or body quickly, so as to avoid being hit by something; **2** to go under the water for a short moment

duckling _noun_ a young duck

due (_say_ **dyoo**) _adjective_
1 owing; to be paid;
2 expected; **3** because of; caused by !! **dew**

dull _adjective_ **1** not bright, strong, or sharp; **2** cloudy; grey; **3** not interesting or exciting

dumb (_say_ **dum**) _adjective_ unable to speak

dumpling _noun_ a ball of dough cooked with meat in a stew or filled with jam or fruit

during _preposition_ all through, or at some point in the course of

dusk _noun_ the time when daylight is fading

¹**dust** _noun_ powder made up of very small pieces; **dusty** _adjective_

²**dust** _verb_ **1** to clean the dust from something; **2** to cover with a fine powder

dustbin _noun_ a container with a lid, for holding rubbish

duty _noun_ **1** what you must do either because of your job or because you think it right; **2** a tax; **dutiful** _adjective_

duvet (_say_ **du-vay**) _noun_ a large bag filled with soft warm material, such as feathers, to keep you warm in bed

dwarf _noun_ **1** a person, animal, or plant of much less than the usual size; **2** a small imaginary person in fairy stories

Ee

each *adjective, pronoun, adverb* every one separately; for or to every one

eager *adjective* wanting to do something very much; keen; **eagerly** *adverb*; **eagerness** *noun*

eagle *noun* a large strong bird that hunts other birds and animals

¹**ear** *noun* **1** the part of the body with which you hear: **earache 2 all ears** listening eagerly

²**ear** *noun* the seeds at the top of a stalk of corn, wheat, etc

early *adverb, adjective* **1** before the usual or right time; **2** near the beginning of the day or another period of time

earn *verb* **1** to get money by working; **2** to get something that you deserve; !! **urn**

earring *noun* a piece of jewellery worn on the ear

earth *noun* **1 Earth** the planet on which we live; **2** soil; **3** the wire connecting a piece of electrical equipment to the ground; **4** the hole where certain wild animals live, such as foxes

earthquake *noun* a sudden shaking of the Earth's surface, that may cause great damage

earwig *noun* a thin brown insect

east *noun* one of the four main points of the compass; the direction in which the sun rises; **east** *adjective, adverb*; **easterly** *adjective*; **eastern** *adjective*

Easter *noun* the time when Christians remember the death of Jesus Christ and his coming back to life

easy *adjective* able to be done without much trouble; not difficult; **easily** *adverb*

eat *verb* (**eats, eating, ate, eaten**) to take food into the mouth and swallow it

eclipse *noun* the blocking off of the sun's light when the moon passes between it and the Earth, or of the moon's light when the Earth passes between it and the sun

in this solar eclipse the moon is passing between the Earth and the sun

ecology *noun* the way that the Earth, plants, animals, and people live together and can change one another

edge *noun* **1** the place or line where something begins or ends; **2** the thin sharp cutting part of a knife, saw, etc

edit *verb* to correct, rearrange and put something together, such as a piece of writing or a film

educate *verb* to teach; to train the character or mind of something; **education** *noun*

eel *noun* a long slippery fish that looks like a snake

effect *noun* **1** a result; **2** a result produced on the mind or feelings; **effective** *adjective*

efficient *adjective* quick and very organised

effort *noun* **1** a show of strength; **2** to try hard using body or mind

e.g. for example

egg *noun* **1** a round or oval object that comes out of the body of a female bird, fish, or reptile and contains new life; **2** a chicken's egg eaten for food; **3** the seed of life in a woman or female animal, which joins with the male seed to make a baby

eight *adjective, noun* the number 8; **eighth** *adjective, adverb*

eighteen *adjective, noun* the number 18; **eighteenth** *adjective, adverb*

eighty *adjective, noun* the number 80; **eightieth** *adjective, adverb*

either *adjective, pronoun* **1** one or the other of two; **2** one and the other of two; each

elastic *noun* a stretchy material that springs back into its original shape after being pulled; **elastic** *adjective*

elbow *noun* the joint where the arm bends

elder *adjective, noun* the older of two

eldest *adjective, noun* the oldest of three or more

electricity *noun* the power produced by a battery or sent along wires which gives us heat and light and makes machines work; **electric** or **electrical** *adjective*; **electrically** *adverb*; **electrician** *noun*

electronic *adjective* connected with anything that works by electronics

electronics *noun* the science concerned with computers, radio and television

elephant *noun* a very large animal with two long curved tusks and a long trunk with which it can pick things up

African elephant

eleven *adjective, noun* the number 11; **eleventh** *adjective, adverb*

else *adverb* **1** besides; as well; **2** different; other; **3 or else** or something different will happen

e-mail *noun* a system of computers by which people write messages to one another through their computers, either inside their company or round the world

embarrass *verb* to make somebody feel awkward or silly; **embarrassment** *noun*

emerald *noun* **1** a bright green jewel; **2** bright green; **emerald** *adjective*

emergency *noun* something, usually something bad, that happens very suddenly and must be dealt with immediately

employ *verb* to give work to; **employee** *noun*; **employer** *noun*; **employment** *noun*

empty *adjective* containing nothing or nobody; **emptiness** *noun*; **empty** *verb*

enact *verb* to act something out

encourage *verb* to give courage, praise, or hope to somebody so that he or she will do something; **encouragement** *noun*; **encouragingly** *adverb*

encyclopaedia *noun* a book that contains factual information often listed alphabetically

¹**end** *noun* **1** the furthest part of anything; the point where something stops; **2** the latest point; the time when something stops

²**end** *verb* to come to an end; to finish

enemy *noun* **1** a country against another country in a war; **2** a person who does not like another person and is not friendly to him or her

energy *noun* **1** the power to do things; being full of life and strength; **2** the power that does work and drives machines: **atomic/electrical energy**

engine *noun* **1** a machine that uses fuel, such as petrol or electricity, to make something move; **2** the front part of a train that pulls the carriages: **engine driver**

George Stephenson's Rocket - an early steam engine

engineer *noun* a person who plans, makes, or looks after machines, roads, bridges, etc; **engineering** *noun*

enjoy *verb* to get happiness from; **enjoyable** *adjective*; **enjoyment** *noun*

enormous *adjective* very big

enough *adjective, adverb* as much or as many as may be needed

enter *verb* to come or go in or into; **entry** *noun*

entertain *verb* **1** to have people as guests or give a party; **2** to make somebody amused or interested; **entertainment** *noun*

entire *adjective* whole, complete; **entirely** *adverb*

entrance *noun* a way into a place

envelope *noun* a paper cover for a letter

environment *noun* the air, water, and land in which people, plants, and animals live

equal *adjective* the same in number, size, etc; as good, big, many as; **equal** *noun*; **equal** *verb*; **equally** *adverb*

Equator *noun* an imaginary line drawn round the world halfway between its North and South Poles

equipment *noun* the things that are necessary for doing something; **equip** *verb* **(equipped)**

equivalent *noun* an object or amount considered to be of the same value or significance as another

escape *verb* to get free from something or somebody; **escape** *noun*

especially *adverb* **1** more than usual; particularly; **2** specially

estimate *noun* an informed guess

etc also **et cetera** and other similar things; and so on

euro *noun* a type of money used by most of Europe

evaluate *verb* to estimate the amount or value of something

¹**even** *adjective* **1** smooth, flat, level; **2** equal; **3** **even number** a number that can be divided exactly by two; **evenly** *adverb*; **evenness** *noun*

²**even** *adverb* **1** used to show that something is more than you expect: *It's* **even** *colder than yesterday*; **2** **even if** whether something happens or not; **3** used when a statement is surprising: **Even** *I don't know the answer!*

evening *noun* the end of the day and early part of the night

event *noun* **1** a happening; **2** a race, competition, etc, arranged as part of a day's sports

ever *adverb* **1** at any time; **2** always; **3** **ever so/such** very

evergreen *noun* a tree on which the leaves remain green all year round; **evergreen** *adjective*

every *adjective* each one; all

everybody also **everyone** *pronoun* every person

everything *pronoun* all; the whole, made up of a number of things

everywhere *adverb* in or to all places

evil *adjective* very bad; wicked; **evil** *noun*

evolution *noun* the development of the world

exact *adjective* completely correct; **exactly** *adverb*

exaggerate (*say* **egzajerate**) *verb* to say that something is bigger, better, worse, etc, than it really is; **exaggeration** *noun*

exam or **examination** *noun* a test in a school subject such as maths or history

examine *verb* **1** to look at closely, in order to find out something; **2** to ask somebody questions or to do something in order to test knowledge or skill; **examiner** *noun*

example *noun* **1** something taken from a number of things of the same kind, which shows a general rule or what the other things are like; **2** a person or action that you should try to copy

excellent *adjective* very good; **excellence** *noun*; **excellently** *adverb*

except *conjunction, preposition* apart from; leaving out

exciting *adjective* making you feel very lively and active and have strong pleasant feelings; **excite** *verb*; **excited** *adjective*; **excitement** *noun*

exclamation mark *noun* a sign (!) used in writing to show surprise, shock, etc

¹**excuse (***say* **ekskyoose)** *noun*
the reason given when asking
to be forgiven or not to be
blamed

²**excuse (***say* **ekskyooz)** *verb*
1 to forgive somebody for
a small fault; to say that
somebody is not to blame;
2 to free somebody from
something he or she should do

exercise *noun* **1** the use of your
body so as to strengthen it and
keep fit; **2** something, such as a
piece of schoolwork, that is
done for practice: **exercise
book**; **exercise** *verb*

exist *verb* to live or to be real

exit *noun* a way out of a place

expect *verb* **1** to think or believe
that something will happen; to
suppose; **2** to wait for

expensive *adjective* costing a lot
of money

experience *noun* **1** knowledge
or skill that comes from
doing things rather than
from books; **2** something
that happens to you and
has an effect on your mind;
experience *verb*; **experienced**
adjective

explain *verb* **1** to say what
something means; **2** to be
the reason for something;
explanation *noun*

explode *verb* to blow up or
burst with a loud noise;
explosion *noun*

explore *verb* to investigate a
place or subject

¹**express** *noun* **1** also **express
train** a fast train that does
not stop at many stations;
2 a service given by the post
office, railways, etc, for carrying
things faster

²**express** *verb* to show a feeling
or opinion in some way

expression *noun* **1** the look
on somebody's face; **2** a word
or phrase that is spoken

extend *verb* to make longer;
extension *noun*

eye *noun* **1** the part of the body
with which you see: **eyebrow,
eyelash, eyelid, eyesight**; **2** the
hole in a needle through which
the thread passes; **3** the dark
spot on a potato, from which
a new plant can grow; **4** the
small loop of metal or thread
into which a hook fits for
fastening a piece of clothing

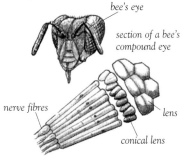

bee's eye

*section of a bee's
compound eye*

nerve fibres

lens

conical lens

human eye

eyebrow

eyelashes

eyelid

iris

pupil

Ff

fable *noun* a story written to make a moral point

¹**face** *noun* **1** the front part of the head from the chin to the hair; **2** a look or expression; **3** the front part of something

²**face** *verb* **1** to turn the face towards something; **2** to look at and not try to avoid

fact *noun* something that is known to be true; something that has actually happened

factor *noun* one of the numbers in a mulitiplication sum

factory *noun* a building where things are made in large quantities, usually by machines

fade *verb* to lose colour through being in the light too long

Fahrenheit *noun* a scale of temperature in which water freezes at 32° and boils at 212°; compare CELSIUS

fail *verb* **1** not to succeed, or not to do what you wanted; **2** not to pass an exam; **failure** *noun*

¹**faint** *adjective* **1** not clear, loud, or strong enough to see, hear, or feel; **2** weak and about to lose your senses; **faintly** *adverb*

²**faint** *verb* to feel weak and lose your senses; **faint** *noun*

¹**fair** *adjective* **1** treating people equally, according to the rules; **2** good, but not very good; average; **3** light in colour; not dark; **fairly** *adverb*; !! **fare**

²**fair** *noun* an outdoor show with rides, games, and other things to amuse you: **fairground**; !! **fare**

fairy *noun* a small imaginary person with wings and magical powers

faith *noun* belief in something; **faithful** *adjective*; **faithfully** *adverb*

fall *verb* (**falls, falling, fell, fallen**) **1** to drop to a lower place; **2** to come down, like prices; **3** to become lower; **fall** *noun*

false *adjective* **1** not true or correct; **2** not faithful or loyal; **3** not real; **falsely** *adverb*

familiar *adjective* something or somewhere that you know and have been or seen before

family *noun* a group made up of a parent or parents and their children; a group of people related by blood or marriage

famous *adjective* being well known and talked about; **fame** *noun*; **famed** *adjective*

¹**fan** *noun* an instrument used to make air move to cool you

²**fan** *verb* (**fanned**) to cause air to blow on something or somebody

³**fan** *noun* someone who admires a pop star, footballer, etc

¹**fancy** *adjective* more decorated, brightly coloured, or expensive than ordinary things; **fancily** *adverb*

²**fancy** *verb* **1** to have a liking for or wish for; **2** to believe without being certain; **3** to form a picture of; to imagine; **fancy** *noun*

far *adverb* (**farther** *or* **further, farthest** *or* **furthest**) **1** at or to a great distance; **2** very much

fare *noun* the price charged to carry a person on a bus, train, plane or taxi; !! **fair**

farm *noun* land and buildings used for growing crops and/or keeping animals; **farm** *verb*; **farmer** *noun*

fashion *noun* the way of dressing or behaving that is considered the best at a certain time; **fashionable** *adjective*

fast *adjective* **1** moving quickly; **2** showing a time that is later than the true time; **3** firmly fixed; **fast** *adverb*

fasten *verb* to make or become firmly fixed or closed; **fastener** *noun*; **fastening** *noun*

¹**fat** *adjective* (**fatter**) **1** having too much or a lot of fat; **2** thick and round; **fatness** *noun*

²**fat** *noun* **1** the material under the skin of people and animals that helps to keep them warm; **2** the white part of meat that can be used for cooking; **3** butter or oil, used in food; **fatty** *adjective*

fate *noun* the power that seems to cause everything to happen; **fateful** *adjective*; !! **fête**

father *noun* a man with children

fault *noun* **1** a mistake that someone can be blamed for; responsibility; **2** a bad point in your character; **3** a problem with a machine; **faulty** *adjective*

favour *noun* **1** something kind done for somebody; **2 in favour of** believing in or choosing; on the side of

favourite *noun* something that is liked more than others; **favourite** *adjective*

fax *noun* a letter that is sent from one machine using a phone line to another, which prints it out; **fax** *verb*; **fax machine**

fear *noun* the feeling that you have when danger is near or when you are afraid; **fear** *verb*; **fearful** *adjective*; **fearless** *adjective*

feat *noun* a clever action, showing strength, skill, or courage; !! **feet**

feather *noun* one part of the soft, light covering of a bird's body; **feathery** *adjective*

feature *noun* a detail, such as parts of the face: eyes, nose etc

February *noun* the second month of the year

feed *verb* (**feeds, feeding, fed**) to give food to

feel *verb* (**feels, feeling, felt**) **1** to touch; **2** to know through your senses; **3** to think; **feel** *noun*; **feeling** *noun*

¹**felt** *noun* a cloth made of wool

²**felt** *see* FEEL

felt-tip pen *noun* a pen with a soft tip made of felt

female *noun* a girl or a woman; any person or animal that gives birth to young

feminine *adjective* like girls or women

¹**fence** *noun* a wall made of wood or wire, round a garden, field, etc

²**fence** *verb* **1** to fight with a sword as a sport; **2** to put a fence round something

maiden hair fern

fern *noun* a plant with feathery leaves and no flowers

ferret *noun* a small animal used for catching rats and rabbits

ferry *noun* a boat for carrying people and things across a narrow stretch of water

fetch *verb* to go and get and bring back

fête (*say* **fate**) *noun* a large outdoor entertainment usually held to collect money for a special purpose; !! **fate**

fever *noun* an illness in which you develop a very high temperature

few *adjective, pronoun, noun* 1 not many; not enough; 2 a small number

fiction *noun* a story which is made up

fidget *verb* to move about and be restless

¹**field** *noun* 1 a piece of land on a farm usually surrounded by a fence or wall, and used for animals or crops; 2 any open area where games or sports are played, or a certain activity is done: **airfield, oilfield**

²**field** *verb* to catch or stop the ball in games like cricket

fierce *adjective* angry, wild, and cruel; **fiercely** *adverb*; **fierceness** *noun*

fifteen *adjective, noun* 1 the number 15; 2 a complete team of fifteen players in rugby union football; **fifteenth** *adjective, adverb*

fifty *adjective, noun* the number 50; **fiftieth** *adjective, adverb*

¹**fight** *verb* (**fights, fighting, fought**) 1 to use your body or weapons against somebody or something; 2 to argue against somebody, or what somebody wants to do

²**fight** *noun* an act of fighting; a battle or struggle

figure *noun* 1 the shape of a person's body; 2 a number or amount; 3 a drawing or diagram

file *noun* 1 an arrangement of drawers, shelves, boxes, or cases for storing papers in an office; 2 a collection of information used or stored in a computer; 3 a metal instrument with a rough edge for making things smooth: **nail file**; 4 a line of people one behind the other; **file** *verb*

fill *verb* 1 to make something full; to become full; 2 to block up a gap or a hole

¹**film** *noun* 1 a story shown in a cinema or on television; 2 the material in a camera on which you take photographs; 3 a thin layer of any material

²**film** *verb* to make a cinema picture

filthy *adjective* very dirty

fin *noun* a part of a fish that helps it to swim

final *adjective* last; coming at the end; **finally** *adverb*

find *verb* (**finds, finding, found**) 1 to discover something after you have been looking for it; 2 **find out** to learn; 3 to discover something by chance

¹**fine** *adjective* 1 beautiful and good; 2 very thin; 3 in very small bits; 4 bright and sunny; not wet; **finely** *adverb*

²**fine** *noun* money paid as a punishment; **fine** *verb*

finger *noun* 1 one of the five movable parts at the end of your hand: **fingernail**; 2 **keep your fingers crossed** to hope for the best

¹**finish** *verb* to bring something to an end; to stop

²**finish** *noun* the end or last part

fir also **fir tree** *noun* a straight tree that has leaves shaped like needles, and cones; !! **fur**

¹**fire** *noun* 1 the heat and light given off by things that are burning: **fire engine, fire escape, fire alarm, firework**; 2 a heap of burning wood or coal for cooking, heating, etc: **fireplace, firelight**; 3 a small gas or electric heater; 4 shooting from guns: **gunfire**; 5 **catch fire** to begin to burn; 6 **set on fire** also **set fire to** to light something not really meant to burn

²**fire** *verb* to shoot a gun

firefighter *noun* a person trained to put fires out and save lives

¹**firm** *adjective* 1 strong; solid; hard; 2 steady and not easily moved; **firmly** *adverb*; **firmness** *noun*

²**firm** *noun* a business

first *adjective, noun, adverb* 1 before any others; 2 the person, thing, or group to do or be something first; 3 for the first time; 4 **at first** at the beginning

¹**fish** *noun* (*plural* **fish** *or* **fishes**) a creature that lives in water and uses its fins and tail to swim

tropical fish

²**fish** *verb* to try to catch fish; to look for something; **fisherman** *noun*; **fishing** *noun*

fist *noun* the hand with the fingers closed in tightly when you are going to hit somebody

¹**fit** *verb* (**fitted**) to be the right size, shape, or kind

²**fit** *adjective* (**fitter**) 1 in good health; 2 suitable; good enough; **fitness** *noun*

³**fit** *noun* 1 a sudden short attack of an illness; 2 a strong feeling

five *adjective, noun* the number 5; **fifth** *adjective, adverb*

fix *verb* 1 to fasten firmly; 2 to arrange; 3 to cook or prepare; 4 to put in order or mend

Union Jack
(United Kingdom)

Rising Sun
(Japan)

Stars and Stripes
(USA)

flag *noun* a piece of cloth with a pattern or picture on it, used as the sign of a country, club, etc

flake *noun* a small thin piece

flame *noun* a bright red or yellow piece of burning gas

¹**flap** *noun* a wide flat thin part of anything that folds or hangs down over an opening

²**flap** *verb* **(flapped)** to wave slowly up and down or to and fro, making a noise

¹**flash** *verb* **1** to shine for a moment; **2** to move very fast

²**flash** *noun* a sudden quick bright light

¹**flat** *adjective* **(flatter) 1** smooth and level with no pieces sticking out; **2** below the true note (music); **3** not having enough air in it (tyre); **flatten** *verb*; **flatness** *noun*

²**flat** *also* **apartment** *noun* a set of rooms on one floor of a building

flavour *noun* a taste; **flavour** *verb*; **flavouring** *noun*; **flavourless** *adjective*

flaw *noun* a small mark or crack, that makes something not perfect; **flaw** *verb*; **flawless** *adjective*; !! **floor**

flea *noun* a small jumping insect that bites people, dogs, etc; !! **flee**

flee *verb* **(fleeing, fled)** to escape quickly; !! **flea**

flesh *noun* **1** the soft substance, including fat and muscle, that covers the bones and lies under the skin; **2** the meat of animals used as food; **3** the soft part of a fruit or vegetable that can be eaten; **fleshy** *adjective*

flex *noun* a length of wire for carrying electricity

flexible *adjective* something that can bend easily

flight *noun* **1** the act of flying; **2** a trip by plane; **3** a group of birds or aircraft flying together; **4** a set of stairs

float *verb* to stay at the top of liquid or to be held up in air without sinking

¹**flood** *noun* the covering with water of a place that is usually dry

²**flood** *verb* to fill or become covered with water

floor *noun* **1** the part of a room on which you stand; **2** one level of a building; !! **flaw**

flour *noun* powder made from grain and used for making bread and cakes; **floury** *adjective*; !! **flower**

f

flow *verb* to run or spread smoothly; to pour; **flow** *noun*; **flowing** *adjective*

flowchart also **flow diagram** *noun* a drawing in which lines and arrows are used to show the order of the actions needed to do something or to solve a problem

fold *verb* to turn or bend one part of something onto another part of it; **fold** *noun*

follow *verb* **1** to come or go after somebody or something; **2** to go in the same direction; **3** to understand; **follower** *noun*

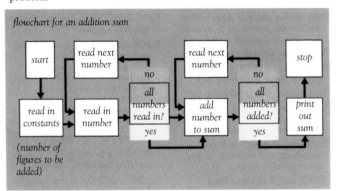

flowchart for an addition sum

start → read next number

read next number → stop

no

read in constants → read in number → all numbers read in? → add number to sum → all numbers added? → print out sum

no

yes

yes

(number of figures to be added)

¹**flower** *noun* the part of a plant that makes the seeds and is usually coloured; !! **flour**

²**flower** *verb* to produce flowers; !! **flour**

fluent *adjective* to speak, write or read easily; **fluently** *adverb*

flute *noun* a musical instrument that you blow

¹**fly** *verb* (**flies, flying, flew, flown**) **1** to move through the air using wings or in a machine; **2** to go quickly

²**fly** *noun* a small insect with wings

¹**focus** *verb* to concentrate

²**focus** *noun* a point or place which attention is diverted towards

fond *adjective* **1** loving; **2** to be **fond of** to have a great liking or love for; **fondly** *adverb*

food *noun* something for eating

¹**fool** *noun* a silly person; **foolish** *adjective*; **foolishly** *adverb*

²**fool** *verb* **1** to deceive or trick; **2** to behave in a silly way

foot *noun* (*plural* **feet**) **1** the part of the body at the end of the leg, on which a person or an animal stands: **footpath, footstep; 2** the lowest or bottom part of anything; **3** a measure of length equal to 12 inches or 30.48 centimetres

football *noun* a game in which two teams kick a ball and try to score goals; **footballer** *noun*

for *preposition* **1** meant to belong to, be given to, or be used in this way; **2** in order to reach, get, or have; **3** as a sign of; instead of; **4** in support of; **5** because of; **6** at the price of; **7** the length or distance of; **!! four**

forbid *verb* (**forbids, forbidding, forbade** *or* **forbad, forbidden**) to tell somebody not to do something

force *noun* **1** strength or power; **2** a group of specially trained people; **force** *verb*

forecast *verb* to say what you think will happen; **forecast** *noun*

forehead *noun* the part of the face above the eyes and below the hair

foreign *adjective* of or from another country; **foreigner** *noun*

forest *noun* a large area of land covered with trees and bushes

forever also **for ever** *adverb* always; for all time

forget *verb* (**forgets, forgetting, forgot, forgotten**) not to remember; to no longer have the memory of something

forgive *verb* (**forgives, forgiving, forgave, forgiven**) to say or feel that you are no longer angry about something and will not punish somebody

fork *noun* **1** an instrument with a handle at one end and two or more points at the other; **2** a place where something divides, or one of the divided parts

¹**form** *noun* **1** shape or appearance; **2** a kind or sort; **3** a special paper on which certain things must be written down; **4** a long wooden seat without a back; **5** a class in a school

²**form** *verb* **1** to take shape or appear; **2** to make; **3** to make up

fortnight *noun* two weeks

fortune *noun* **1** a great amount of money; **2** whatever happens in the future to a person by good or bad luck; **fortunate** *adjective*; **fortunately** *adverb*

forty *adjective, noun* the number 40; **fortieth** *adjective, adverb*

¹**forward** also **forwards** *adverb* **1** towards the front in the direction you are facing; **2** to an earlier time; **3** look forward to to think something will be pleasant; **forward** *adjective*

²**forward** *verb* to send on letters or parcels to a new address

fountain *noun* a stream of water that shoots straight up into the air from a pipe

a fountain in Florence, Italy

four *adjective, noun* the number 4; **fourth** *adjective, adverb*; !! **for**

fourteen *adjective, noun* the number 14; **fourteenth** *adjective, adverb*

fox *noun* (*female* **vixen**, *young* **cub**) a small wild animal like a dog, with a bushy tail and reddish fur

fraction *noun* a very small piece or amount; a part of a whole number (2/3, 7/16, etc)

frame *noun* **1** the rods and bars that are fitted together to make something or round which something is built: **framework**; **2** the pieces of wood, plastic, or metal round a picture; **frame** *verb*

free *adjective* **1** able to do what you like; not tied up or in prison; **2** not costing any money; given away; **3** not busy; not being used; **free** *verb*; **freedom** *noun*

freeze *verb* (**freezes, freezing, froze, frozen**) **1** to harden or become solid as a result of great cold; **2** to keep and store food by freezing it

freezer also **deep freeze** *noun* a large refrigerator for frozen food

frequency *noun* **1** the number of times something happens or is repeated during a certain amount of time; **2** a particular number of radio waves per second at which a radio signal is broadcast

frequent *adjective* something that happens often

fresh *adjective* **1** new or different; **2** newly made; **3** newly picked, grown, or supplied; **4** not preserved in tins, bottles, etc; not frozen; **5** clean or pure; **6** not tired; healthy; **freshness** *noun*; **freshly** *adverb*

Friday *noun* the sixth day of the week

fridge a machine in which food and drinks can be kept cool

friend *noun* a person you like and enjoy talking to and going out with; somebody who is kind and helpful; **friendliness** *noun*; **friendly** *adjective*; **friendship** *noun*

frighten *verb* to make somebody afraid

frog *noun* a small animal that can live in water and on land and has long back legs for swimming and jumping

South American poison arrow frog

from *preposition* **1** beginning at; **2** given or sent by; **3** out of; **4** using; **5** because of

front *noun* **1** the position directly before somebody or something; **2** the surface or part facing forwards, outwards, or upwards; **3** the most forward or important position; **4 in front of** in the position facing forward; whilst somebody is present; **front** *adjective*

frost _noun_ white powdery ice that forms on outside surfaces when the weather is very cold; **frosty** _adjective_

frown _verb_ to draw your eyebrows down and wrinkle your forehead when angry or worried; **frown** _noun_

fruit _noun_ the part of a tree or bush that contains seeds and is often sweet and used for food

fry _verb_ to cook in hot fat or oil

fuel _noun_ material that is used for producing heat or power by burning

full _adjective_ holding as much or as many people, objects, liquids, etc, as possible; **fully** _adverb_

full stop _noun_ the mark (.) at the end of a sentence or a shortened form of a word

fun _noun_ amusement and enjoyment

funeral _noun_ the time when a dead person is buried

fungus _noun_ (_plural_ **fungi** _or_ **funguses**) a type of plant without flowers, leaves, or greenery

fly agaric toadstool - a very poisonous fungus

funny _adjective_ **1** amusing; **2** strange; unusual

fur _noun_ the soft hair that covers the body of animals such as bears, rabbits, cats, etc; **furry** _adjective_; !! **fir**

furniture _noun_ all the things used in a house or room such as beds, chairs, tables, etc

a Tudor four poster bed

fuse _noun_ a short thin piece of wire placed in something electrical, which melts if too much power is used and prevents fires or other damage

¹**future** _noun_ **1** the time that will come; **2** things that will happen to somebody or something

²**future** _noun, adjective_ an action that will happen later: _the_ **future tense**

Gg

galaxy *noun* a very large group of stars

gale *noun* a strong wind

gallon *noun* a measure for liquids equal to eight pints or 4.546 litres

gallop *noun* the fastest movement of a horse; **gallop** *verb*

game *noun* **1** something you play, with rules that tell you what to do; **2** wild animals or birds that are hunted for food

gander *noun* a male goose

gang *noun* a group of people who go around together

gap *noun* an empty space; a narrow opening

garage *noun* a place where cars are kept or repaired

garden *noun* a piece of land, near a house or in a public place, on which flowers, trees, and vegetables may be grown; **garden** *verb*; **gardener** *noun*; **gardening** *noun*

gas *noun* (*plural* **gases**) **1** a substance like air, which is not solid or liquid; **2** a substance like this which is used for heating and cooking

gate *noun* a sort of door which closes an opening in a fence or wall

gather *verb* to come or bring together; **gathering** *noun*

gauge (*say* **gage**) *noun* an instrument for measuring such things as the amount of rain or the width of wire

Geiger counter for measuring radioactivity

gaze *verb* to look steadily at something for a long time; **gaze** *noun*

gear *noun* **1** a set of toothed wheels in an engine or a machine, which help to control the power, speed, or direction of movement; **2** clothes and things for doing an activity, such as swimming

general *adjective* about, for, or by everybody or everything

generally *adverb* usually

generous *adjective* ready to give money or be helpful or kind; **generously** *adverb*

genre *noun* a single category within a wide range of artistic material, such as crime, non-fiction and romance are all written **genres**

gentle *adjective* kind and friendly; soft and quiet; **gentleness** *noun*; **gently** *adverb*

gentleman *noun* a man who behaves well and can be trusted

geography *noun* the study of the world and its countries, seas, rivers, towns, etc; **geographer** *noun*; **geographical** *adjective*; **geographically** *adverb*

g

gerbil *noun* a small jumping animal like a large mouse, often kept as a pet

get *verb* (**gets, getting, got**) **1** to have; to receive; **2** to obtain or buy; to take; **3** to become; **4** to make happen; **5** to cause somebody to do something; **6** to arrive; **7** to catch an illness; **8 have got to** must

ghost *noun* the spirit of a dead person or animal that appears again; **ghostly** *adjective*

giant *noun* a very big, strong person who is written about in fairy stories; **giant** *adjective*

gift *noun* something that is given; a present

giraffe *noun* an animal with a very long neck and legs and a yellowish coat with dark spots

giraffe

girl *noun* a young female person

give *verb* (**gives, giving, gave, given**) **1** to hand something over to somebody; **2** to let somebody have something; **3** to pay; **4** to cause to experience; **5** to produce or supply; **6** to show; to tell in words; **7** to do: **give** *a speech*

glad *adjective* pleased and happy; **gladly** *adverb*; **gladness** *noun*

glance *verb* to look quickly; **glance** *noun*

glass *noun* **1** a hard clear material used for windows; **2** a drinking container made of this material

glasses *noun* two pieces of specially shaped glass held in a frame and worn in front of the eyes to help somebody to see better

glider *noun* a plane that flies on a current of air

glossary *noun* a list of words used in a book

glove *noun* a covering for the hand

glow *verb* **1** to give out heat and/or light without flames or smoke; **2** to look or feel warm or excited; **glow** *noun*

¹**glue** *noun* a sticky substance used for joining things together

²**glue** *verb* (**glues, gluing** *or* **glueing, glued**) to join with glue

gnaw (*say* **naw**) *verb* to keep biting something until it is worn away; !! **nor**

go *verb* (**goes, going, went, gone**) **1** to leave; **2** to travel or move; **3** to reach; **4** to do or start something: **go** *swimming*; **5** to have a usual or proper place; **6** to work properly; **7** to become; **8** to wear out; to disappear; to die

goal *noun* the place where the ball must go for a point to be won in football, hockey, etc: **goalkeeper**

goat *noun* (*female* **nanny**, *male* **billy**, *young* **kid**) an animal like a sheep, with horns and that gives milk and a hairy sort of wool

god *noun* **1** (*feminine* **goddess**) a being to whom people pray because they feel he or she has power over people and the world; **2 God** the being to whom Christians, Jews, and Muslims pray

gold *noun* **1** a yellow metal that costs a lot of money and is used for making jewellery, coins, etc; **2** the colour of this metal; **gold, golden** *adjective*

goldfish *noun* a small fish that is often kept as a pet

golf *noun* a game in which a small hard ball is hit with special golf clubs into holes on a golf course; **golfer** *noun*

¹**good** *adjective* (**better, best**) **1** having the right qualities; **2** kind; helpful; **3** well-behaved; **4** useful or suitable; **5** enjoyable; **6** able to do something; **7** large in size, amount, etc; **8** used in greetings: **Good morning, Goodbye; goodness** *noun*

²**good** *noun* what is right or useful

goods *noun* things that are bought, sold, or owned

goose *noun* (*plural* **geese**, *male* **gander**, *young* **gosling**) a large bird with webbed feet

gooseberry *noun* a small round green berry that grows on a bush

gorilla *noun* a large animal with human features, that is very strong, and lives in Africa; !! **guerrilla**

government *noun* the people who rule a country

grab *verb* (**grabbed**) to take hold of something with a sudden, rough movement; **grab** *noun*

gradual *adjective* happening slowly and little by little; **gradually** *adverb*

grain *noun* **1** a seed of rice, wheat, etc; **2** a small piece

gram *noun* a measure of weight equal to 0.035 ounces

grammar *noun* the way words are used together to make sense

grand *adjective* very large and fine

grandchild *noun* (*plural* **grandchildren**) the child of your child: **granddaughter, grandson**

grandparent *noun* the father or mother of your father or mother: **grandfather, grandmother**

grand prix *noun* a car race often around a track

grape *noun* a small round juicy fruit, usually green or dark purple, that grows in bunches and is used for making wine

grapefruit *noun* a large yellow fruit that is like an orange but is sour

grapefruit - a citrus fruit

graphics *noun* pictures in a computer program or game

grass *noun* a green plant that grows close to the ground and has thin leaves that cattle eat; **grassy** *adjective*

grasshopper *noun* a jumping insect that makes a sharp noise by rubbing parts of its body together

¹**grate** *verb* 1 to rub food on a hard rough surface so as to break it into small pieces; 2 to make a sharp unpleasant sound; **grater** *noun*; **grating** *noun*; !! **great**

²**grate** *noun* the bars and frame that hold the wood, coal, etc, in a fireplace; !! **great**

grateful *adjective* feeling or showing thanks to somebody; **gratefully** *adverb*

¹**grave** *noun* the place in the ground where a dead person is buried

²**grave** *adjective* serious; **gravely** *adverb*

gravity *noun* the natural force of the Earth, which makes things fall to the ground

gravy *noun* a sauce made from the juice which comes out of meat as it cooks

grease *noun* oil or fat; **grease** *verb*; **greasy** *adjective*

great *adjective* 1 very large, important, etc; 2 very good, enjoyable, or pleasant; 3 unusually good at something; **greatly** *adverb*; !! **grate**

great-grandchild *noun* the son or daughter of a grand-child: **great-granddaughter**, **great-grandson**

great-grandparent *noun* the father or mother of a grandparent: **great-grandfather**, **great-grandmother**

greed *noun* a wish to obtain more of something than you need, such as food or money; **greedy** *adjective*; **greedily** *adverb*

green *noun* 1 a colour between yellow and blue, which is that of leaves and grass; 2 a smooth piece of grass used for a special purpose; **green** *adjective*; **greenish** *adjective*

greengrocer *noun* a person who sells vegetables and fruit

greenhouse *noun* a building made of glass or plastic used to protect growing plants

greenhouse   sun's rays

glass lets sunlight through

heated interior helps plants to grow

glass prevents warm air escaping

greet *verb* to welcome with words or actions; **greeting** *noun*

grey *noun* a colour like black mixed with white, which is that of ashes and of rain clouds; **grey** *adjective*; **greyish** *adjective*

grin *noun* a wide smile that shows your teeth; **grin** *verb*

grip *verb* (**gripped**) to take a very tight hold of something; **grip** *noun*

groan *verb* to make a deep low sound to show you are in pain or are very sad; **groan** *noun*

grocer *noun* a shop that sells foods, like flour, sugar, rice, and other things for the home, such as matches and soap

ground *noun* **1** the surface of the Earth; **2** soil; earth

group *noun* a number of people or things placed together; a set; **group** *verb*

grow *verb* (**grows, growing, grew, grown**) **1** to get bigger, taller, or longer; **2** to live and be able to develop; **3** to cause to or allow to grow; **4** to become; **growth** *noun*

grown-up *noun* a fully grown person; **grown-up** *adjective*

grubby *adjective* dirty

grunt *noun* a short deep rough sound like that of a pig; **grunt** *verb*

guarantee *noun* a promise to repair or replace something if it does not work; **guarantee** *verb*

¹**guard** *noun* **1** a person who guards; **2** somebody in charge of a train; **3** something which covers and protects: **fireguard, mudguard**

²**guard** *verb* to watch over and keep safe; **guardian** *noun*

guerrilla also **guerilla** *noun* a person who fights secretly against the government or against an army; !! **gorilla**

guess *verb* to say something is correct or not correct without really knowing; **guess** *noun*

guest *noun* **1** a person you invite to stay in your home; **2** someone who stays at a hotel

guide *noun* something or somebody that shows the way or gives directions; **guide** *verb*; **guidance** *noun*

guilt *noun* knowing you have done wrong; **guiltily** *adverb*; **guiltless** *adjective*; **guilty** *adjective*

guinea pig *noun* **1** a small furry animal, often kept as a pet; **2** someone used as a test of something, such as a new drug or way of doing things

guitar *noun* a musical instrument usually with six strings played by plucking or strumming

electric base guitar

¹**gum** *noun* the part of the mouth in which your teeth are fixed

²**gum** *noun* **1** a substance used to stick things together; **2** a type of sweet

gun *noun* a weapon from which bullets are fired

gutter *noun* an open pipe at the edge of a roof or a channel at the side of the road to carry away water

gymnastics, gym *noun* the training of the body by exercises; **gymnasium** *noun*; **gymnast** *noun*

Hh

habit *noun* **1** something you always do; **2** a special kind of clothing, especially that worn by monks and nuns

hacker *noun* someone who breaks into a computer system; **hack** *verb*

haddock *noun* a common sea fish that is eaten

hail *noun* little balls of ice that fall from the clouds; **hail** *verb*

hair *noun* the fine threads that grow from the skin of a person or animal: **hairbrush, haircut, hairdresser**; **hairy** *adjective*; **hairless** *adjective*; !! **hare**

¹half *noun, pronoun (plural* **halves**) one of the two equal parts into which something is divided; 1/2; 50%; **half** *adjective*; **halfway** *adjective, adverb*

²half *adverb* **1** partly; not completely; **2 half past** thirty minutes after: **half past** *six*

hall *noun* **1** a large room in which meetings, dances, etc, can be held; **2** the space just inside the front door of a house, from which the rooms open; !! **haul**

Hallowe'en also **Halloween** *noun* the night of 31st October

ham *noun* meat from a pig's leg

hammer *noun* a tool with a heavy metal head for hitting in nails, or for breaking things; **hammer** *verb*

¹hand *noun* **1** the movable part at the end of the arm, including the fingers, with which you hold things; **2** a pointer or needle on a clock or machine; **handful** *noun*

²hand *verb* to give from your own hand into somebody else's: **hand over**

handbag *noun* a small bag for money and personal things

handkerchief *noun (plural* **handkerchiefs** *or* **handkerchieves**) a piece of cloth or thin soft paper for drying the nose, eyes, etc

¹handle *noun* a part of something for holding it or for opening it: **handlebars**

²handle *verb* **1** to feel or move with your hands; **2** to deal with; to control

handsome *adjective* good-looking and attractive; **handsomely** *adverb*

¹hang *verb* (**hangs, hanging, hung**) **1** to fix something at the top so that the lower part is free; **2** to be in such a position

²hang *verb* (**hangs, hanging, hanged**) to kill or die, as a punishment for a crime, by dropping with a rope round the neck

h

pumpkin lantern for Hallowe'en

happen *verb* **1** to take place; to be; **2** to do by chance; **happening** *noun*

happy *adjective* feeling very pleased; giving pleasure; **happily** *adverb*; **happiness** *noun*

harass *verb* to annoy or trouble somebody; **harassment** *noun*

harbour *noun* an area of sheltered water where ships are safe from rough seas

a harbour wall keeps out rough seas so that boats can be harboured safely

¹**hard** *adjective* **1** firm, solid, and not easily broken, pressed down, bent, etc; **2** difficult to do or understand; **harden** *verb*

²**hard** *adverb* **1** with great effort; **2** a lot; very much

hardly *adverb* almost not at all; only just

hardware *noun* **1** the machines that make up a computer; **2** goods for the home and garden, such as pans, tools, etc

hare *noun* (young **leveret**) an animal like a rabbit, with long ears and long back legs that make it able to run fast; !! **hair**

harm *noun* damage; wrong; **harm** *verb*; **harmful** *adjective*; **harmfully** *adverb*; **harmfulness** *noun*

harp *noun* a large musical instrument with strings, played by stroking or plucking with the hands; **harpist** *noun*

harvest *noun* **1** the time of year when crops are picked; **2** the amount picked; **harvest** *verb*

hat *noun* a covering placed on top of the head

hate *verb* to have a strong dislike for something or somebody; **hate** *noun*; **hateful** *adjective*; **hatred** *noun*

haul *verb* to pull hard; !! **hall**

haunt *verb* to appear in a place as a ghost

have *verb* (**has, having, had, haven't, hasn't, hadn't**) **1** also **have got** to possess or own; **2** to receive or take; **3** to enjoy or experience; **4** to cause to be done; **5** **had better** ought to; **6** **have to** also **have got to** must

hay *noun* grass that has been cut and dried and is used as food for horses, sheep, and cows: **haystack, haymaking**

he *pronoun* (**him, himself**) that male person or animal

h

¹**head** *noun* **1** the part of the body that contains the eyes, ears, nose and mouth, and the brain – in people on top of the body, in other animals in front: **headache, headband, headfirst**; **2** the chief person; a ruler or leader; **3** the front side of a coin which often has a picture of the ruler's head: *heads or tails?*; **4** the top or front part of something; **5 head over heels** turning over in the air headfirst

²**head** *verb* **1** to be at the front or in charge of something; **2** to strike a ball with the head; **header** *noun*

heading *noun* a title of a story or letter that stis at the top or beginning of the page

headphones *noun* a piece of apparatus made to fit over the ears, for listening to a radio, cassette player, etc

headphones

heal *verb* to make or become better; !! **heel**

health *noun* **1** the state of being well, without any illness; **2** the condition of the body; **healthily** *adverb*; **healthiness** *noun*; **healthy** *adjective*

heap *noun* a pile or mass of things one on top of another; **heap** *verb*

hear *verb* (**hears, hearing, heard**) **1** to receive and understand by using the ears; **2** to get news of; to be told; !! **here**

heart *noun* **1** the organ inside the chest that pumps the blood round the body: **heartbeat, heart attack**; **2** the centre of your feelings; your true nature; **3** a playing card with one or more figures of this shape printed on it in red; **4** the centre or middle of something; **heartless** *adjective*; **hearty** *adjective*

¹**heat** *noun* **1** hotness; warmth; **2** a part of a race or competition to decide who will be in the final

²**heat** *verb* to make or become warm or hot; **heater** *noun*

heaven *noun* the place where God or the gods are said to live and where good people are believed to go after they die

heavy *adjective* **1** of great weight, and not easy to move or lift; **2** of unusual force or amount; **heavily** *adverb*; **heaviness** *noun*

hedge *noun* a row of bushes or small trees acting as a fence

hedgehog *noun* a small insect-eating animal that comes out only at night. It rolls itself into a ball and sticks up sharp spines when it is afraid

heel *noun* **1** the back part of the foot; **2** the part of a shoe, sock, etc, that covers this; the raised part of a shoe underneath the foot; !! **heal**

height *noun* how tall or high something is

heir (*say* **air**) (*feminine* **heiress**) *noun* a person who gets money, property, or a title when somebody dies; !! **air**

helicopter *noun* a type of aircraft that is made to fly by a set of large fast-turning metal blades, and that can land in a small space, take off straight from the ground, and hover or hang in the air

passenger helicopter

hell *noun* the place where the Devil is said to live and where bad people are believed to go after they die

hello used as a greeting

helmet *noun* a hard covering to protect the head, worn by soldiers, policemen, etc

¹**help** *verb* **1** to do part of the work for somebody; **2** to be of use; **3 can't help** can't avoid or prevent; **helper** *noun*

²**help** *noun* **1** the act of helping; **2** something or somebody that helps; **helpful** *adjective*; **helpfully** *adverb*; **helpfulness** *noun*

hem *noun* the sewn bottom edge of a skirt, dress, etc; **hem** *verb*

hen *noun* (*male* **cock**; *young* **chick**) a female chicken often kept for its eggs on farms

¹**her** *adjective* belonging to her

²**her** *see* SHE

herb *noun* a plant used to flavour food. Can also be used in medicines or perfumes

herd *noun* a group of animals of one kind that live and feed together; **herd** *verb*

here *adverb* **1** at, in, or to this place; **2** at this point of time; !! **hear**

herring *noun* a fish which swims in large shoals in the sea and is eaten for food

hers *pronoun* that/those belonging to a female person

hibernate *verb* to be in a state like a long sleep during the winter, as some animals do; **hibernation** *noun*

hide *verb* (**hides, hiding, hid, hidden**) to put or keep out of sight; to make or keep secret

high *adjective, adverb* **1** at a point well above the ground; **2** important; chief; **3** near the top of the set of sounds that the ear can hear

high chair *noun* a chair with long legs and a tray in which a baby or small child can sit

hijack *verb* to force the driver of a plane, train, etc, to take you somewhere or give you something; **hijacker** *noun*

hill *noun* a raised piece of ground; a small mountain: **uphill, downhill; hilly** *adjective*

Hindu *noun* a person who follows the religion Hinduism

hip *noun* the fleshy part of either side of the human body above the legs

hippopotamus, hippo *noun* (*plural* **hippopotamuses** *or* **hippopotami, hippos**) a large animal with a thick skin, that lives near water

¹**his** *adjective* belonging to a male person

²**his** *pronoun* that/those belonging to a male person

history *noun* the study of past events; **historical** *adjective*; **historically** *adverb*

¹**hit** *verb* (**hits, hitting, hit**) to strike; to come against something with force

²**hit** *noun* **1** a blow; a stroke; **2** a successful song, film, etc

hive also **beehive** *noun* a place where bees live, like a small hut or box

hobby *noun* an enjoyable activity you do in your free time

hockey *noun* a game played by two teams of eleven players each, on a field with sticks and a ball

hold *verb* (**holds, holding, held**) **1** to keep or support with the hands; **2** to contain; **3** to possess; **4** to arrange and give an event, such as a party; **hold** *noun*; **holder** *noun*

hole *noun* **1** an empty space or opening within something; **2** the home of a small animal; !! **whole**

holiday *noun* **1** a time of rest from work or school; **2** going away to another country or place for a time to rest and enjoy yourself

hollow *adjective* having an empty space inside; not solid

holly *noun* a small tree with dark green prickly leaves and red berries

hologram, holograph *noun* a picture, that looks very real produced by lasers; **holograph** *verb*; **holography** *noun*

holy *adjective* of God and religion

home *noun* the house or place where somebody lives; **home** *adjective*; **homeless** *adjective*; **homelessness** *noun*

homonym *noun* a word which has the same spelling and sound as another, but a different meaning

honest (*say* **onest**) *adjective* not telling lies or deceiving people; fair and true; **honestly** *adverb*; **honesty** *noun*

honey *noun* the sweet sticky material produced by bees

honeycomb with worker bee

h

French horn

honour (*say* **onor**) *noun* great respect; **honour** *verb*; **honourable** *adjective*

hood *noun* **1** a covering for the head and neck usually fastened to the back of a coat; **2** a folding cover over a car, pram, etc

hoof *noun* (*plural* **hoofs** *or* **hooves**) the hard foot of certain animals, such as horses and cows

¹**hook** *noun* a curved piece of metal, plastic, etc, for catching something on or hanging things on

²**hook** *verb* **1** to catch with a hook; **2** to hang on or fasten with a hook

hoop *noun* a round band of wood or metal; a ring

hop *verb* (**hopped**) **1** to jump on one leg; **2** to move along by jumping, like some birds and small creatures

hope *verb* to wish for and expect; **hope** *noun*; **hopeful** *adjective*; **hopefully** *adverb*; **hopeless** *adjective*; **hopelessly** *adverb*

horizon *noun* the line that represents the furthest distance that you can see to

horizontal *adjective* something which is flat: a line that goes from left to right

horn *noun* **1** one of two hard pointed growths on the top of the heads of some animals such as cattle, sheep, and goats; **2** the material that these growths are made of; **3** a musical instrument that you blow; **4** an instrument in a car, bus, etc, that makes a noise to warn people; **horned** *adjective*; **hornless** *adjective*

horrendous *adjective* really terrible; causing great fear

horrible *adjective* very unkind, unpleasant, or ugly; **horribly** *adverb*

horror *noun* great shock, fear, and dislike; **horrid** *adjective*; **horridly** *adverb*; **horridness** *noun*

horse *noun* a large strong animal with a mane, tail, and hooves, that people ride and used for pulling and carrying heavy things in old times: **horseback, horsehair, horseshoe**

hose *also* **hosepipe** *noun* a piece of rubber or plastic tube that can direct water onto fires, a garden, etc

hospital *noun* a place where ill people stay and have treatment

host (*feminine* **hostess**) *noun* a person who receives and looks after guests

hot *adjective* (**hotter**) **1** having a lot of heat; **2** having a burning taste; **hotness** *noun*

hotel *noun* a building where people can stay if they pay

h

hour (*say* **our**) *noun* a measure of time; sixty minutes; **hourly** *adverb*; !! **our**

house *noun* a building for people to live in: **household, housekeeper, housewife, housework**

House of Commons *noun* the lower, but more powerful, of the two parts of the British Parliament

House of Lords *noun* the upper, but less powerful, of the two parts of the British Parliament

hover *verb* to stay in the air in one place

hovercraft *noun* (*trademark*) a sort of boat that moves over land or water by means of a strong force of air underneath

how *adverb* **1** in what way or by what means; **2** in what condition of health or mind; **3** by what amount

howl *noun* a long loud cry like that made by wolves and dogs; **howl** *verb*

hug *verb* (**hugged**) to hold tightly in the arms; **hug** *noun*

huge *adjective* very big; **hugeness** *noun*

hum *verb* (**hummed**) **1** to make a buzzing sound like a bee; **2** to sing with the lips closed; **hum** *noun*

¹**human** *adjective* of or like a person

²**human** also **human being** *noun* a man, woman, or child, not an animal

humour *noun* the ability to laugh at things or make other people laugh; **humorous** *adjective*

this warning road sign shows a hump-back bridge ahead

hump *noun* a lump or round part that sticks out

hundred *adjective, noun* the number 100; **hundredth** *adjective, adverb*

hunger *noun* the wish or need for food; **hungrily** *adverb*; **hungry** *adjective*

hunt *verb* **1** to chase and kill animals and birds either for food or sport; **2** to search for; **hunt** *noun*; **hunter** *noun*

hurricane *noun* a violent wind storm

hurry *verb* to move or do something quickly; **hurry** *noun*

hurt *verb* (**hurts, hurting, hurt**) to cause pain and/or injury; to damage; **hurt** *noun*; **hurtful** *adjective*

husband *noun* the man to whom a woman is married

hut *noun* a small building, often made of wood

hutch *noun* a small box or cage for keeping rabbits in

hydrogen *noun* a colourless gas that is lighter than air and burns very easily

hymn *noun* a song to or about God; !! **him**

hyphen *noun* a short line (-) that joins words or parts of words

Ii

I *pronoun* (**me, myself**) the person speaking

ice *noun* water that has frozen to a solid; **icy** *adjective*

iceberg *noun* a large piece of ice that has broken away from a very big ice glacier

ice cream *noun* a sweet frozen mixture, usually containing milk products

icicle *noun* a pointed stick of ice formed when running water freezes

stalactites and stalagmites look like stone icicles - they form in caves from the constant dripping of water

icing *noun* a sweet and either creamy or hard covering for cakes, biscuits, etc

idea *noun* a picture in the mind; a thought of something new to do

ideal *adjective* perfect; the best possible

identical *adjective* exactly the same

identify *verb* to say who somebody is or what something is; **identification** *noun*; **identity** *noun*

idle *adjective* **1** not working; not doing anything; **2** lazy; **idleness** *noun*; **idly** *adverb*; !! **idol**

idol *noun* **1** a statue worshipped as a god; **2** somebody who is greatly loved or admired; !! **idle**

i.e. that is to say

if *conjunction* on condition that; whether

ignorant *adjective* not knowing much; not having been taught; **ignorance** *noun*

ignore *verb* to take no notice

¹**ill** *adjective* not well

²**ill** *adverb* (**worse, worst**) badly, cruelly, or unpleasantly: *The child has been ill-treated*

illness *noun* a disease; sickness

illustration *noun* a picture to go with the words of a book, a speaker, etc; **illustrate** *verb*; **illustrator** *noun*

image *noun* a picture

imagine *verb* **1** to form a picture of something in the mind; **2** to suppose or have an idea about; **imaginary** *adjective*; **imagination** *noun*; **imaginative** *adjective*

immediate *adjective* done or needed at once; **immediately** *adverb*

impatient *adjective* not able to wait for something to happen; **impatience** *noun*; **impatiently** *adverb*

important *adjective* powerful; having a big effect; **importance** *noun*; **importantly** *adverb*

impossible *adjective* not possible; not able to be done; **impossibility** *noun*; **impossibly** *adverb*

impress *verb* to cause admiration; to have a strong effect on the mind; **impression** *noun*; **impressive** *adjective*; **impressively** *adverb*

improve *verb* to make or get better; **improvement** *noun*

in *preposition, adverb* **1** contained or surrounded by something; within; inside; **2** during; at the time of; !! **inn**

include *verb* to have or put in as a part; to contain

increase *verb* to make or become larger in amount or number; **increase** *noun*; **increasingly** *adverb*

incredible *adjective* too strange or good to be believed; **incredibly** *adverb*

indeed *adverb* really; certainly

independent *adjective* not needing other things or people; **independence** *noun*; **independently** *adverb*

index *noun* an alphabetical list in the back of a book which tells you the page number and topic so that you can find what you are looking for easily

indigo *noun* a dark purple-blue colour

indoor *adjective* done, used, etc, indoors

indoors *adverb* to, in, or into the inside of a building

industry *noun* the making of machines, getting oil out of the ground, or other activities when employing lots of people: *the computer* **industry**; **industrial** *adjective*

infant *noun* a very young child

infect *verb* to put disease into a person's body; **infection** *noun*; **infectious** *adjective*

influence *verb* to have an effect on; **influence** *noun*

inform *verb* to tell

information *noun* **1** facts or other things that people know; **2** these things stored in a computer

initial *noun* a large letter at the beginning of a name, used to stand for the name

inject *verb* to give medicine through the skin, with a needle; **injection** *noun*

injure *verb* to hurt; **injury** *noun*

ink *noun* coloured liquid used for writing or drawing; **inky** *adjective*

inn *noun* a pub or small hotel; !! **in**

inner *adjective* inside; closest to the centre

input *verb* to put data into a computer; **input** *noun*

insect *noun* a small creature with six legs and a body divided into three parts, such as an ant or fly

¹**inside** *noun* the area within something else; that part that is nearest to the centre, or that faces away from other people or from the open air

²**inside** *preposition, adjective, adverb* in; on or to the inside of something

instead *adverb* in place of somebody or something

instruct *verb* **1** to teach; **2** to order; **instruction** *noun*

instructions *noun* a list of directions which tell you how to do something

instrument *noun* **1** a tool; **2** an object such as a piano, horn, etc, played to give music *an integrated circuit as on a microchip*

integrated circuit *noun* a tiny electronic circuit on a single computer chip

intelligence *noun* the ability to learn and understand; **intelligent** *adjective*

intend *verb* to plan to do something; **intention** *noun*

interest *noun* wanting to know more about something; getting pleasure from studying something; **interest** *verb*; **interesting** *adjective*; **interestingly** *adverb*

interfere *verb* to get in the way; to prevent somebody from doing something; **interference** *noun*; **interfering** *adjective*

international *adjective* involving several nations **internationally** *adverb*

internet *noun* an electronic system that allows people to search the world-wide-web and communicate with one another through computers

interrupt *verb* to stop something continuing; to break in on somebody who is already speaking; **interruption** *noun*

into *preposition* to the inside of; in

introduce *verb* **1** to make two people known for the first time to each other; **2** to bring in a new thing; **introduction** *noun*

invent *verb* to make up or produce something new; **invention** *noun*; **inventor** *noun*

invisible *adjective* not able to be seen

invite *verb* to ask somebody to do something or go somewhere, such as to a party; **invitation** *noun*

involve *verb* to be part of something

inwards *adverb* towards the inside

¹iron *noun* **1** a useful grey-white metal; **2** a heavy metal object with a handle, pointed at the front and flat underneath, used for making clothes smooth: **ironing board**

²iron *verb* to make smooth with an iron

irritate *verb* **1** to annoy; **2** to make sore; **irritation** *noun*

island *noun* a piece of land surrounded by water

it *pronoun* (**itself**) **1** that thing already mentioned; **2** that person or animal whose sex is not known or not thought important

italics *noun* a style of handwriting in which the letters slant to one side

itch *verb* to feel or cause a soreness which you want to scratch; **itch** *noun*; **itchy** *adjective*; **itchiness** *noun*

its *adjective* belonging to it; !! **it's**

it's it is; it has; !! **its**

ivy *noun* a plant which climbs up walls and has shiny leaves

Jj

jack *noun* **1** an apparatus for lifting something heavy, such as a car, off the ground; **2** also **knave** any of the four playing cards with a picture of a man, that comes between the 10 and the queen

car jack

jacket *noun* a short coat

jail also **gaol** *verb* to put in prison; **jail** *noun*

¹**jam** *noun* sweet food made of fruit boiled in sugar, for spreading on bread

²**jam** *noun* a mass of people or things: *a traffic* **jam**

³**jam** *verb* (**jammed**) **1** to pack tightly into a small space; to push or press together; **2** to get stuck

January *noun* the first month of the year

jar *noun* a container like a bottle with a short neck and wide mouth

javelin *noun* a light throwing spear used in sport

jaw *noun* either of the two face bones which hold the teeth

jazz *noun* a type of music with a strong beat

jealous *adjective* **1** wanting to get what somebody else has; **2** being afraid of losing what you have; **jealously** *adverb*; **jealousy** *noun*

jeans *noun* strong cotton trousers that are often blue

jelly *noun* a soft food that shakes when moved

jersey *noun* a sweater

jet *noun* **1** a type of aircraft that has a jet engine; **2** a narrow stream of liquid, gas, etc, forced through a small hole

Jew *noun* a person belonging to the worldwide group descended from the people of ancient Israel and practising their religion; **Jewish** *adjective*

jewel *noun* a precious stone, used as an ornament

jewellery or **jewelry** *noun* ornaments with jewels

jigsaw puzzle or **jigsaw** *noun* a picture made up of pieces that have to be fitted together

job *noun* **1** a piece of work; **2** regular work for which you are paid

jockey *noun* a person who rides in horse races

jog *verb* (**jogged**) **1** to run slowly and steadily; to run like this to keep fit; **2** to shake or push slightly; **jog** *noun*; **jogger** *noun*; **jogging** *noun*

join *verb* **1** to fasten together; to connect; **2** to become a member of a group; **join** *noun*

j

joint *noun* **1** a join; a thing used for making a join; **2** a place where two or more bones fit together; **3** a large piece of meat

joke *noun* anything said or done to cause amusement; **joke** *verb*; **jokingly** *adverb*

journey *noun* (*plural* **journeys**) a trip of some distance

joy *noun* great happiness

joystick *noun* a lever in a control box that is connected to a computer to move figures, pictures, etc, about on a computer screen, especially in computer games

¹**judge** *verb* **1** to act as a judge; **2** to give a decision about somebody or something; **3** to give an opinion about

²**judge** *noun* **1** the person who has the power to decide questions brought before a court of law; **2** a person who decides who has won a competition; **judgement, judgment** *noun*

jug *noun* a pot for liquids, with a handle and a lip for pouring

juggle *verb* to keep several things in the air at the same time, throwing them up and catching them; **juggler** *noun*

juggler

juice *noun* the liquid part of fruit, vegetables, and meat; **juiciness** *noun*; **juicy** *adjective*

July *noun* the seventh month of the year

¹**jump** *verb* **1** to move your body suddenly and quickly off the ground, into the air, or over something; **2** to make a quick sudden movement

²**jump** *noun* **1** an act of jumping; **2** something you jump over in a race

June *noun* the sixth month of the year

junior *adjective* **1** younger; **2** of lower importance or position; **junior** *noun*

junk food *noun* food that does not have much nutritional value

Jupiter *noun* the largest planet of the solar system

*the planet Jupiter -
the red spot is a violent storm*

¹**just** *adverb* **1** exactly; **2** **just now** very near the present time; **3** hardly; almost not; **4** only

²**just** *adjective* fair and honest; **justice** *noun*; **justly** *adverb*

justify *verb* to support a choice or actions with evidence

Kk

kaleidoscope *noun* a tube fitted with mirrors and pieces of coloured glass, which shows coloured patterns when turned

kangaroo *noun* (*young* **joey**) an animal that jumps along on large back legs and carries its young in a special pocket

red kangaroo with a joey in its pouch

kebab *noun* pieces of meat and vegetables that are put on a skewer and grilled

keen *adjective* eager to do something; liking to do something; **keenly** *adverb*; **keenness** *noun*

keep *verb* (**keeps, keeping, kept**) **1** to have without giving back; **2 keep on** to do again and again; **3** to have or hold for some time; **4** to take care of; **5** to own; to have the use of; **6** to cause to continue, to stay, or to remain

kennel *noun* a small house for a dog

kerb *noun* a line of raised stones separating the footpath from the road

ketchup *noun* a sauce, made usually of tomatoes, for flavouring food

kettle *noun* a pot with a lid, handle, and spout for heating water to make tea, coffee, etc

key *noun* **1** a metal instrument for locking or unlocking a door, winding a clock, etc: **keyhole, key ring**; **2** a part of a piano, computer, etc, that is pressed with the finger: **keyboard**; **3** something that explains or helps you to understand, such as the list of symbols or abbreviations on a map; **4** a set of musical notes with a certain starting note

kick *verb* **1** to hit with the foot; **2** to move the feet backwards and forwards; **kick** *noun*; **kicker** *noun*

kid *noun* **1** a child or young person; **2** a young goat

kidnap *verb* to take somebody away and ask for money in return for bringing him or her back safely; **kidnapper** *noun*

kill *verb* to cause somebody or something to die; **killer** *noun*

kilogram also **kilo** *noun* a measure of weight equal to 1000 grams or 2.21 pounds

kilometre *noun* a measure of length equal to 1000 metres or 0.62 miles

¹**kind** (*say* **kynd**) *noun* a group that are alike; type; sort

²**kind** (*say* **kynd**) *adjective* helpful; gentle and wanting to do good; **kindness** *noun*

k

king *noun* **1** the male ruler of a country: **kingdom**; **2** any of the four playing cards with a picture of a king

kipper *noun* a smoked salted herring used for food

kiss *verb* to touch with the lips as a greeting or sign of love; **kiss** *noun*

kitchen *noun* a room used for cooking

kite *noun* a very light frame covered with paper or cloth for flying at the end of a long string

kitten *noun* a young cat

knee *noun* the middle joint of the leg

kneel *verb* (**kneels, kneeling, knelt**) to go down on the knees

knife *noun* (*plural* **knives**) a blade fixed in a handle for cutting

knight *noun* **1** a man given the title 'Sir' by the king or queen of Great Britain; **2** a soldier on horseback serving a ruler; **!! night**

knight - a chess piece: the horses head symbolises a soldier on horseback

knit *verb* (**knits, knitting, knitted** *or* **knit**) **1** to make a sort of cloth or a piece of clothing by joining threads using long knitting needles; **2** to join together closely; **knitter** *noun*; **knitting** *noun*

knob *noun* a round lump, handle, or control button; **knobbly** *adjective*

¹**knock** *verb* **1** to strike something so that it makes a noise; **2** to hit hard

²**knock** *noun* **1** a sound caused by knocking; **2** a hit

knot *noun* **1** a fastening formed by tying two ends of something together; **2** a hard mass in wood where a branch has come off a tree; **3** a measure of the speed of a ship, 1852 metres or 6076.12 feet per hour; **knot** *verb*; **!! not**

figure of eight knot

know *verb* (**knows, knowing, knew, known**) **1** to have in the mind; **2** to have learnt; **3** to have seen, heard, etc, before; to recognise somebody or something; **knowledge** *noun*; **!! no**

knuckle *noun* a joint in the finger

Ll

label *noun* a piece of paper fixed to something, on which is written what it is, where it is to go, etc; **label** *verb*

lace *noun* **1** a string for fastening the edges of something together: **shoelaces**; **2** pretty cloth with a pattern of holes in it

ladder *noun* a frame of two bars or ropes of equal length joined by shorter bars that form steps for climbing

lady *noun* **1** a polite way of saying woman; **2 Lady** the wife of a Lord or knight; the daughter of an earl, duke, etc

ladybird *noun* a small round beetle, usually red with black spots

lake *noun* a large mass of water surrounded by land

lamb (*say* lam) *noun* **1** a young sheep; **2** the meat of sheep

lamp *noun* an object for giving light: **table lamp; street lamp**

lamppost *noun* a tall post with a light at the top

¹**land** *noun* **1** the solid dry part of the Earth's surface; **2** a country

²**land** *verb* to come to, bring to, or put on land

landing *noun* the level space or passage at the top of stairs

lane *noun* **1** a narrow, often winding, road; **2** any of the parallel parts into which wide roads are divided; **!! lain**

language *noun* **1** the words people use in speaking or writing; **2** a system of signs for use in a computer

laptop *noun* a small computer that you can carry round with you

laptop computer

large *adjective* more than usual in size, number, or amount; big; **largely** *adverb*

lark *noun* a small light brown bird with long pointed wings

laser *noun* a machine with a very strong, very narrow beam of light used to cut materials, send messages, etc

argon laser beam - for measuring distances to objects in space

¹**last** *adjective, adverb, pronoun* **1** after all others; **2** the one before now; most recent

²**last** *verb* to continue

late *adjective, adverb* arriving, developing, happening, etc, after the expected time; **lateness** *noun*

lately *adverb* recently

laugh *verb* to make a sound to show that you are pleased, happy, amused, etc; **laugh** *noun*; **laughter** *noun*

launch *verb* **1** to set a boat into the water; **2** to send a rocket into space: **launch pad, launching site**

launching the American space shuttle

launderette *noun* a place where the public can wash clothes in machines that work when coins are put into them

laundry *noun* **1** a place where clothes are washed and ironed; **2** clothes, sheets, etc, that need washing or have just been washed

lava *noun* very hot liquid rock that comes out of a volcano

lavatory *noun* **1** a large seatlike bowl connected to a drain, used for passing body waste; **2** a room or building containing this

law *noun* a rule made by the government that everybody must follow; **lawful** *adjective*; **lawyer** *noun*

lawn *noun* a stretch of smooth ground covered with short grass: **lawn mower**

¹**lay** *verb* (**lays, laying, laid**) **1** to place or set; to put in a certain position; **2** to produce an egg or eggs

²**lay** *see* LIE

layer *noun* a thickness of some material laid over something or put between two things

layout *noun* the way something, such as a garden, is arranged

lazy *adjective* not wanting to work; **lazily** *adverb*; **laziness** *noun*

¹**lead** (*say like* need) *verb* (**leads, leading, led**) **1** to show somebody the way; to guide; **2** to be the chief person in doing something; to be first, especially in a race or competition; **leader** *noun*

²**lead** (*say like* need) *noun* **1** the first or front place; a guiding example; **2** the chief acting part in a play or film; **3** *also* **leash** a length of leather, chain, etc, tied to a dog to control it; **4** a wire that carries electrical power

³**lead** (*say like* dead) *noun* **1** a soft heavy metal, sometimes used as a covering for roofs; **2** the black substance in the middle of pencils; !! **led**

leaf *noun* (*plural* **leaves**) one of the flat parts of a plant that grow from a stem or branch

leak *noun* a hole or crack through which a liquid or gas may pass in or out; **leak** *verb*; **leaky** *adjective*; !! **leek**

¹**lean** *verb* (**leans, leaning, leant** *or* **leaned**) **1** to bend forwards, backwards, sideways, or towards; **2** to rest something against or on another

²**lean** *adjective* without much fat; thin; **leanness** *noun*

leap *verb* (**leaps, leaping, leapt** *or* **leaped**) to jump; **leap** *noun*

learn *verb* (**learns, learning, learned** *or* **learnt**) **1** to get knowledge or skill; **2** to find out; **learner** *noun*; **learning** *noun*

least *noun, adjective, adverb* **1** the smallest thing, amount, etc; **2** *see* LITTLE

leather *noun* animal skin treated for use in shoes, jackets, etc

¹**leave** *verb* (**leaves, leaving, left**) **1** to go away from; **2** to allow something to stay somewhere; **3** to let things stay as they are

²**leave** *noun* a short time away from work

leek *noun* a vegetable like an onion, with a long white fleshy stem; !! **leak**

¹**left** *noun, adjective* the side or direction opposite to right

²**left** *see* LEAVE

leg *noun* **1** the part of the body on which an animal walks and which supports its body; **2** the part of a piece of clothing that covers the leg; **3** one of the pieces of wood, metal, or plastic on which a table, chair, etc, stands

legal *adjective* allowed by the law; **legally** *adverb*

legend *noun* a story that has been told and retold for a long time, often supposed to be based on something real

legible *adjective* readable

lemon *noun* **1** a fruit with a yellow skin and sour juice; **2** a light bright yellow colour; **lemon** *adjective*

lemonade *noun* a drink tasting of lemons and usually containing bubbles of gas

lend *verb* (**lends, lending, lent**) to give somebody the use of something, such as money or a book for a short time, after which he or she must give it back; **lender** *noun*

length *noun* the measurement from one end of something to the other; **lengthen** *verb*; **lengthy** *adjective*

lens *noun* (*plural* **lenses**) a piece of glass or plastic with curved surfaces, used in cameras, telescopes, microscopes, glasses, etc, for seeing things clearly

a fisheye lens creates a curved, slightly distorted picture

Lent *noun* the forty days before Easter, during which many Christians give up some of their usual pleasures

leopard *noun* (*female* **leopardess**) a large meat-eating wild animal of the cat family, that is yellowish with black spots

leotard *noun* a piece of clothing that fits tightly, worn when doing exercise, etc

less *noun, adjective, adverb* **1** a smaller amount; not so much; **2** *see* LITTLE

lesson *noun* **1** part of a school day, when a pupil or class studies a subject; **2** something that we must learn

let *verb* **(lets, letting, let) 1** to allow to do or happen; **2** to give the use of a room, a building, land, etc, in return for money; **3 let's** let us; used when you ask somebody to do something with you

letter *noun* **1** a written or printed message sent to somebody, usually in an envelope; **2** one of the signs we use in writing

lettuce *noun* a garden plant with large pale green leaves which are used in salads

¹level *adjective* **1** having a surface that is the same height above the ground all over; **2** flat; smooth; **3** equal

²level *verb* **(levelled)** to make or become flat

a carpenter's spirit level

lever *noun* a long bar used for lifting or moving something heavy

leveret *noun* a young hare

library *noun* **1** a room or a building that contains books that may be looked at or borrowed: **public library**; **2** someone's collection of books

licence *noun* a written or printed paper which allows you to do something: **driving licence**; !! **license**

license *verb* to give or get permission to do something; !! **licence**

lick *verb* to move the tongue across something in order to taste, clean, make wet, etc; **lick** *noun*

lid *noun* **1** the top of a box or other hollow container, that can be taken off; **2** an eyelid

¹lie *verb* **(lies, lying, lay, lain) 1** to have your body in a flat resting position on something such as the ground or a bed; **2** to be or stay in a certain place

²lie *noun* something said that is not true; **lie** *verb*

life *noun* **(***plural* **lives) 1** the active force that makes humans, animals, and plants able to grow and produce young ones, and that makes them different from stones, machines, objects, etc; **2** the time that humans, animals, and plants are alive; **3** the way somebody lives or spends their time; **4** activity; strength; cheerfulness

life-cycle *noun* the entire process of any life, whether animal or plant, from beginning to end

¹lift *verb* to pick up; to pick up and put in a higher place; to raise

²lift *noun* **1** a machine in a building for taking people and goods from one floor to another; **2** a free ride in a vehicle

lift-off *noun* the start of the flight of a spacecraft

¹light *noun* **1** that which makes you able to see things; **2** something that gives out light such as a lamp or torch; **3** something that will make something else start burning

²light *adjective* **1** having light; not dark; bright; **2** not deep or dark in colour; pale

³**light** *verb* (**lights, lighting, lit** *or* **lighted**) **1** to make a fire, match, etc, start to burn; **2** to give light to something

⁴**light** *adjective* of little weight; not heavy; **lightly** *adverb*; **lightness** *noun*

lighten *verb* to make or become brighter or less dark; **lightening** *noun*; !! **lightning**

lighthouse *noun* a tower with a powerful flashing light that guides ships or warns them of dangerous rocks

lightning *noun* a powerful flash of light in the sky, usually followed by thunder; !! **lightening**

forked lightening

light year *noun* a unit of length in astronomy equal to the distance that light travels in one year in a vacuum: 9460 thousand million kilometres (5878 thousand million miles)

¹**like** *verb* **1** to be fond of; to find pleasant; **2** to wish; **liking** *noun*

²**like** *adjective, preposition* **1** in the same way as; of the same kind; **2** for example; **likeness** *noun*; **likewise** *adverb*

likely *adjective* **1** expected; **2** suitable

lilac *noun* a tree with pinkish purple or white flowers giving a sweet smell

lily *noun* a plant with large white flowers

limb (*say* lim) *noun* a part of the body, such as an arm or a leg

lime *noun* a fruit like a small green lemon

¹**limp** *verb* to walk as if your leg or foot has been hurt; **limp** *noun*

²**limp** *adjective* not stiff or firm

line *noun* **1** a long very thin mark which can be drawn on a surface; **2** a piece of string, wire, or thin cord: **fishing line**; **3** a set of people or things one after the other or beside each other; a row

lion *noun* (*female* **lioness**, *young* **cub**) a large wild animal of the cat family. The male has a thick mane over the head and shoulders

lion cub

lip *noun* **1** one of the two soft pink edges of the mouth: **lipstick**; **2** the edge of something such as a cup

liquid *noun* a substance, like water, that is not solid or gas, that flows and has no fixed shape

list *noun* a set of names of things written one after the other, so as to remember them

listen *verb* to try to hear; to pay attention to what someone is saying; **listener** *noun*

literacy *noun* the ability to read

litre *noun* a measure of liquid equal to 1.759 pints

litter *noun* **1** waste paper and other things thrown away; **2** a group of young animals born at the same time

¹**little** *adjective* small; not big; young

²**little** *adjective, adverb, noun* (**less, least**) **1** a small amount, but at least some; **2** not much; not enough

¹**live** (*say* **liv**) *verb* **1** to be alive; to have life; **2** to have your home somewhere; to stay in a place or at a house; **3** to keep yourself alive by eating food or by working

²**live** (*say* **like dive**) *adjective* **1** having life; not dead; **2** seen and/or heard as it happens; not recorded: *a live television programme*; **3** carrying electricity which can kill anyone who touches it

lizard *noun* a reptile with a rough skin, four legs, and a long tail

a cave lizard from Chile, South America

¹**load** *verb* **1** to put a full load on or in something; **2** to put bullets into a gun or film into a camera; **3** to put a program onto a computer

²**load** *noun* things that are carried by train, ship, or lorry

loaf *noun* (*plural* **loaves**) bread shaped and baked in one large piece

lobster *noun* a sea animal with a shell, eight legs, and a pair of powerful claws, eaten as food

local *adjective* in a certain place that is near the place or area in which you live

location *noun* where something is

lock *noun* a thing for closing and fastening something by means of a key or special number; **lock** *verb*

log *noun* a thick piece of wood from a tree

lollipop *noun* a sweet on a stick

lonely *adjective* unhappy because of being on your own or without friends; **loneliness** *noun*

¹**long** *adjective* **1** measuring a great distance or time from one end to the other; **2** covering a certain distance or time

²**long** *adverb* for a long time

³**long** *verb* to want very much; **longing** *noun, adjective*; **longingly** *adverb*

long wave *noun* radio broadcasting on waves of 1000 metres or more in length

look *verb* **1** to try to see; to use your eyes; **2** to seem to be; **look** *noun*

loop *noun* a ring made by a piece of rope, string, etc, crossing itself

loose *adjective* **1** not tied up, shut up, etc; **2** not firmly fixed; not tight; **loosely** *adverb*; **loosen** *verb*; **looseness** *noun*; !! **lose**

lord *noun* **1** a man who rules people; a master; **2 Lord** a title for a man of high position

lorry also **truck** *noun* a large motor vehicle for carrying goods

car transporter

lose *verb* (**loses, losing, lost**) **1** not to keep; not to have something any more; not to find; **2** not to win; not to do well; !! **loose**

lost *adjective* not able to find your way

lot *noun* **a lot** a large number or amount; much

loud *adjective* being or producing much sound; not quiet; noisy; **loudly** *adverb*; **loudness** *noun*

loudspeaker also **speaker** *noun* an apparatus that turns electrical current into sound

love *noun* **1** a strong warm feeling of liking somebody or something very much; **2** a person who is loved; **lovable** *adjective*; **love** *verb*; **loving** *adjective*; **lovingly** *adjective*

lovely *adjective* **1** beautiful, attractive, etc; **2** very pleasant; **loveliness** *noun*

low *adjective* **1** near the ground; not high; **2** not loud; soft; not high in sound; **lower** *verb*; **lowness** *noun*

loyal *adjective* true to our friends, country, etc; faithful; **loyally** *adverb*; **loyalty** *noun*

luck *noun* good or bad things which happen to you by chance; fate; **luckily** *adverb*; **lucky** *adjective*

luggage *noun* the cases and bags that you take with you when you travel

lukewarm *adjective* not much hotter than cool

lump *noun* **1** a mass of something solid without a special size or shape; **2** a hard swelling on the body

lunar *adjective* of the moon; made for use on or around the moon: **lunar module**

lunch *noun* a meal eaten in the middle of the day

lung *noun* either of the two organs for breathing in the chest of humans and certain other creatures

luxury *noun* **1** great comfort; **2** something not necessary and not often had or done but which is very pleasant

Mm

macaroni *noun* a food made of thin tubes of pasta

machine *noun* an instrument or apparatus that uses power (such as electricity) to do work; **machinery** *noun*

mackerel *noun* a sea fish with green and dark blue stripes on its back

mad *adjective* 1 very foolish; 2 angry

magazine *noun* a thin book with a paper cover that contains articles or stories, pictures, and advertisements, and that is sold usually every week or month

magic *noun* 1 the use of spells, spirits, secret forces, etc, to try to control events; 2 the skill used by a conjuror who produces unexpected results by tricks; **magical** *adjective*; **magician** *noun*

magnet *noun* an object, such as a piece of iron, steel, etc, that can draw iron towards it; **magnetic** *adjective*; **magnetism** *noun*

magpie *noun* a noisy black and white bird that often takes small bright objects

maid *noun* a female servant; !! **made**

¹**mail** *noun* letters and anything else sent or received by post; !! **male**

²**mail** *noun* armour made of pieces or rings of metal; !! **male**

main *adjective* chief; first in importance or size: **main road**; **mainly** *adverb*; !! **mane**

maintain *verb* to keep in good condition; **maintenance** *noun*

¹**make** *verb* (**makes, making, made**) 1 to produce or form something, especially by work or action; 2 to earn, get, or win; 3 to force or cause a person to do something or a thing to happen; **maker** *noun*

²**make** *noun* the type to which a set of man-made objects belongs, especially the name of the makers: *a foreign **make** of car*

male *noun* a boy or a man; any person or animal of the sex that does not give birth to young; **male** *adjective*; !! **mail**

electro-magnet used in a scrapyard

mammal *noun* an animal that feeds its young on milk from the mother's body

¹**man** *noun* (*plural* **men**) **1** a fully grown human male; **2** a human being; **3** also **mankind** the human race

²**man** *verb* (**manned**) to provide with people for an activity

manage *verb* **1** to succeed in dealing with something; **2** to control or be in charge of something or somebody; **management** *noun*; **manager** *noun*

mane *noun* the long hair on the back of a horse's neck, or around a lion's face; !! **main**

man-made *adjective* made by people; not growing or produced by nature

manner *noun* the way in which anything is done or happens

manners *noun* the way you behave, especially the correct way to behave when you are with other people

many *adjective, pronoun, noun* (**more, most**) a great number

map *noun* **1** a drawing of the Earth's surface or of a part of it, showing the shape of countries, the position of towns, the height of land, etc; **2** a plan of the stars in the sky or of the surface of the moon or a planet

marble *noun* **1** a hard stone that can be polished to make it smooth, which is used for building; **2** a small hard glass ball used in the game of marbles

¹**march** *verb* to walk with a regular step like a soldier

²**march** *noun* **1** the act of marching; **2** a piece of music that can be marched to

March *noun* the third month of the year

¹**mark** *noun* **1** a spot or line on something by which it can be recognised; **2** something like this which spoils it or makes it dirty; **3** a number, sign or letter that shows something, such as how well somebody has done a piece of work

²**mark** *verb* **1** to make or put a mark on something, especially one that spoils the appearance; **2** to give a mark to a person, piece of work, etc

market *noun* a place where people bring goods to sell

marmalade *noun* a type of jam usually made from oranges

marry *verb* **1** to become the husband or wife of somebody; **2** to join two people as husband and wife; **marriage** *noun*

Mars *noun* the planet that is fourth in order from the sun

map of the moon

marvellous *adjective* wonderful

masculine *adjective* concerning boys or men

mask *noun* a covering for the face that hides or protects it; **masked** *adjective*

Aztec mask

mass *noun* 1 a quantity or heap of something; 2 a large number of people or things

master *noun* a person in control of people, animals, or things; the chief person

mat *noun* a small piece of material for covering part of a floor or for putting under an object such as a plate

¹**match** *noun* a short thin stick with one end covered by chemicals that catch fire when rubbed or struck against a rough surface

²**match** *verb* to be like or suitable for use with something else

³**match** *noun* 1 something that is like or that is suitable to be used with something else; 2 a game or sports event between two teams or people

¹**mate** *noun* 1 a friend; 2 one of a male-female pair of animals

²**mate** *verb* to join together as a pair to have young

material *noun* 1 anything from which something can be made; 2 cloth from which clothes, curtains, etc, can be made

mathematics *also* **maths** *noun* the study or science of numbers; **mathematical** *adjective*; **mathematically** *adverb*; **mathematician** *noun*

¹**matter** *noun* 1 **What's the matter?** What is wrong? 2 a subject to which you give attention; 3 the material that makes up the world and everything which can be seen or touched

²**matter** *verb* to be important

mattress *noun* a large bag filled with soft material, on which you sleep

may *verb* (**might**) 1 to be possible or likely to: *She* **may** *come, or she* **may** *not*; 2 to have permission to do something: **May** *I come in?* 3 used to show a hope that something will happen: **May** *the best team win!* NB Used correctly, **may have** and **might have** mean different things. Compare: *he* **may** *have been* (=perhaps he was) *drowned/he* **might** *have been* (=but he was not) *drowned*

May *noun* the fifth month of the year

maybe *adverb* perhaps

mayor *noun* the chief person of a city or town

meal *noun* an amount of food eaten at one time

¹**mean** *adjective* **1** not generous; not willing to give or help; **2** nasty; spiteful; **meanly** *adverb*; **meanness** *noun*

²**mean** *verb* (**means, meaning, meant**) **1** to be the same as; to have as a meaning; **2** to plan or want to do or say something

³**mean** *noun* a number which is midway between the highest and lowest numbers in a sequence

meaning *noun* the idea that is intended to be understood

measles *noun* an infectious disease that causes a temperature and small red spots on the face and body

¹**measure** *noun* **1** a unit used for calculating amount, size, weight, etc; **2** an instrument used for measuring: **tape measure**

²**measure** *verb* **1** to find the size, weight, amount, etc, of something; **2** to be of a certain size; **measurement** *noun*

meat *noun* the parts of an animal's body that are eaten; ‼ **meet**

medal *noun* a piece of metal in the shape of a coin, cross, etc, given to somebody for something he or she has done, such as a brave action or for winning a race; ‼ **meddle**

Olympic medal

meddle *verb* to interest yourself in something that is nothing to do with you; to interfere; **meddler** *noun*; **meddling** *adjective*; ‼ **medal**

media *noun* the newspapers, television, and radio

medial *adjective* something in the middle, especially the middle letter in a three-letter word

medicine *noun* **1** a substance used for treating disease; **2** the science of treating and understanding diseases; **medical** *adjective*; **medically** *adverb*

medium *adjective* of middle size, amount, etc

medium wave *noun* radio broadcasting on waves of about 200 to 700 metres in length

meet *verb* (**meets, meeting, met**) **1** to get to know or be introduced to somebody for the first time; **2** to come together; **meeting** *noun*; ‼ **meat**

melon *noun* a large very juicy round or oval fruit with a thick skin

melt *verb* to become or cause to become liquid

member *noun* a person who belongs to a club, group, etc: **Member of Parliament**

memorise *verb* to learn by heart

memory *noun* **1** the ability to remember things; **2** something remembered; **3** the part of a computer in which information is stored

mend *verb* to put something back into its proper condition

m

mental *adjective* any process of activity that uses the mind, such as mental maths

menu *noun* **1** a list of the foods that are available in a restaurant or at a meal; **2** a list of the choices that are available in a computer program

mercury *noun* a silver-white metal that is liquid at ordinary temperatures and is used in thermometers

Mercury *noun* the planet that is nearest to the sun

mercy *noun* kindness shown by somebody who has the power to hurt or punish; **merciful** *adjective*; **merciless** *adjective*

mermaid *noun* an imaginary creature with the head and body of a woman and a fish's tail instead of legs

merry *adjective* full of laughter; cheerful; happy; **merrily** *adverb*; **merriness** *noun*

mess *noun* a dirty or untidy state; **messy** *adjective*

message *noun* a spoken or written piece of information passed from one person to another

messenger *noun* a person who brings a message

metal *noun* one of a group of usually solid shiny substances such as tin, gold, silver, and iron

meteor *noun* a small piece of matter in space that glows as it falls into the Earth's atmosphere

meteorite *noun* a meteor that has fallen onto the Earth

metre *noun* a measure of length equal to 3.28 ft; **metric** *adjective*

metric system *noun* a system of measurement that uses the metre for measuring length and the kilogram for measuring weight

microchip *noun* a tiny electronic device that is used in computers

microphone or **mike** *noun* an instrument for recording sounds or carrying them over a distance, or for making sounds louder

microprocessor *noun* a chip in a computer

microscope *noun* an instrument that makes very small close objects look larger

muscle fibres as seen under a microscope

microwave also **microwave oven** *noun* an oven in which food is cooked very quickly by radio waves of very short length entering the food

microwave oven

midday *noun* the middle of the day; 12 o'clock in the day

middle *noun* the part, point, or position which is an equal distance from the two ends or sides of something; **middle** *adjective*

middle-aged *adjective* neither old nor young

midnight *noun* 12 o'clock at night

¹**might** **1** *see* MAY; **2** to be possible or likely to: *Jane **might** come later, but I don't think she will*

²**might** *noun* power; strength; force

mile *noun* a measure of length or distance equal to 1760 yards or 1.609 kilometres

¹**milk** *noun* a white liquid produced by female mammals for feeding their young, especially cow's milk

²**milk** *verb* to take milk from a cow, goat, or other animal

Milky Way *noun* the galaxy to which the sun and solar system belong

mill *noun* **1** a place where grain is made into flour; **2** a place, such as a factory, where something is produced or made; *a steel **mill***; **3** a small machine in which something, such as coffee, can be ground into smaller pieces

million *adjective, noun* the number 1,000,000; a thousand thousand; **millionth** *adjective*

¹**mince** *verb* to cut food, especially meat, into very small pieces; **mincer** *noun*

²**mince** *noun* minced meat

mincemeat *noun* a mixture of spices and dried fruits such as raisins and currants that is used as a filling for mince pies

¹**mind** *noun* **1** thoughts; a person's way of thinking or feeling; **2 make up your mind** to reach a decision

²**mind** *verb* **1** to be careful of; to take notice of; **2** to dislike or to have a reason against something; **3** to take care or charge of; look after

¹**mine** *pronoun* that or those belonging to me

²**mine** *noun* a hole, usually under the ground, from which coal, gold, tin, etc, are dug; **mine** *verb*; **miner** *noun*

minerals *noun* natural substances that are found in the earth

mineral water *noun* **1** water that comes from a natural spring and contains minerals, often drunk for health reasons; **2** a drink with a sweet taste and bubbles in it

minibus *noun* a small bus

¹**minute** (*say* min-it) *noun* one of the sixty parts into which an hour is divided

²**minute** (*say* my-newt) *adjective* very small; tiny

mirror *noun* a piece of glass with a silvery back in which you can see things reflected

mischief *noun* naughty behaviour, such as playing tricks on people; **mischievous** *adjective* (*say* mis-chuvus)

miss *verb* **1** to fail to hit, catch, find, meet, see, etc; **2** to feel sorry or unhappy because somebody or something is not there; **3** to discover that somebody or something is lost or is not there

Miss *noun* a title placed before the name of a girl or a woman who is not married

mist *noun* thin cloud near the ground; thin fog; **mist** *verb*; **misty** *adjective*

¹**mistake** *noun* a wrong thought, act, etc; something done, said, believed, etc, as a result of wrong thinking or understanding

²**mistake** *verb* (**mistakes, mistaking, mistook, mistaken**) to have a wrong idea about somebody or something; to understand wrongly

mistletoe *noun* a white berry with green leaves that is used as a symbol at Christmas

mitten

mitt

mitten *noun* a type of glove having one part for all of the fingers and one part for the thumb

mix *verb* **1** to put different things together so that the separate parts no longer have a separate shape, appearance, etc, or cannot easily be separated; **2 mix up** to mistake one thing for another; to confuse in your mind; **mixer** *noun*; **mixture** *noun*

moan *verb* **1** to make a low sound of pain; **2** to complain; **moan** *noun*

moat *noun* a deep ditch, often filled with water, surrounding a castle

mode *noun* **1** a way of doing something; **2** the way a computer works: *in print* mode

model *noun* **1** a small copy of something or a small object, such as a building, which is to be made in a large size; **2** a person whose job is to wear clothes and to show them to possible buyers; **3** a person who is painted by an artist or photographed by a photographer; **4** an object, such as a car, which is one of a number of objects of a standard pattern; **model** *verb*

m

98

lunar module used for the first landing on the moon

modem *noun* a small machine that sends information from one computer to another one far away through a phone line

modern *adjective* of the present time; not old

module *noun* **1** a part of a space vehicle that can be used on its own without the rest of the vehicle: **command module, lunar module**; **2** a part of a school course, treating a particular subject

¹**mole** *noun* a small animal with soft fur that digs holes in the ground

²**mole** *noun* a small dark spot on the skin

³**mole** *noun* a spy

moment *noun* **1** a short period of time; **2** the time for doing something

Monday *noun* the second day of the week

money *noun* metal coins or paper notes with their value printed on them, used in buying and selling

monkey *noun* any of several types of long-tailed active tree-climbing animals, belonging to that class most like humans

monster *noun* a creature that is unusual in shape or qualities, and that is often very large and ugly

month *noun* one of the twelve parts into which the year is divided; about four weeks

moon *noun* a body that moves round a planet, especially the body that moves round the Earth once every 28 days, and can be seen in the sky at night: **moonlight**

¹**moor** *noun* a wide open area covered with rough grass or bushes; !! **more**

²**moor** *verb* to fasten (a boat, an airship, etc) to land, the sea bed, etc, by means of ropes, an anchor, etc; !! **more**

m

mop *noun* a long stick with threads of thick string or a sponge on one end for washing floors

more *adjective, pronoun, adverb* **1** *see* MANY, MUCH; **2 more or less** nearly; about; !! **moor**

morning *noun* **1** the first part of the day from sunrise until midday; **2** the part of the day from midnight until midday; !! **mourning**

mosquito *noun* (*plural* **mosquitoes**) a small fly that pricks the skin and then drinks blood

moss *noun* a small flat green or yellow plant that grows in a thick furry mass on damp surfaces; **mossy** *adjective*

moth *noun* an insect like a butterfly but not usually so brightly coloured, that flies mainly at night and is attracted by lights

mother *noun* **1** a woman who has children; **2** a female animal that has young

¹**motor** *noun* a machine that changes power, especially electrical power, into movement and makes cars go and other machines work

outboard motor on a rubber dinghy

²**motor** *adjective* driven by an engine: **motorboat, motorbike, motorcycle**

motorist *noun* a person who drives a car

motorway *noun* a very wide road for fast long-distance vehicles

mountain *noun* a very high hill

mourn *verb* to be very sad when somebody dies; **mourning** *noun*; !! **morning**

mouse *noun* **1** (*plural* **mice**) a small furry animal with a long tail; **2** a small electronic machine that you move with your hand to move something on a computer screen

mouth *noun* **1** the opening in the face through which a person eats and makes sounds; **2** an opening: *the* **mouth** *of the cave*

move *verb* **1** to go from one place to another; **2** to change the position of something; to put something in a different place; **3** to cause a person to have certain feelings, such as sadness; **movable, moveable** *adjective*; **move** *noun*; **movement** *noun*

mow *verb* (**mows, mowing, mowed, mown** *or* **mowed**) to cut grass; **mower** *noun*

Mr *noun* a title placed before the name of a man

Mrs *noun* a title placed before the name of a married woman

Ms *noun* a title placed before the name of a woman instead of Mrs or Miss

much *adjective, noun, adverb* (**more, most**) **1** a large quantity or amount; **2** often

mud *noun* very wet sticky earth or soil; **muddy** *adjective*

muddle *noun* a confused, untidy, or mixed-up state; **muddle** *verb*

¹**mug** *noun* a big cup usually with straight sides and a handle, that is not normally used with a saucer

²**mug** *verb* (**mugged**) to attack and rob somebody, as in a dark street; **mugger** *noun*; **mugging** *noun*

mule *noun* an animal that is a cross between a horse and a donkey

mule

multimedia *noun* computer programs using sound, pictures and words to give information; **multimedia** *adjective*

¹**multiple** *adjective* several

²**multiple** *noun* in maths, a product of two other numbers multiplied together

multiply *verb* **1** to increase a number by a certain number of times; **2** to increase; to make more; **multiplication** *noun*

mumble *verb* to speak in a way that is hard to hear

mumps *noun* an infectious disease which causes swelling of the face and neck

murder *verb* to kill somebody on purpose; **murder** *noun*; **murderer** *noun*

muscle *noun* one of the pieces of elastic material in the body that tighten to produce movement; !! **mussel**

museum *noun* a building where interesting objects are kept and shown to the public

mushroom *noun* a fungus that can be eaten

music *noun* **1** sounds arranged in pleasant patterns and tunes produced by singing or playing instruments; **2** a written set of musical notes; **musical** *adjective*

musical symbols

musician *noun* somebody who plays a musical instrument

Muslim also **Moslem** *noun* a person of the religion started by Mohammed

mussel *noun* a type of shellfish; !! **muscle**

must *verb* (**mustn't**) **1** to have to because it is necessary; **2** to be sure or likely to

mustard *noun* a hot-tasting yellow powder used in cooking, or a thick mixture of this powder with water, eaten with food

my *adjective* belonging to me

mystery *noun* something strange that cannot be easily explained; **mysterious** *adjective*; **mysteriously** *adverb*

myth *noun* an old story about fictional events **mythical** *adjective*

m

Nn

nail *noun* **1** a thin piece of metal with a point at one end and a flat head at the other for hammering into a piece of wood or other material; **2** a fingernail or toenail; **nail** *verb*

naked *adjective* **1** not wearing any clothes; **2** not covered: *a naked flame*

name *noun* the word or words that somebody or something is called by; **name** *verb*

narrative *noun* a story, or retelling of an event; **narrator** *noun* the person who tells a story

narrow *adjective* **1** small from one side to the other; not wide; **2** almost not enough or only just successful: *a narrow escape*; **narrowness** *noun*

nasty *adjective* unpleasant; unkind; ugly; **nastily** *adverb*; **nastiness** *noun*

nation *noun* people living in one place or area or with the same history; **national** *adjective*

natural *adjective* **1** to do with nature; not made by people; **2** usual; normal; **naturally** *adverb*

nature *noun* **1** the qualities that make somebody or something different from others; the character of somebody or something; **2** the whole world and everything in it that is not made or changed by people, such as the mountains, sea, sky, animals, and plants

naughty *adjective* badly behaved; not obeying a parent, teacher, set of rules, etc; **naughtily** *adverb*; **naughtiness** *noun*

navy *noun* **1** the ships, people, etc, which make up the power of a country for war at sea; **2** a dark blue colour

near *adjective, adverb, preposition* not far from in distance, time, etc; close

nearly *adverb* almost but not quite

neat *adjective* showing care in appearance; liking order; clean and tidy; **neatly** *adverb*; **neatness** *noun*

necessary *adjective* something that must be had or done; **necessarily** *adverb*; **necessity** *noun*

neck *noun* **1** the part of the body between the head and shoulders; **2** the narrow part of something that is shaped like this: *the neck of a bottle*

necklace *noun* a string of jewels or beads worn round the neck

need *verb* **(needn't) 1** to want or not have something necessary or very useful; **2 need to** to have to; **need** *noun*

needle *noun* **1** a long thin pointed piece of metal with a hole in one end, for carrying thread through material in sewing; **2** a thin pointed object: *a pine needle*; **3** any of various thin rods with points or hooks used in working with wool, cloth, etc: *knitting needles*; **4** the small pointed marker that moves along a row of marks to show how fast a car is going, etc

negative *adjective* a number below zero

neighbour *noun* somebody who lives very near you

neither *adjective, pronoun, adverb* **1** not one and not the other of two; **2** also not

nephew *noun* the son of your brother or sister

Neptune *noun* the planet eighth in order from the sun

nerve *noun* any of the threadlike parts of the body that form a system to carry feelings and messages to and from the brain

nervous *adjective* slightly afraid; anxious; worried; **nervously** *adverb*; **nervousness** *noun*

nest *noun* **1** a hollow place built or found by a bird as a home; **2** the home of certain animals or insects; **nest** *verb*

birds' nests

longtailed tit's nest

thrush eggs

net *noun* **1** a material of strings, wires, threads, etc, twisted, tied, or woven together with regular equal spaces between them; **2** any of various objects made from this, such as a fishing net or the goal in football

netball *noun* a game in which two teams of seven people try to score goals by throwing a large ball through a ring on a high post

nettle *noun* a wild plant covered with stinging hairs

network *noun* **1** a set of lines, wires, or roads that are linked and work together; **2** all the parts of a TV channel; **3** a set of computers that are linked

neutral *adjective* **1** neither for nor against something; not taking sides; **2** in a position between opposites; not one thing or the other; **3** not electrically live; being the wire in a plug that is neither live nor earth

never *adverb* **1** not ever; not at any time; **2 never mind** do not worry, it does not matter

new *adjective* **1** not used by anyone before; **2** different from the earlier thing or things; not seen or known before; **newly** *adverb*; **newness** *noun*; !! **knew**

news *noun* **1** new information; **2** any of the regular reports of recent events broadcast on radio and television

newsagent *noun* a person in charge of a shop selling newspapers and magazines

newspaper or **paper** *noun* a paper printed usually daily or weekly, with news, notices, etc

newt *noun* a small animal that can live both on land and in water

next *adjective, adverb* **1** without anything coming between; **2** following nearest in time

n

nibble *verb* to eat with small bites; **nibble** *noun*

nice *adjective* good; kind; pleasant; **nicely** *adverb*

niece *noun* the daughter of your brother or sister

night *noun* the dark part of each day: **nighttime**; !! **knight**

nightingale *noun* a bird with a beautiful song

nightmare *noun* an unpleasant and frightening dream

nil *noun* nothing, zero

nine *adjective, noun* the number 9; **ninth** *adjective, adverb*

nineteen *adjective, noun* the number 19; **nineteenth** *adjective, adverb*

ninety *adjective, noun* the number 90; **ninetieth** *adjective; adverb*

no *adverb, adjective* **1** a word used in an answer to show that you refuse or do not agree with something; **2** not one; not any; !! **know**

noble *adjective* **1** brave and not selfish; **2** belonging to the group of people who have titles, such as Lord and Lady: **nobleman**

nobody *also* **no one** *pronoun* not anybody; no person

nod *verb* (**nodded**) to bend the head forwards and down, especially to show agreement or give a greeting or sign; **nod** *noun*

noise *noun* a loud sound that is often unpleasant; **noisily** *adverb*; **noisy** *adjective*

none *pronoun* not one; not any; !! **nun**

non-fiction *adjective* books or programmes showing facts or information

nonsense *noun* something that is said that is not sensible

nor *conjunction* used between the two choices after neither: *just warm, neither cold* **nor** *hot*; !! **gnaw**

normal *adjective* usual; expected; ordinary; **normally** *adverb*; **normality** *noun*

north *noun* one of the four main points of the compass; the direction which is on the left of a person facing the rising sun; **north** *adjective, adverb*; **northerly** *adjective*; **northern** *adjective*

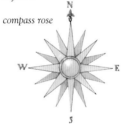

compass rose

northeast *noun* the direction of the point of the compass which is halfway between north and east

northwest *noun* the direction of the point of the compass which is halfway between north and west

nose *noun* **1** the part of the face above the mouth through which we breathe and with which we smell things; **2 turn your nose up at** to consider something not good enough to eat, take part in, etc

not *adverb* used for changing a word or sentence to one with the opposite meaning; !! **knot**

¹**note** *verb* to look or listen carefully and remember

²**note** *noun* **1** a single particular musical sound; **2** a reminder of something in writing: **notebook**; **3** a short letter or written message; **4** a piece of paper money

a Jamaican bank note

nothing *pronoun* no thing; not any thing

¹**notice** *verb* to see, feel, hear, etc, something; **noticeable** *adjective*

²**notice** *noun* **1** a written message in a public place for people to see; **2** warning or information about something that is going to happen

nought *noun* the figure 0; zero

noun *noun* a word that is the name of a person, place, animal, or thing

November *noun* the eleventh month of the year

now *adverb* at this time; at present

nowhere *adverb* not anywhere; in, at, or to no place

nuclear *adjective* using or to do with the energy that comes from splitting atoms or joining them together: **nuclear weapon, nuclear power**

nude *adjective* when a person or object has no clothes on

number *noun* **1** a member of the system used in counting and measuring; a word or figure for one of these; **2** a quantity or amount; **number** *verb*

numeracy *noun* the ability to use numbers

nun *noun* one of a group of women who live together and have given their lives to God; !! **none**

nurse *noun* a person who cares for sick, hurt, old, or very young people; **nurse** *verb*

nursery *noun* **1** a place where small children are looked after for a short time; **2** a place where young plants and trees are grown for sale

nut *noun* **1** a dry fruit or seed with a hard shell; **2** a block, usually of metal, with a hole in the centre for screwing onto a bolt

nuts
brazil nut
hazelnut
almond
pistachio

nutrition *noun* relating to food and how food makes people healthy or unhealthy

nylon *noun* a strong man-made material, often made into cloth or thread

n

Oo

oak _noun_ a large tree with hard wood

oar _noun_ a pole with a wide flat blade, used for rowing a boat

oats _noun_ a plant which produces grain that can be eaten

obey _verb_ to do what somebody tells you; **obedient** _adjective_; **obedience** _noun_

¹**object** (_say_ ob-ject) _noun_ 1 a thing; 2 an aim or purpose

²**object** (_say_ ob-ject) _verb_ to be against something or somebody; **objection** _noun_

oblong _noun_ a shape with four straight sides that is longer than it is wide

oboe _noun_ a musical instrument that you blow

observatory _noun_ a place from which the stars can be watched using a telescope

Mauna Kea observatory, Hawaii

observe _verb_ to watch; to see; **observation** _noun_; **observer** _noun_

obtain _verb_ to get

occasion _noun_ a particular or special time; a time when something happens; **occasional** _adjective_; **occasionally** _adverb_

occur _verb_ (**occurred**) to happen; **occurrence** _noun_

ocean _noun_ a very large sea

o'clock _adverb_ used in telling the time to say what hour it is

October _noun_ the tenth month of the year

odd _adjective_ 1 strange; unusual; 2 not matching; not part of a set; left over; 3 not regular or planned: **odd** jobs; 4 **odd number** a number that cannot be divided by two; **oddly** _adverb_

of _preposition_ 1 belonging to; 2 made from; 3 containing; 4 that is one or some from the whole or all; 5 connected or concerned with; to do with

off _adverb, preposition, adjective_ 1 away; from a place or position; 2 not to be working or in use; 3 to or at a distance away; 4 no longer keen on or fond of: _He's_ **off** _his food_; 5 no longer good to eat or drink; not fresh; 6 not going to happen after having been arranged

offend _verb_ 1 to do wrong; 2 to cause somebody to feel annoyed or unhappy; **offence** _noun_; **offender** _noun_; **offensive** _adjective_

offer _verb_ to say or show that you are ready to give or do something; **offer** _noun_

office _noun_ 1 a place where business, or written work connected with a business, is done; 2 a part of the government: _the Foreign_ **Office**

officer _noun_ 1 a person who gives orders to others in the army, navy, etc; 2 a police officer

often *adverb* many times

oil *noun* any of several types of liquid used for burning, for making machines run easily, or for cooking; **oily** *adjective*

ointment *noun* a sticky substance that is rubbed on the skin to heal wounds

old *adjective* **1** used when asking or showing the age of somebody or something; **2** having lived, been in use, or continued for a long time; not young or new

on *preposition, adverb, adjective* **1** to be above or supported from below; at or covering the top; **2** attached to or touching; **3** towards; by; near to; **4** about; to do with; **5** at the time of; **6** by means of; using; **7** further; forwards; **8** in use; working; **9** happening or about to happen

once *adverb* **1** one time; **2** some time ago; **3** all at once suddenly; **4** at once immediately; at the same time

¹**one** *adjective, noun* the number 1; !! **won**

²**one** *pronoun* a single thing or person; any person; !! **won**

onion *noun* a round white vegetable with a strong smell, that is much used in cooking

only *adjective, adverb* **1** having no others in the same group; **2** and nothing more; and no one else: *Only the goalkeeper can handle the ball*

onset *noun* the first sound in a word

onto *preposition* to a position or point on

¹**open** *adjective* **1** not shut; **2** ready for business: *The bank is* **open**; **3** not covered; not fastened; **4** not surrounded by other things

²**open** *verb* **1** to make or become open; **2** to start or cause to start

operation *noun* **1** a state of working; the way a thing works; **2** a carefully planned action or activity; **3** an act of using instruments on a person's body in order to set right or cut out a diseased part; **operate** *verb*

opinion *noun* what a person thinks about something

opponent *noun* somebody who is on the opposite side in a fight, game, argument, etc

opportunity *noun* a chance or time to do something

¹**opposite** *noun* a person or thing that is as different as possible from another

²**opposite** *adjective* **1** as different as possible; **2** facing

or *conjunction* **1** and not; **2** used to show that there is a choice

orange *noun* **1** a round sweet juicy fruit with an orange coloured peel; **2** a colour between red and yellow; **orange** *adjective*

o

moon orbiting Earth

orbit *noun* the path of one thing, such as a planet, moon, or satellite, round another in space; **orbit** *verb*; **orbital** *adjective*

orbital *noun* a big road that goes round a town to take the traffic away from the centre

orchard *noun* a place where fruit trees are grown

orchestra *noun* a large group of people who play music together on different instruments; **orchestral** *adjective*

order *noun* 1 neatness; tidiness; 2 fitness for working or use; 3 a special way in which a group of people, objects, etc, are arranged: *alphabetical* **order**; 4 the condition in which laws and rules are obeyed; 5 a command to do something; 6 a request to supply something; 7 **in order that** so that; 8 **in order to** with the purpose of; so as to; 9 **out of order** not working; **order** *verb*

ordinary *adjective* not unusual; common; **ordinarily** *adverb*; **ordinariness** *noun*

organ *noun* 1 a part of an animal or plant that has a special purpose, especially the heart, liver, etc; 2 a musical instrument consisting of pipes through which air is forced to make the sounds

organise *verb* to plan something properly and put things in a clear order

origin *noun* a place or time at which something begins; a starting point

original *adjective* 1 earliest; first; 2 new; different from others; not copied; **originally** *adverb*

ornament *noun* an object that we have for its beauty; **ornamental** *adjective*

ostrich *noun* a very large bird with long legs and a long neck, that runs very quickly but cannot fly

other *adjective, pronoun* the remaining one or ones of a set; a different one from that spoken of

otherwise *adverb* 1 if not; 2 apart from that

otter *noun* an animal with dark brown fur that swims well and eats fish

ought *verb* 1 should; 2 will probably

our *adjective* belonging to us; !! **hour**

ours *pronoun* that or those belonging to us

out *adverb* **1** in or to the open air, the outside, etc; away from the inside or centre; **2** not at home; **3** no longer in a game; **4** no longer lit or shining

outdoor *adjective* existing, happening, done, or used not in a building

outdoors *adverb* in the open air; not in a building

outing *noun* a pleasure trip

output *noun* something that is produced; the quantity of things produced

¹**outside** *noun* the part furthest from the centre

²**outside** *adverb, preposition, adjective* **1** in, on, or to the outside; out; **2** not in a building; in the open air

outwards *adverb* towards the outside

oval *adjective* shaped like an egg or flattened circle; **oval** *noun*

oven *noun* a machine that can be made hot to cook food in

over *adverb, preposition* **1** directly above; **2** completely or partly covering; **3** to or on the other side of; across; **4** downwards from an upright position; **5** right through; from the beginning to the end; **6** more; more than; **7** remaining; **8** finished; at an end

overalls *noun* loose clothes worn over other clothes to keep them clean

overflow *verb* to be so full that the contents flow over the edges; **overflow** *noun*

owe *verb* **1** to have to pay; **2** to feel grateful to somebody for what he or she has done for us or given to us

owl *noun* a bird with large eyes that flies at night

¹**own** *adjective, pronoun* **1** belonging to the particular person spoken of and to nobody else; **2 on your own** alone or without help

²**own** *verb* to have; to possess; **owner** *noun*

oxygen *noun* a colourless gas that is present in the air and is needed by plants and animals in order to live

ozone layer *noun* a layer of gas in the sky that protects the Earth from the harmful rays of the sun

harmful sun rays

a cross-section of Earth's atmosphere showing the protective ozone layer which absorbs harmful rays from the sun

Pp

¹**pack** *noun* **1** a number of things put together; **2** a group of animals, such as wolves, that hunt together

²**pack** *verb* **1** to put things into containers; **2** to crush or crowd together into a space

package *noun* a parcel

packet *noun* a small parcel or container

pad *noun* **1** a mass of soft material used to protect something or make it more comfortable, or to fill out a shape; **2** a number of sheets of paper fastened together along one edge

¹**paddle** *noun* a short pole with a wide flat end used for pushing and guiding a small boat, such as a canoe

²**paddle** *verb* **1** to move a boat through water using a paddle; **2** to walk about in shallow water; **3** to swim about in water as a dog or duck does

¹**page** *noun* one side of a sheet of paper in a book, newspaper, etc

²**page** *noun* a boy servant

pail *noun* a bucket; !! **pale**

pain *noun* a feeling of hurt or suffering; **painful** *adjective*; **painfully** *adverb*; !! **pane**

¹**paint** *verb* **1** to put on a surface, such as a wall; **2** to make a picture using paint; **painter** *noun*

²**paint** *noun* liquid colouring matter for putting or spreading on a surface

painting *noun* a painted picture

pair *noun* **1** two things that are alike or of the same kind, and are used or thought of together; **2** something made up of two parts that are alike and that are joined and used together: *a **pair** of trousers*; !! **pear**

palace *noun* a very large grand house in which an important person, such as a king or queen, lives

pale *adjective* **1** light in colour; not bright; **2** with a white face through feeling ill; **paleness** *noun*; !! **pail**

¹**palm** *noun* the inside part of a hand between the fingers and the wrist

²**palm** *noun* usually a very tall tree with large leaves at the top and no branches

palm trees in a desert oasis

pan *noun* a round metal container with a handle, used in cooking food: **saucepan**

pancake *noun* a very thin cake made from batter and cooked in a frying pan

pane *noun* a flat piece of glass in a window; !! **pain**

panic *verb* to lose control through fear or worry

pansy *noun* a small plant with wide flat flowers

pant *verb* to breathe quickly, taking short breaths, especially after exercise or in great heat

pantomime *noun* a play, usually telling an old story, which includes singing and dancing

pants *noun* underpants or trousers

paper *noun* **1** material made in the form of sheets from very thin threads of wood or cloth, used for writing or printing on, covering parcels or walls, etc; **2** a newspaper

parable *noun* a short story used to teach people, sometimes religious

parachute *noun* a large piece of material that is fastened to people or objects dropped from aircraft in order to make them fall slowly

parachute

parallel *adjective* running side by side but staying the same distance apart: *parallel* lines

paramedic *noun* a person who is sent to help when there is a medical emergency

parcel *noun* a thing or things wrapped in paper and tied or fastened for posting or carrying

parent *noun* a father or mother

park *noun* **1** a large garden or grass place in a town, used by the public; **2** a piece of land with grass and trees round a large country house

park *verb* to stop or leave a vehicle for a time; **parking** *noun*

parliament *noun* the group of people who make the laws of a country: *Member of Parliament* (MP)

parrot *noun* a brightly coloured tropical bird that has a curved beak and can be taught to copy human speech

part *noun* **1** any of the pieces that make up a whole; some of a thing; **2** a share in some activity: take part in; **3** a character acted by an actor in a play or film; the words and actions of an actor in a play or film

part *verb* to separate or no longer be together

particular *adjective* separate or different from others; special; **particularly** *adverb*

parting *noun* the line on the head where the hair is parted

partition *verb* to divide into parts or shares

partly *adverb* in some way but not completely

partner *noun* one or two, or sometimes more, people who share in the same activity; **partnership** *noun*

party *noun* **1** a meeting of people, usually by invitation, to eat, drink, and enjoy themselves; **2** a group of people doing something together; **3** a group of people having the same political opinions

¹**pass** *verb* **1** to reach and move beyond; **2** to go forward, through, across, over, or between; **3** to give: *Please pass the bread*; **4** to succeed in an examination or test; **5** to go by: *several years passed*; !! **past**

²**pass** *noun* **1** an act of passing something, such as the ball in various sports; **2** a way by which one may pass, especially through mountains; **3** a printed piece of paper, which shows that one is permitted to do a certain thing; **4** a successful result in an examination

passage *noun* **1** a narrow and often long connecting way or path, especially inside a building; **2** a part of a speech or of a piece of writing or music

passenger *noun* a traveller in a vehicle

passport *noun* a small book or card with your photograph and information about you in it, which you need if you are travelling to some countries

European community passport

¹**past** *noun* the time before the present; !! **passed**

²**past** *adjective* to do with or belonging to the past; in the past; !! **passed**

³**past** *preposition, adverb* **1** after: *ten past seven*; **2** up to and beyond; !! **passed**

⁴**past** *noun, adjective* talking about an action that has already happened: *past tense*; !! **passed**

pasta *noun* a food made from flour and water that is formed into many different shapes, such as spaghetti

paste *noun* **1** a thin mixture used for sticking paper; **2** a soft mixture that is easily shaped or spread; **paste** *verb*

pastry *noun* a baked mixture of flour, fat, and milk or water that is used for pies

pat *verb* (**patted**) to touch or strike gently with the palm of the hand; **pat** *noun*

patch *noun* **1** a piece of material used to cover a hole; **2** a part of a surface that is different from the space round it; **patch** *verb*

path *noun* a track for walking or riding along

¹**patient** (*say* **payshunt**) *adjective* able to bear trouble without complaining or to wait for something calmly; **patience** *noun*; **patiently** *adverb*

²**patient** (*say* **payshunt**) *noun* a sick person who is being treated by a doctor or nurse

patio *noun* a paved stone area in a garden

pattern *noun* **1** a regularly repeated arrangement of shapes and colours; **2** something that can be copied and used as a guide for making something

pause *verb* to stop for a short time; pause *noun*; !! **paws**

pavement *noun* a hard path at the side of a road

paw *noun* an animal's foot with nails or claws; !! **poor, pore, pour**

¹**pay** *verb* (**pays, paying, paid**) to give money for something bought, work done, etc; **payment** *noun*

²**pay** *noun* money received for work

pea *noun* a round green seed eaten as a vegetable

peace *noun* **1** a state or time in which there is no war or fighting; **2** calmness; quietness; **peaceful** *adjective*; **peacefully** *adverb*; !! **piece**

peach *noun* a round fruit with soft yellowish-red skin, sweet juicy flesh, and a large rough seed (stone)

peacock *noun* **1** (*female* **peahen**) the male of a large bird (**peafowl**) whose long tail feathers can be spread out to show beautiful colours and patterns; **2** a butterfly with large colourful wings

peacock

peal *noun* a ringing noise, or loud noise: a peal of bells; **peal** *verb*; !! **peel**

pear *noun* a sweet juicy fruit that is narrower at the stalk end; !! **pair**

pearl *noun* a hard silvery white ball formed inside shellfish, especially oysters, which is very valuable as a jewel

pebble *noun* a small stone

peck *verb* to eat or strike at something with the beak; **peck** *noun*

peculiar *adjective* strange; odd; unusual

¹**pedal** *noun* a part of a machine that can be pressed with the foot to control or move the machine

²**pedal** *verb* (**pedalled**) to work the pedals of a machine; to move a machine, e.g. a bike, by using pedals

pedestrian *noun* someone travelling on foot

¹**peel** *verb* to remove or lose the peel or an outer covering; !! **peal**

²**peel** *noun* the outer covering of a fruit or vegetable; !! **peal**

peep *verb* to look at something quickly and secretly; **peep** *noun*

¹**peer** *verb* to look at something very carefully or hard

²**peer** (*feminine* **peeress**) *noun* **1** a person of high position, such as an earl or a duke; **2** a person who has the right to sit in the House of Lords

peg *noun* **1** a short piece of metal, plastic, etc, fixed to a wall or door for hanging coats and hats on; **2** a wooden or plastic clip for fastening wet washing to a line

p

¹**pen** *noun* an instrument for writing or drawing with ink

²**pen** *noun* a small place with a fence round it for keeping animals in

pencil *noun* a narrow pointed instrument containing a thin stick of lead or coloured material, for writing or drawing

penguin *noun* a large black and white seabird from cold regions that swims well but cannot fly

penicillin *noun* a type of antibiotic

penny *noun* (*plural* **pence** or **pennies**) a small coin. In Britain, 100 pence equal one pound

people *noun* men, women, and children; human beings

pepper *noun* **1** a hot-tasting spice used for flavouring food; **2** a green or red vegetable that can be eaten cooked or raw

per *preposition* for each; during each; !! **purr**

percentage *noun* a number or amount represented as part of a whole amount, if the whole amount is taken as being 100

perfect *adjective* of the very best possible kind; without any faults; **perfection** *noun*; **perfectly** *adverb*

perform *verb* **1** to act, dance, play a musical instrument, etc, in front of an audience; **2** to do something; to carry out a piece of work; **performance** *noun*; **performer** *noun*

perfume *noun* **1** a pleasant-smelling liquid that is put on the skin; **2** a sweet smell

perhaps *adverb* it may be; possibly

period *noun* a length of time

permanent *adjective* lasting for a long time or for ever; **permanently** *adverb*

permit *verb* (**permitted**) to allow; **permission** *noun*

person *noun* a man, woman, or child; a human being

personal *adjective* belonging to, or for, one person; of your own; private: *a* **personal** *letter*; **personally** *adverb*

persuade (*say* perswade) *verb* to cause somebody to do or to believe something

pet *noun* **1** an animal you look after and keep in your house; **2** a favourite person

petal *noun* one of the usually coloured leaflike parts of a flower

petrol *noun* a liquid used as a fuel for producing power in car engines

PG *noun, adjective* In Britain, a film that can be watched by anybody but for which you should ask your parents' permission if you are under 15

phantom *noun* a ghost

pharaoh *noun* a ruler of ancient Egypt

pheasant *noun* a large bird with a long tail

phobia *noun* a fear of something specific, such as spiders or flying

phone *noun* a machine that you use to speak to someone who is somewhere else. It works by electricity; **phone** *verb*

phoneme *noun* a single speech sound, which can be represented by letters

p

114

phonics *noun* the process of learning to read by recognising the sounds made by letters and letter combinations within words

photograph also **photo** *noun* a picture obtained with a camera and film; **photograph** *verb*; **photographer** *noun*; **photographic** *adjective*

phrase *noun* a group of words that does not make a full sentence

physical *adjective* **1** of or about the body: **physical education**; **2** of or about the natural world

physics *noun* the science of matter and natural forces, such as light, heat, and sound

piano *noun* (*plural* **pianos**) a large musical instrument that is played by pressing keys which cause soft little hammers to hit wires; **pianist** *noun*

grand piano

pick *verb* **1** to choose; **2** to take up or pull off with the fingers

picnic *noun* a meal eaten outside, usually away from home; **picnic** *verb* (**picnicked**); **picnicker** *noun*

picture *noun* **1** a painting, drawing, or photograph; **2 the pictures** the cinema

pie *noun* a pastry case filled with meat or fruit, baked usually in a deep dish

piece *noun* **1** a part of something; a part that is separated from a whole; **2** a single object: *a piece of furniture*; !! **peace**

pig *noun* (*male* **hog**, *female* **sow**, *young* **piglet**) a short-legged animal with a curly tail and thick skin, kept on farms for food

pigeon *noun* a quite large short-legged bird

piglet *noun* a young pig

pile *noun* a heap of things on top of one another; **pile** *verb*

pill *noun* a small ball of solid medicine to be swallowed

pillar *noun* a tall upright usually round post made of concrete, stone, etc

pillow *noun* an oblong cloth bag filled with soft material, for supporting the head in bed: **pillowcase**

pilot *noun* **1** a person who flies an aircraft; **2** a person who guides ships in and out of a harbour; **pilot** *verb*

pimple *noun* a small raised diseased spot on the skin; **pimply** *adjective*; **pimpled** *adjective*

pin *noun* a short thin stiff sharp piece of metal for fastening cloth, paper, etc; **pin** *verb*

p

¹**pinch** *verb* **1** to press tightly and often painfully between the thumb and finger or between two hard surfaces; **2** to steal

²**pinch** *noun* an amount that can be picked up between the thumb and a finger; a small amount

¹**pine** *noun* a tall tree with thin sharp leaves (**pine needles**), which bears cones

²**pine** *verb* to feel great longing or desire for something that is unobtainable

pineapple *noun* a large yellow juicy tropical fruit with thin stiff leaves on top

pineapple

pink *noun, adjective* pale red; **pinkish** *adjective*

¹**pip** *noun* a small fruit seed

²**pip** *noun* a short high-sounding note, as given on the radio to tell the time

pipe *noun* **1** a tube for carrying a liquid or gas: **oilpipe 2** a small tube with a bowl-shaped container at one end, for smoking tobacco; **3** a tube-shaped musical instrument, played by blowing

pirate *noun* **1** a person who robs a ship at sea; **2** a person who uses or sells the work of other people such as books or videos without permission or payment; **piracy** *noun*

pit *noun* **1** a hole, usually in the ground; **2** a coal mine

¹**place** *noun* **1** a particular area, part of space, or position; **2** a position in the result of a competition, race, etc; !! **plaice**

²**place** *verb* to put in a certain place or position; !! **plaice**

plaice *noun* a flat bony sea fish; !! **place**

¹**plain** *adjective* **1** easy to see, hear, or understand; **2** simple; without decoration; **plainly** *adverb*; !! **plane**

²**plain** *noun* a large area of flat land; !! **plane**

plait (*say* **plat**) *noun* a length of something, especially hair, made by twisting three or more pieces over and under one another; **plait** *verb*

plan *noun* **1** a carefully worked out arrangement for something to be done in the future; **2** a drawing of a building or room showing the shape, measurements, etc; **plan** *verb*

plane *noun* a flying vehicle that has wings and at least one engine; !! **plain**

planet *noun* a large body in space that moves round a sun

planetarium *noun* a building containing a machine that throws spots of light onto a surface to show the movements of the stars and planets

¹**plant** *verb* to put plants or seeds in the ground to grow

²**plant** *noun* **1** a living thing that has leaves and roots and grows, usually in the ground; **2** the buildings and machines used in making something; a factory

plaster *noun* **1** a soft mixture that hardens when dry and is spread on walls to give a smooth surface; **2** a piece of sticky tape put on the body to protect a wound; **3** also **plaster cast** a special covering for protecting a broken bone in an arm, leg, etc, while it heals

leg in a plaster cast

plastic *noun* a man-made material that can be made into different shapes

plate *noun* **1** a flat dish from which food is eaten or served; **2** a flat thin piece of metal

platform *noun* **1** a raised floor or stage; **2** a raised surface along the side of the track at a railway station

¹**play** *verb* **1** to have fun; to take part in a game: **playground**; **2** to perform a part in a film or play; **3** to make sounds on a musical instrument; **4** to reproduce the sounds recorded on a record, cassette, etc; **player** *noun*; **playful** *adjective*; **playfully** *adverb*

²**play** *noun* a story performed in a theatre or on the radio or television

pleasant *adjective* enjoyable; nice; **pleasantly** *adverb*

please *verb* **1** to make somebody happy; **2** used to make a request more polite; **pleasure** *noun*

plenty *noun* a large quantity or number; enough; **plentiful** *adjective*

plough (*say like* **cow**) *noun* a farming tool for breaking up and turning over soil and earth; **plough** *verb*

pluck *verb* **1** to pull the feathers off a bird; **2** to play a musical instrument by pulling the strings and letting go quickly

an eastern musical instrument played by plucking - a sitar

plug *noun* **1** a plastic object with metal pieces that connects a television set, iron, vacuum cleaner, etc, to an electrical socket; **2** something used for blocking a hole, especially a round piece of rubber or plastic for stopping water from running out of a sink or bath

plum *noun* a sweet juicy fruit with a smooth skin and large stone; the tree on which this grows

plumber *noun* somebody who fits and mends water pipes, central heating, etc

plus *preposition* with the addition of; and

Pluto *noun* the planet furthest from the sun

p m after midday (short for *post meridiem*)

pocket *noun* a small flat cloth bag sewn into or onto a piece of clothing for putting money, a handkerchief, etc, in

poem *noun* a piece of writing in patterns of lines and sounds, expressing something in powerful or beautiful language, often using rhymes

poet *noun* a person who writes poems; **poetic** *adjective*

poetry *noun* poems

¹**point** *noun* **1** a sharp end; **2** the importance or purpose of something said or done; **3** an exact moment; **4** a mark or position on a compass, measuring instrument, etc; **5** a single quantity used in deciding the winner in a game, quiz, etc; a mark

²**point** *verb* to hold out a finger, a stick, etc, in a direction; to show where something is with the finger; **pointer** *noun*

poison *noun* a substance that harms or kills if it is taken into the body; poison *verb*; **poisonous** *adjective*

poke *verb* to push a pointed thing into or at somebody or something; **poke** *noun*

¹**pole** *noun* a long often thin round stick or post: **flagpole, telegraph pole**

²**pole** *noun* **1** either end of an imaginary straight line (**axis**) round which a solid round mass, such as the Earth, turns: *North* **Pole 2** a point at the ends of a magnet where its power is greatest

French flag flying from a flagpole

police *noun* a body of men and women whose duty is to protect people and buildings, to make everyone obey the law, to catch criminals, etc: **police force, policeman, police station, policewoman**

¹**polish** *verb* to make something smooth and shiny by rubbing

²**polish** *noun* a liquid, paste, etc, used in polishing a surface

polite *adjective* having good manners; **politely** *adverb*; **politeness** *noun*

politics *noun* the study of government; how countries should be governed; **political** *adjective*

pollution *noun* bad chemicals, smells, sounds and objects which spoil the air and can be dangerous to health

polyester *noun* man-made fabric

polystyrene *noun* a crumbly cardboard used in packaging

polythene *noun* light plastic often used for shopping bags

pond *noun* a small area of water, in a garden, for example

pony *noun* a small horse

pool *noun* **1** a small area of water; a pond; **2** a small amount of any liquid poured or dropped on a surface; **3** a swimming pool

poor *adjective* **1** having very little money; **2** low in quality or quantity; not good; **3** needing kindness; unlucky; !! **paw, pore, pour**

¹**pop** *noun* a sudden noise like the sound of the top being pulled out of a bottle

²**pop** *noun* modern popular music and songs

³**pop** *verb* (**popped**) **1** to make a popping noise; **2** to go: *pop along to the shops*; **3** to put: *pop it on the table*

Pope *noun* head of the Roman Catholic Church

poppy *noun* a plant that has a milky juice in its stem and bright, usually red flowers

popular *adjective* liked by many people

population *noun* the whole number of people living in a place

pore *noun* any of the tiny holes in the skin through which you sweat; !! **paw, poor, pour**

pork *noun* meat from a pig

porridge *noun* a soft breakfast food made by boiling oats in milk or water

¹**port** *noun* a harbour or a town with a harbour

²**port** *noun* the left side of a ship or aircraft as you face forward

porter *noun* a person who carries luggage at airports, etc

position *noun* **1** the place where somebody or something is or stands; **2** the place where somebody or something belongs; **3** the way in which somebody or something is placed or moves, stands, sits, etc; **4** a condition or state; **5** a job

possess *verb* to have or own; **possession** noun

possible *adjective* that may exist, happen, or be done; **possibility** *noun*; **possibly** *adverb*

¹**post** *noun* a strong thick upright pole or bar made of wood, metal, etc, fixed into the ground or some other base especially as a support: **gatepost**

²**post** *noun* the system for collecting, carrying, and delivering letters, parcels, etc: **postbox, postman, post office, postwoman**

³**post** *verb* to send something by post

⁴**post** *noun* **1** a special place of duty, especially on guard or on watch; **2** a job

postage stamp *noun* a stamp for sticking on things to be posted

one of the first postage stamps - a Penny Black

postcard *noun* a small card, often with a picture on one side, on which a message may be written and sent by post

poster *noun* a large printed notice or drawing put up in a public place

postpone *verb* to put off until a later time or day; **postponement** *noun*

pot *noun* a container, especially a round one, made from baked clay, metal, etc

potato *noun* (*plural* **potatoes**) a vegetable with a thin usually brown skin that is cooked and served in many ways

pottery *noun* pots, dishes, etc, made from baked clay

pound *noun* **1** a measure of weight equal to 0.454 kilograms; **2** the standard unit of money in Britain, which is divided into 100 pence

pour *verb* **1** to flow or make a liquid flow; **2** to rain hard and steadily; !! **paw, poor, pore**

powder *noun* a substance in the form of very small dry grains; **powdery** *adjective*

power *noun* **1** strength, force, or energy; **3** a person, group, government, etc, that has control; **powerful** *adjective*

practice *noun* the doing of something, especially again and again to become better at it; !! **practise**

practise *verb* to do something regularly or over and over again, especially in order to become better at it; !! **practice**

praise *verb* to speak well of; to say that you admire; **praise** *noun*

prawn *noun* a shellfish that looks like a large shrimp

pray *verb* to speak, often silently, to God or a god; !! **prey**

prayer *noun* the act of praying; what you say when you are praying

a mosque, where Muslims pray

precede *verb* to come before or in front

precious *adjective* very valuable

predict *verb* to say what is going to happen before it happens

prefer *verb* **(preferred)** to like better; **preference** *noun*

prefix *noun* letters put at the beginning of a word to alter the meaning, such as *un*happy

pregnant *adjective* about to have a baby; **pregnancy** *noun*

prehistoric *adjective* to do with or belonging to time in history before there were written records

prepare *verb* to get ready or make something ready; **preparation** *noun*

preposition *noun* a word like to, for, on, by, etc; a word that is put in front of a noun to show where, when, how, etc

¹**present** (*say prez-*ent) *noun* a gift

²**present** (*say prez-*ent) *verb* to give; to offer

³**present** (*say prez-*ent) *adjective* **1** in the place talked of; there; here; **2** existing or happening now

⁴**present** (*say prez-*ent) *noun* the present time; this time

⁵**present** (*say prez-*ent) *noun*, *adjective* talking about an action that is happening now: **present tense**

presenter *noun* a person who introduces a show

preserve *verb* to keep safe or in good condition; **preservation** *noun*

president *noun* **1** the head of government in many countries that do not have a king or queen: *the* **President** *of France*; **2** the head of a company, club, etc

¹**press** *verb* **1** to push firmly and steadily; **2** to make flat or smooth, as by ironing; **pressure** *noun*

²**press** *noun* **1** an act of pressing something; **2** newspapers and magazines in general; **3** a machine for printing books, newspapers, etc

pretend *verb* **1** to act in a deceiving way; **2** to imagine as a game

¹**pretty** *adjective* pleasing to look at; **prettily** *adverb*; **prettiness** *noun*

²**pretty** *adverb* quite though not completely; fairly

prevent *verb* to stop something from happening; **prevention** *noun*

prey *noun* an animal that is hunted by another; !! **pray**

price *noun* an amount of money for which a thing is bought or sold

prick *verb* to make a very small hole or wound in something with a sharp-pointed object

prickle *noun* a small sharp part of a plant or animal; **prickly** *adjective*

pride *noun* **1** the feeling of having a good opinion of yourself or being satisfied with yourself; being proud; **2** a group of lions

p

121

priest *noun* a person trained for various religious duties

primary *adjective* earliest; first; most important

primary school *noun* a school for children aged between five and eleven

prime *adjective* the first or the best

Prime Minister *noun* the head of government

primrose *noun* **1** a pale yellow flower that grows in the spring; **2** its colour

prince *noun* the son or grandson of a king or queen

princess *noun* **1** a daughter or granddaughter of a king or queen; **2** the wife of a prince

¹**print** *noun* **1** a mark on a surface showing the shape, pattern, etc, of the thing pressed into it: **footprint**; **2** printed letters; **3** a photograph printed from a camera film

²**print** *verb* **1** to make a book, magazine, etc, by putting words and pictures on paper using a special machine; **2** to make or copy a photograph on paper from film; **3** to write without joining the letters; **4** to make a paper copy of work done on a computer

printer *noun* **1** a person whose job is printing; **2** a machine for making photographic prints; **3** a machine connected to a computer, for printing out paper copies of writing, pictures, etc

printout *noun* information produced and printed on paper by a computer

prism *noun* a block of clear glass that breaks up light into its separate colours

a prism, which divides light into different parts

prison *noun* a large building where criminals are kept locked up; **prisoner** *noun*

private *adjective* belonging to or to do with one person or one group of people; not for everybody; **privacy** *noun*; **privately** *adverb*

prize *noun* something of value given to the winner of a competition, game, etc; a reward for doing well or for good work

probably *adverb* almost but not quite certainly; likely

problem *noun* a difficulty that needs attention; a question for which an answer is needed

procession *noun* a line of people or vehicles moving slowly forwards

¹**produce** (*say* pro-duce) *verb* **1** to show or bring out; **2** to make or cause to exist; **product** *noun*; **production** *noun*

²**produce** (*say* prod-uce) *noun* something produced, especially by growing or farming

product *noun* **1** something that has been made **2** in maths, the answer when you mulitply two or more numbers together

¹**professional** *noun* someone who does a job for money

²**professional** *adjective* to do your job responsibly

profit *noun* money you get when you sell something for more than it cost to buy or make; **profitable** *adjective*; !! **prophet**

¹**program** *noun* a set of instructions for a computer; !! **programme**

²**program** *verb* (**programmed**) to provide a computer with a program; !! **programme**

programme *noun* 1 a show, story, etc, on radio or television; 2 a list of things to be done or that will happen; !! **program**

project *noun* a piece of work in which a subject is studied in close detail

promise *verb* to say that you definitely will or will not do something; **promise** *noun*

pronoun *noun* a word, like he, she, it, they, etc, that is used instead of using a noun again

pronounce *verb* to make the sound of a letter or a word; **pronunciation** *noun*

proof *noun* a way of showing that something is true

propel *verb* to drive or push something forward; **propulsion** *noun*

propeller *noun* a set of specially shaped blades that turn rapidly to drive a plane or ship

proper *adjective* suitable; correct; right; **properly** *adverb*

property *noun* 1 something that is owned; 2 land, buildings, or both together

prophet *noun* a person directed by God to make known God's wishes or to teach a religion; !! **profit**

prose *noun* non-rhyming, non-rhythmic writing

protect *verb* to keep safe; to prevent somebody or something from being hurt or damaged; **protection** *noun*

protein *noun* something found in certain foods such as meat, fish, nuts and many other things that makes us strong and healthy

protest *verb* to strongly disagree with something

proud *adjective* having a high opinion of yourself or of something connected with yourself; **proudly** *adverb*

prove *verb* to show that something is true

provide *verb* to supply

prune *noun* a dried plum

pub also **public house** *noun* a building where alcohol may be bought and drunk

¹**public** *adjective* for or to do with people in general; for everyone to use

²**public** *noun* 1 people in general; 2 **in public** with many people present

publisher *noun* a person or company whose business it is to produce books, newspapers, magazines etc for sale to the public **publish** *verb*

ship's propellor

pudding *noun* **1** a dessert; **2** a sweet food made with pastry, rice, bread, etc, and served hot; **3** a meat dish boiled with a pastry cover

puddle *noun* a small pool of water, especially rainwater

puff *noun* a sudden rush of air, smoke, etc; **puff** *verb*

pull *verb* **1** to draw something along behind; **2** to move or draw something towards yourself

pump *noun* a machine for forcing a liquid or gas into or out of something; **pump** *verb*

pumpkin *noun* a large round dark yellow vegetable

punch *verb* to strike hard with the fist; **punch** *noun*

punctuation *noun* in grammar, the separation of writing, using marks like commas, colons and full stops

puncture *noun* a small hole, especially in a tyre; **puncture** *verb*

punish *verb* to cause somebody to suffer for a fault or crime; **punishment** *noun*

¹**pupil** *noun* a person, especially a child, who is being taught

²**pupil** *noun* the small round opening in the middle of your eye, that looks black and which can grow larger or smaller

puppet *noun* **1** a small toy figure of a person or an animal that can be made to move by pulling wires or strings; **2** also **glove puppet** a hollow cloth figure into which you put your hand to move the figure with your fingers

puppy also **pup** *noun* a young dog

pure *adjective* without anything mixed with it; clean; **purely** *adverb*; **purity** *noun*

purple *noun* a dark colour between red and blue; **purple** *adjective*; **purplish** *adjective*

purpose *noun* a reason for doing something

purr *noun* a low sound produced by a cat when it is pleased; **purr** *verb*; !! **per**

purse *noun* a small bag for carrying money

push *verb* to move somebody or something forward, away, or to a different position by pressing with your hands; **push** *noun*

pushchair *noun* a light folding chair on wheels for pushing a small child along

put *verb* (**puts, putting, put**) to move, place, or fix somebody or something in, on, or to a certain place

¹**puzzle** *noun* **1** something that you cannot understand or explain; a difficult question to answer; **2** a game or toy in which parts must be fitted together correctly: **crossword puzzle, jigsaw puzzle**

²**puzzle** *verb* to think hard about a problem; **puzzled** *adjective*

pyjamas *noun* a loose shirt and trousers that you wear in bed

pyramid *noun* a solid object or shape with straight flat triangular sides that slope upwards and meet in a point at the top

Qq

quack *noun* the sound that ducks make; **quack** *verb*

quality *noun* 1 how good something is; 2 something typical of a person or thing

quantity *noun* the amount of something or the number of things

quarrel *noun* an argument; **quarrel** *verb*

quarter *noun* 1 one of four parts of anything; $\frac{1}{4}$; 2 15 minutes before or after the hour: **quarter past, quarter to**

quartet *noun* a group of four musicians or singers

queen *noun* 1 a female ruler of a country or the wife of a king; 2 any of the four playing cards with a picture of a queen, that comes between the jack and the king

queer *adjective* strange; unusual; **queerly** *adverb*

¹question *noun* 1 a sentence that asks something and needs an answer; 2 a problem; something to be talked about

²question *verb* 1 to ask a question; 2 to raise doubts about somebody or something; **questioner** *noun*

question mark *noun* the mark (?) used in writing or printing at the end of a sentence that asks a question

queue (*say* kyoo) *noun* a line of waiting people, cars, etc; **queue** *verb*; !! **cue**

quick *adjective* fast; not slow; soon finished; **quickly** *adverb*

quiet *adjective* 1 having or making very little noise; 2 calm; peaceful; **quiet** *noun*; **quietly** *adverb*; **quietness** *noun*

quilt *noun* a thick cover for a bed, often a warm one

quintet *noun* a group of five musicians

quit *verb* to leave, especially a computer program

quite *adverb* 1 rather; 2 completely; perfectly

quiz *noun* a competition or game in which questions are asked

quotation mark *noun* either of a pair of marks (" ") or (' ') showing the beginning and end of words said or written by somebody else

q

traffic jam

125

Rr

rabbit *noun* (*male* **buck**, *female* **doe**) a small long-eared animal of the hare family that lives in a burrow

¹**race** *noun* a competition to see who can do something fastest

²**race** *verb* **1** to try to run or go faster than somebody else; **2** to go very fast; **racer** *noun*

³**race** *noun* a group of people who have the same colour of skin or other similarities about their faces or bodies; **racial** *adjective*; **racially** *adverb*

racist *noun* someone who hates people of other races; **racist** *adjective*

rack *noun* a frame with bars, hooks, etc, for holding things: **luggage rack**

¹**racket, racquet** *noun* a net, usually of nylon, stretched in a frame with a handle, for hitting the ball in games such as tennis

²**racket** *noun* a loud noise

radar *noun* a way of finding the position of solid objects, such as ships, aeroplanes, etc, by using radio waves

radiate *verb* to send out light or heat

radiation *noun* **1** the sending out of heat, light, etc; **2** the giving off of harmful rays from the sun or a radioactive substance

radiator *noun* **1** an object for sending out heat in a house; **2** a machine for cooling the engine of a car

radio *noun* **1** the sending or receiving of sounds through the air by electrical waves; **2** a machine to receive sounds sent out in this way; **radio** *verb*

radioactive *adjective* giving out energy or rays; **radioactivity** *noun*

rag *noun* **1** a small piece of old cloth; **2** an old worn-out piece of clothing

rail *noun* **1** a fixed bar to hang things on or for protection; **2** one of the pair of metal bars along which a train runs: **railway**

rain *noun* water falling in drops from the clouds: **raindrop, rainwater; rain** *verb*; **rainy** *adjective*; !! **reign, rein**

rainbow *noun* an arch of different colours that often appears in the sky when it is both sunny and rainy

rainforest *noun* a thick forest found in hot and wet tropical countries

raise *verb* **1** to lift, push, or move up; **2** to make greater; **raise prices**

raisin *noun* a dried grape

rake *noun* a gardening tool with a row of teeth at the end of a long handle, for levelling soil, gathering up leaves; **rake** *verb*

ram *noun* a male sheep

RAM *also* **random access memory** *noun* a type of computer memory that holds information and programs

random *adjective* made or done without a fixed plan; by chance; **randomly** *adverb*

range *noun* **1** a line of mountains or hills; **2** the distance that a gun can fire; **3** a set of different objects of the same kind

rapid *adjective* very fast; **rapidly** *adverb*

rare *adjective* not happening often; not often seen; **rarely** *adverb*

¹**rash** *noun* a set of red spots on the skin, caused by illness

²**rash** *adjective* acting quickly without thinking enough of what might happen; **rashly** *adverb*

raspberry *noun* a soft sweet red berry; the bush on which this grows

rat *noun* a long-tailed animal with strong sharp teeth, related to but larger than the mouse

a black rat

rather *adverb* **1** a little; quite: *rather cold weather*; **2** sooner; more willingly: *I'd rather play tennis than swim*

¹**rattle** *verb* to make a lot of quick little noises

²**rattle** *noun* a baby's toy that makes a rattling noise when it is shaken

raw *adjective* not cooked; !! **roar**

ray *noun* a line of light, heat, or other form of energy

razor *noun* a sharp instrument for shaving

reach *verb* **1** to stretch out your hand or arm; **2** to be big enough to touch; to stretch out as far as; **3** to get to; to arrive at

read *verb* **(reads, reading, read)** to look at and understand printed or written words; **reading** *noun*; !! **reed**

ready *adjective* **1** prepared; in the right way or order for use; **2** willing; **readily** *adverb*

real *adjective* actual; true; not imagined; !! **reel**

realise *verb* to understand and believe something as a fact; **realisation** *noun*

really *adverb* in fact; truly; very

reason *noun* **1** what makes you decide to do something; why something happens; **2** the power to think and understand; **reasonable** *adjective*; **reasonably** *adverb*

receipt (*say* re-seet) *noun* a written or printed note saying that something has been paid for or that something has been received

receive *verb* to get something given or sent to you; **receiver** *noun*

recent *adjective* having happened only a short time ago; **recently** *adverb*

recipe (*say* ressipee) *noun* a set of instructions for cooking food

r

recite *verb* to repeat from memory or read aloud to an audience

recognise *verb* **1** to know again somebody or something you have met before; **2** to agree that something is true; **recognisable** *adjective*; **recognition** *noun*

¹**record** (*say* re-kord) *verb* **1** to write down so that it will be known; **2** to keep sounds or pictures on tape, CDs, etc, so that they can be heard or seen again; **recording** *noun*

²**record** (*say* rek-ord) *noun* **1** information that is written down and kept; **2** the best yet done; **3** a circular piece of plastic on which sound or music is recorded

recorder *noun* **1** a wooden or plastic musical instrument like a whistle, which is played by blowing; **2** an instrument for recording: **tape recorder, cassette recorder**

descant recorder

recycle *verb* to reuse what would otherwise be thrown away, such as waste paper, glass etc

red *noun* the colour of blood; **red** *adjective*; **reddish** *adjective*; **redness** *noun*

reduce *verb* to get or make smaller or less; **reduction** *noun*

reed *noun* a tall grasslike plant that grows in wet places; !! **read**

reel *noun* a round object on which cotton, wire, fishing line, recording tape, etc, can be wound; !! **real**

referee *noun* somebody who makes sure that the rules are not broken in some sports, such as football

reference *noun* information contained in books, on the internet or in any other form that can be used to check facts and find out information

reflect *verb* to throw back light, heat, sound, or a picture; **reflection** *noun*

refrigerator *noun* the full name for a fridge

¹**refuse** (*say* re-fyooz) *verb* not to allow; not to accept, do, or give

²**refuse** (*say* reff-yoos) *noun* rubbish

register *noun* a list of names; **register** *verb*; **registration** *noun*

regret *verb* (**regretted**) to be sorry about something; **regret** *noun*

regular *adjective* **1** done or happening at fixed times; **2** normal; proper; correct; **regularly** *adverb*

reign (*say* rane) *verb* **1** to be king or queen; **2** to exist noticeably: *quietness reigned*; **reign** *noun*; !! **rain, rein**

rein *noun* a long narrow band of leather by which a horse is controlled; !! **rain, reign**

reindeer *noun* a deer with long branching horns

reject (*say* re-ject) *verb* to refuse to accept; to throw away; **reject** (*say* ree-ject) *noun*; **rejection** *noun*

r

related *adjective* of the same family or kind

relation *noun* a member of your family

relative *noun* a relation

relax *verb* 1 to make or become less active; to stop worrying; 2 to make or become less stiff or tight; **relaxation** *noun*

release *verb* 1 to set free; to allow to come out; 2 to let a new film or record be shown to or bought by the public; **release** *noun*

reliable *adjective* fit to be trusted; **reliability** *noun*; **reliably** *adverb*

relief *noun* 1 a feeling of comfort at the ending of worry or pain; 2 help for people in trouble: *famine relief*; **relieve** *verb*

religion *noun* 1 belief in one or more gods; 2 a particular set of beliefs and the worship, behaviour, etc, connected with them; **religious** *adjective*

rely *verb* 1 to depend on something or something happening; 2 to trust somebody or trust them to do something

remain *verb* to stay or be left behind after others have gone; **remainder** *noun*

remark *noun* something said; an opinion; **remark** *verb*

remember *verb* to keep in the memory; to not forget

remind *verb* to cause somebody to remember; **reminder** *noun*

remote control *noun* a hand-held device that controls things such as a TV, stereo, etc

remove *verb* to take away; to take off; **removal** *noun*

¹**rent** *noun* money paid for the use of a house or office

²**rent** *verb* 1 to have the use of or allow somebody to use a house, room, etc, in return for money; 2 to pay to use a video, car, etc, for a short time

¹**repair** *verb* to mend

²**repair** *noun* 1 mending; 2 **in good/bad repair** in good/bad condition

repeat *verb* to say or do again; **repeat** *noun*; **repetition** *noun*

replace *verb* 1 to put something back in its place; 2 to take the place of somebody or something; **replacement** *noun*

reply *verb* to answer; **reply** *noun*

report *verb* to give the story of; to say what has happened; **report** *noun*; **reporter** *noun*

represent *verb* to stand on behalf of something

reproduce *verb* 1 to produce young; 2 to make a copy of; **reproduction** *noun*

reptile *noun* a cold-blooded animal, such as a snake, tortoise, or crocodile, that has a body covered in scales

request *verb* to ask politely; **request** *noun*

rescue *verb* to save from harm or danger; to set free; **rescue** *noun*; **rescuer** *noun*

research *noun* the study of a subject, so as to learn new facts; **research** *verb*

resources *noun* equipment available for your use

respect *noun* 1 admiration; feeling of honour; 2 attention; care; **respect** *verb*

r

response *noun* an answer or reply; an action done in answer to something

responsible *adjective* **1** having the duty of looking after somebody or something, so that you can be blamed if things go wrong; **2** able to be trusted; **responsibility** *noun*; **responsibly** *adverb*

¹**rest** *noun* **1** freedom from anything tiring; sleep; **2** a support; **rest** *verb*; **restful** *adjective*; **restless** *adjective*

²**rest** *noun* what is left

restaurant *noun* a place where food is sold and eaten

result *noun* **1** what happens because of an action or event; an effect; **2** a person's or team's success or failure in an examination, match, etc: *the football **results***

retire *verb* to stop working at your job, usually because of old age; **retired** *adjective*; **retirement** *noun*

return *verb* **1** to come or go back; **2** to give or send back; **return** *noun*

revise *verb* to go back and re-read things previously learned

revolution *noun* **1** the changing of a government by force, usually by people who have been badly treated; **2** a complete change; something completely new; **3** one complete circular movement round a fixed point; a full turn of a wheel or other object

reward *noun* something received or given for work, service, finding something, etc

rewind *verb* to wind film, tape, etc, back onto a reel; **rewind** *noun*

rhinoceros also **rhino** *noun* a large heavy thick-skinned animal, with either one or two horns on its nose

rhubarb *noun* a garden plant with thick juicy stems that can be eaten

rhyme *noun* **1** a word that ends with the same sound as another; **2** a short poem or piece of writing, using words that rhyme; **rhyme** *verb*

rhythm *noun* a regular pattern of beats in music, poetry, etc; **rhythmic, rhythmical** *adjective*; **rhythmically** *adverb*

ribbon *noun* a long narrow band of cloth used for tying things, for ornament, etc

rice *noun* a food grain grown in hot wet places, with seeds that can be cooked and eaten

rich *adjective* **1** having a lot of money or property; **2** valuable and beautiful; **3** containing a lot of a particular thing; full of goodness and colour: *rich food*; **riches** *noun* (*plural*); **richly** *adverb*; **richness** *noun*

rid *verb* (**rids, ridding, rid**) **1** to make free of; **2 get rid of** to free yourself from something; to drive or give away

r

riddle *noun* a rhyming verse with a puzzle in the words

¹ride *verb* (**rides, riding, rode, ridden**) **1** to travel along, sitting on a bicycle, in a car, etc; **2** to travel on and control a horse; **rider** *noun*

performing dressage at the Spanish Riding School in Vienna

²ride *noun* a journey on an animal, in a vehicle, etc

rifle *noun* a gun fired from the shoulder, with a long barrel

¹right *noun, adjective* the side or direction opposite to left; !! **rite, write**

²right *adjective* **1** correct; true; **2** good; proper; !! **rite, write**

³right *noun* **1** what is good; **2** something a person can have or do because of the law; !! **rite, write**

⁴right *adverb* **1** towards the right; **2** directly; straight; **3** properly; correctly; **4** all the way; !! **rite, write**

rind (*say* **rynd**) *noun* the thick outer covering of certain fruits, foods, etc: *lemon* **rind**

¹ring *noun* **1** a metal band worn on the finger; **2** a circle; **3** a circular band; something shaped like a circle: **key ring**; **4** any closed-in space where things are shown or performed, as in a circus or for boxing; !! **wring**

²ring *verb* to put or make a ring round something; !! **wring**

³ring *verb* (**rings, ringing, rang, rung**) **1** to cause a bell to sound; **2** to make a sound like a bell; **3** to phone; **4** ring a bell to remind you of something; **ring** *noun*; !! **wring**

rinse *verb* **1** to wash in clean water to remove soap, dirt, etc; **2** to colour the hair; **rinse** *noun*

rip *noun* a long tear; **rip** *verb*

ripe *adjective* fully grown and ready to be eaten; **ripen** *verb*

¹rise *verb* (**rises, rising, rose, risen**) to go up; to get higher; to increase

²rise *noun* **1** an increase in wages, prices, etc; **2** the act of growing greater or more powerful

¹risk *noun* a danger; a chance of losing something; **risky** *adjective*

²risk *verb* **1** to place in danger; **2** to take a chance

rite *noun* a ceremony, especially one that is religious; !! **right, write**

river *noun* a wide natural stream of water

road *noun* a smooth broad prepared track for wheeled vehicles; !! **rode**

roar *noun* a deep loud continuing sound; **roar** *verb*; !! **raw**

roast *verb* to cook meat or other foods by dry heat in an oven or over a fire

rob *verb* (**robbed**) to take money, goods, etc, from a person or place when it is not yours; to steal from; **robber** *noun*; **robbery** *noun*

robin also **robin redbreast** *noun* a fat little bird, with a brown back and a red breast

robot *noun* 1 a machine that can do some human work; 2 an imaginary machine figure that acts as if alive

robotic arm used in industrial assembly

r

¹**rock** *noun* 1 stone forming part of the Earth's surface; 2 a large separate piece of stone; 3 a hard sticky sweet made in long round bars; **rocky** *adjective*

²**rock** *verb* to move backwards and forwards or from side to side

³**rock** *noun* a kind of popular modern music played on electric instruments and with a strong beat

rocket *noun* 1 a kind of firework that shoots high into the air and lets out coloured flames; 2 a machine of this kind driven by burning gases, used for spacecraft

rod *noun* a long thin stiff stick of wood, metal, etc

role *noun* the part taken by somebody in a play or film; !! **roll**

¹**roll** *noun* 1 a flat piece of some material rolled into a tube shape; 2 a small loaf of bread for one person; !! **role**

²**roll** *verb* 1 to turn over and over, round and round, or from side to side; 2 to move steadily and smoothly along as if on wheels; 3 to form into a circular shape by curling round and round; 4 to make flat by passing something over and over: **rolling pin**; 5 to make a long deep sound: *the drums* **rolled**; !! **role**

Roman Catholic *noun* a member of the branch of Christianity (**Roman Catholic Church**) that has the Pope as its head; **Roman Catholic** *adjective*

roof *noun* **1** the outside covering on top of a building; **2** the top covering of a tent, vehicle, etc; **3** the bony upper part of the inside of the mouth

room *noun* **1** a place in a building, with its own walls, floor, and ceiling; **2** space which could be filled

root *noun* **1** the part of a plant that grows down into the soil; **2** the part of a tooth, hair, or organ that holds it to the body; !! **route**

rope *noun* a strong thick cord

¹**rose** *noun* a sweet-smelling flower with prickly stems

²**rose** *see* RISE

rot *verb* (**rotted**) to decay or go bad; **rot** *noun*; **rotten** *adjective*

rough *adjective* **1** not smooth; **2** not gentle; violent; **3** done quickly and not yet in finished form: *a **rough** sketch*; **4** stormy; **roughly** *adverb*; **roughen** *verb*

¹**round** *adjective* **1** shaped like a circle or a ball; **2** curved

²**round** *adverb, preposition* **1** with a circular movement or movements; spinning in a circle; **2** in a circular position; surrounding a central point; **3** all over the place; in or into all parts; **4** so as to face the other way; **5** all the **year round** during the whole year

³**round** *noun* **1** one stage, period, or game in a competition or sport; **2** a regular journey to many houses, offices, etc: *a paper **round***; **3** a complete slice of bread

roundabout *noun* **1** a circular machine on which you can ride, usually at a park or a fairground; **2** a circular place where several roads meet or cross that helps to prevent traffic jams

rounders *noun* a ball game in which a player hits the ball and runs round the sides of a square marked by posts

rounding up/down *verb* making a number bigger or smaller to make it easier to use, for example, rounding up to the nearest ten, 69 becomes 70, or rounding down to the nearest ten, 64 becomes 60

route *noun* a way planned or followed from one place to another; !! **root**

¹**row** (*say like* no) *noun* a neat line of people or things side by side

²**row** (*say like* now) *noun* a quarrel; a loud noise; **row** *verb*

³**row** (*say like* no) *verb* to move through the water with oars; **row** *noun*; **rower** *noun*

royal *adjective* for, belonging to, supported by, or connected with a king or queen; **royally** *adverb*

rub *verb* (**rubbed**) to slide something to and fro or round and round against something else; **rub** *noun*

rubber *noun* **1** a substance, made from chemicals or from the juice of a tropical tree, which keeps out water and springs back into position after being stretched; **2** a piece of this substance used for removing pencil marks; **rubbery** *adjective*

rubbish *noun* **1** waste material to be thrown away; **2** silly remarks; nonsense

rubella *also* **German measles** *noun* a disease in which red spots appear for a short time on your body

rucksack *noun* a cloth bag you carry on your back

rude *adjective* not polite; **rudely** *adverb*; **rudeness** *noun*

rug *noun* **1** a thick floor mat; **2** a warm woollen covering to wrap round yourself when travelling

rugby *also* **rugby football**, **rugger** *noun* a type of game played with an oval ball, by teams of thirteen (**rugby league**) or fifteen (**rugby union**) players

ruin *verb* to destroy and spoil completely; **ruin** *noun*

the ruins of the Inca city Machu Picchu in Peru

¹**rule** *noun* **1** an order, law, etc, that tells you what you must or must not do; **2** government; **3 as a rule** usually; generally

²**rule** *verb* **1** to have and use the highest power over a country, people, etc, especially as a government; **2** to draw a straight line

ruler *noun* **1** a person who rules; **2** a long narrow piece of hard material with straight edges for measuring things or drawing lines

rumour *noun* something that people tell one another but that may not be true

¹**run** *verb* (**runs, running, ran, run**) **1** to move on your legs faster than walking; **2** to move quickly; **3** to be in charge of a shop, business, etc; **4** to flow, pour, drip, etc; **5** to stretch; to continue: *The road **runs** beside the river*; **6** to work or cause to work: *The car **runs** well*

²**run** *noun* **1** the action of running; **2** a journey; **3** a point won in cricket

¹**rung** *noun* one of the bars that form the steps of a ladder

²**rung** *see* RING

runway *noun* an area with a specially prepared hard surface, on which aircraft land and take off

rush *verb* to hurry; to act quickly; **rush** *noun*

rust *noun* the reddish-brown substance that forms on iron when it has been wet; **rust** *verb*; **rusty** *adjective*

r

Ss

¹**sack** *noun* **1** a large bag used for storing or moving goods: **sackful**; **2** the taking away of someone's job by an employer

²**sack** *verb* to take somebody's job away

sad *adjective* (**sadder**) feeling, showing, or causing sorrow; unhappy; **sadly** *adverb*; **sadness** *noun*

saddle *noun* a leather seat that fits on the back of a horse or on a bicycle, for a rider to sit on; **saddle** *verb*

¹**safe** *adjective* out of danger; not able to be hurt; protected; **safely** *adverb*; **safety** *noun*

²**safe** *noun* a box or cupboard with thick metal sides and a lock, used to protect money, jewellery, etc

¹**sail** *noun* **1** a piece of cloth fixed on a boat to move it through the water by the force of the wind; **2** a short trip in such a boat; **3 set sail** to begin a trip at sea; !! **sale**

²**sail** *verb* **1** to travel on water; **2** to direct a ship or boat on water; **sailor** *noun*; !! **sale**

salad *noun* a mixture of lettuce, uncooked vegetables, or fruits, served cold

sale *noun* **1** an act of selling; **2** a time when goods are sold at lower prices than usual; !! **sail**

salmon *noun* a large fish of the northern seas with silvery skin and yellowish-pink flesh, which swims up rivers to breed

salt *noun* a very common colourless or white solid substance used to improve the taste of food, preserve it, etc; **salt** *verb*; **salty** *adjective*

same *adjective* **1** like something else in every way; not different or changed; **2** being always only one single thing, person etc

sand *noun* a loose material of very small fine grains, found along coasts and in deserts; **sandy** *adjective*

sandal *noun* a light open shoe

sandwich *noun* two slices of bread with some other food between them

sardine *noun* a small sea fish used as food

sailing dinghy

jib

mainsail

satellites

Landsat D

Comsat

satellite *noun* **1** a man-made object that travels round the Earth, moon, etc; **2** a small body moving round a planet

satisfy *verb* **1** to make happy; to please; **2** to be or give enough for; **satisfaction** *noun*; **satisfactory** *adjective*; **satisfying** *adjective*

Saturday *noun* the seventh day of the week

Saturn *noun* a planet surrounded by large rings that is sixth in order from the sun

sauce *noun* any of various kinds of usually cooked liquids put on or eaten with food; !! **source**

saucer *noun* a small plate made for putting a cup on

sausage *noun* meat in a tube shape, **sausage roll**

save *verb* **1** to make safe from danger; rescue; **2** to keep for later use; **3** to use less; to stop waste; **4** to keep for later use on a computer; **saver** *noun*; **savings** *noun*

¹**saw** *noun* a tool for cutting materials, having a thin flat blade with a row of V-shaped teeth on the edge; !! **sore**

²**saw** *verb* (**saws, sawing, sawed, sawn** *or* **sawed**) to cut with a saw; !! **sore**

³**saw** *see* SEE; !! **sore**

say *verb* (**says, saying, said**) **1** to pronounce a sound, word, etc; to speak; **2** to give an opinion, ask a question, etc, using words; **3 that is to say** also **i.e.** in other words; **saying** *noun*

scab *noun* a hard mass of dried blood that forms over a wound while it is healing; **scabby** *adjective*

¹**scale** *noun* one of the small nearly flat stiff pieces covering the skin of some animals, especially fish and reptiles

²**scale** *noun* **1** a set of marks on a measuring instrument such as a ruler or a thermometer; **2** a rule or set of numbers comparing measurements on a map or model with actual measurements; **3** a set of musical notes going up or down in order

³**scale** also **scales** *noun* a weighing machine

⁴**scale** *verb* to climb up

scampi *noun* large prawns

scanner *noun* a machine that takes pictures, which can be used by computers

scar *noun* a mark remaining on the skin from a wound, cut, etc; **scar** *verb* (**scarred**)

S

scare *verb* **1** to cause sudden fear to somebody; **2** to become afraid; **scare** *noun*; **scared** *adjective*

scarecrow *noun* a figure in the shape of a person, put in a field to keep birds away from crops

scarf *noun* (*plural* **scarfs** *or* **scarves**) a piece of cloth for wearing round the neck, head, or shoulders

scarlet *noun* a very bright red colour; **scarlet** *adjective*

scatter *verb* **1** to cause a group of people or things to separate widely; **2** to spread widely in all directions

scene *noun* **1** a short part of a play, film, etc; **2** the place where something happens; **3** a view of a place; !! **seen**

scenery *noun* **1** the set of painted backgrounds and other articles used on a theatre stage; **2** a view of the countryside

scent *noun* **1** a liquid with a nice smell; perfume; **2** a smell; !! **cent, sent**

schedule (*say* **shedule**) *noun* a timetable of things to be done or when trains, buses, or planes will come; **schedule** *verb*

¹**school** *noun* a place where people go to learn: **schoolboy, schoolgirl, schoolwork**

²**school** *noun* a large group of one kind of fish, whale, etc

science *noun* **1** the study of knowledge that can be made into a system and that usually depends on testing facts and making general laws; **2** a branch of such knowledge, such as chemistry, physics, or biology; **scientific** *adjective*; **scientist** *noun*

scissors *noun* two sharp blades having handles at one end with holes for the fingers, fastened at the centre so that they open in the shape of the letter X and cut when they close: **pair of scissors**

scold *verb* to speak angrily, especially to blame; **scolding** *noun*

scone (*say* **skon** *or* **skohn**) *noun* a small soft round cake

scooter *noun* **1** a child's vehicle, pushed by one foot touching the ground; **2** also **motor scooter** a low bicycle-like vehicle with an engine, two small wheels, and usually a wide curved front to protect the legs

motor scooter

scorch *verb* to burn something slightly, usually so there is a brown mark; **scorch** *noun*

score *noun* the number of points, runs, goals, etc, made in a game, sport, etc; **score** *verb*

S

scrape *verb* **1** to rub with something hard or sharp; **2** to hurt or damage in this way; **scrape** *noun*

¹**scratch** *verb* to rub and tear or mark with something pointed or rough

²**scratch** *noun* a mark or small wound made by scratching

scream *verb* to cry out loudly on a high note; **scream** *noun*

screen *noun* **1** the front surface of a television, computer, or other instrument on which pictures and information can be shown; **2** a flat surface on which films or slides are shown; **3** a covering frame used for protecting people from cold or heat, for hiding something from view, etc

¹**screw** *noun* an object like a nail with a raised edge **(thread)** going round and round it which helps to hold it in place

²**screw** *verb* **1** to fasten by turning or tightening screws; **2** to move something, such as the top of a jar, in the same way; **3** to make paper, etc, into a small ball

scribble *verb* to write carelessly or in a hurry; **scribble** *noun*

script *noun* written speech made for a play

scrub *verb* **(scrubbed)** to clean by hard rubbing, as with a stiff brush; **scrub** *noun*

scruffy *adjective* if somebody looks messy or untidy

sea *noun* the great body of salty water that covers much of the Earth's surface: **seabird, seashell, seashore, seaside, seaweed**; ‼ **see**

¹**seal** *noun* a large fish-eating animal having broad flat limbs **(flippers)** for swimming

elephant seal

²**seal** *noun* a small piece of paper, wax, etc, which is fixed across an opening, and which must be broken in order to open it

³**seal** *verb* **1** to make or fix a seal onto something; **2** to fasten or close tightly and firmly

seam *noun* a line of stitches joining two pieces of cloth, leather, etc, at or near their edges; **seamless** *adjective*; ‼ **seem**

search *verb* to look at, through, into, etc, to try to find something; **search** *noun*

season *noun* **1** one of the four parts of the year – spring, summer, autumn, or winter; **2** a period of time each year for a particular activity: *the football season*

seat *noun* **1** a place for sitting; **2** a thing to sit on; **3 take/have a seat** please sit down

seat belt *noun* a strap that keeps you safe in a car or aeroplane

S

¹**second** *noun* **1** a length of time equal to 1/60 of a minute; **2** a moment; a very short time

²**second** *adjective, adverb, noun, pronoun* the one after the first; 2nd

secret *noun* something known to only you or just a few other people; **secrecy** *noun*; **secret** *adjective*; **secretly** *adverb*

secretary *noun* a person with the job of preparing letters, keeping records, arranging meetings, etc, for others; **secretarial** *adjective*

see *verb* (**see, seeing, saw, seen**) **1** to use the eyes; to have or use the power of sight; **2** to look at; **3** to understand or recognise; **4** to visit, call upon, or meet; !! **sea**

seed *noun* the part of a plant from which a new plant can grow; **seedless** *adjective*

seek *verb* (**seeks, seeking, sought**) to make a search for; to try to find or get

seem *verb* to appear to be; !! **seam**

seesaw *noun* a board for children to sit on at opposite ends, balanced so that when one end goes up the other goes down

¹**segment** (*say seg-ment*) *noun* a piece of something

²**segment** (*say seg-ment*) *verb* to divide something into parts

self *noun* (*plural* **selves**) your own person

selfish *adjective* thinking only about yourself and not caring for others; **selfishly** *adverb*; **selfishness** *noun*

self-service *noun, adjective* the system in many restaurants, shops, garages, etc, in which customers collect what they want and then pay at special desks

sell *verb* (**sells, selling, sold**) to give to another for money; **seller** *noun*; !! **cellar**

send *verb* (**sends, sending, sent**) to cause or order a person or thing to go or be taken to a place, in a direction, etc; **sender** *noun*

senior *adjective* **1** of higher position or importance; **2** older; **senior** *noun*

¹**sense** *noun* **1** good understanding and reasonable ideas: **common sense**; **2** one of the five powers by which we see, smell, hear, feel, or taste; **sensation** *noun*; **sensitivity** *noun*; **sensitive** *adjective*

²**sense** *verb* to feel; to know through the senses

sensible *adjective* reasonable; having good sense; **sensibly** *adverb*

sentence *noun* a group of words that forms a statement, question, etc, contains a verb and usually a subject, and (in writing) begins with a capital letter and ends with one of the marks .!?"

¹**separate** (*say sepparayt*) *verb* **1** to move apart; to go in different directions; **2** to make or keep in different places

²**separate** (*say sepprut*) *adjective* **1** not the same; different; **2** apart; not joined or shared with another; **separately** *adverb*; **separation** *noun*

S

September *noun* the ninth month of the year

sequel *noun* a play, film or story that follows on from another

sequence *noun* actions or objects in a specific order

sergeant (*say* **sar-junt**) *noun* a person in the army or police force

serial *noun* a story appearing in parts; !! **cereal**

series *noun* a group of things coming one after the other

serious *adjective* **1** not cheerful; not joking; **2** important

seriously *adverb* **1** in a serious way; **2** very; extremely: *seriously* rich

servant *noun* a person who works for another such as a maid

serve *verb* **1** to work for; **2** to give food to people; **3** to look after somebody buying something; **4** to begin play in tennis, badminton, etc, by hitting the ball to the other player; **5 serve somebody right** to be a fair punishment for somebody

service *noun* **1** work or duty done for somebody; **2** helping customers in a shop or guests in a hotel, restaurant, etc; **3** a religious ceremony; **4** a useful business or job that usually does not produce goods: **postal service, train service**

¹**set** *verb* (**sets, setting, set**) **1** to put in a place; **2** to give a piece of work for somebody to do; **3** to put into a position; arrange: *set the table;* **4** to put into action; to make something happen; **5** to pass downwards out of sight: *The sun is setting*

²**set** *noun* **1** a group of things thought of together; **2** a piece of electrical equipment especially a television

settee *noun* a long, comfortable seat with a back; a sofa

settle *verb* **1** to go and live in a place; **2** to bring or place down, often in a comfortable position; **3** to sink or come down, usually to a position of rest; **4** to decide on; to fix or arrange something; **settlement** *noun;* **settler** *noun*

seven *adjective, noun* the number 7; **seventh** *adjective, adverb*

seventeen *adjective, noun* the number 17; **seventeenth** *adjective, adverb*

seventy *adjective, noun* the number 70; **seventieth** *adjective, adverb*

several *adjective, pronoun* more than two but fewer than many; some but not many

severe *adjective* **1** not kind or gentle; strict; **2** hard; difficult; **severely** *adverb*

sew *verb* (**sews, sewing, sewed, sewn**) to join or fasten materials such as cloth, leather, paper, etc, by stitching with thread; to make or mend with a needle and thread: **sewing machine;** !! **so, sow**

electric sewing machine

sex *noun* being male or female

¹**shade** *noun* **1** slight darkness; shelter from the sun or other light; **2** something that keeps out light: **lampshade**; **3** a slightly different colour: *light blue and a deeper* **shade**; **shady** *adjective*; **shadiness** *noun*

²**shade** *verb* to shelter from direct light or heat

shadow *noun* a dark shape made by something when it blocks out light

shake *verb* (**shakes, shaking, shook, shaken**) **1** to move quickly up and down and to and fro; **2 shake hands with somebody** to take somebody's right hand in your own for a moment, moving it up and down, as a sign of greeting, goodbye, agreement, etc; **3 shake your head** to move your head from side to side to show 'no' or disapproval; **shake** *noun*; !! **sheikh, sheik**

hammerhead shark

shall *verb* (**should, shan't**=shall not) **1** used with I and we when asking a question or offering to do something: **Shall** *I get you a chair?* **2** sometimes used instead of *will* with I and we to say what is going to happen: *I* **shall** *have finished my work by next Friday*

shallow *adjective* not deep; not far from top to bottom

shame *noun* the painful feeling you have when you have done something wrong or silly; **shame** *verb*

shampoo *noun* a liquid soap used for washing hair; **shampoo** *verb*

shape *noun* the appearance or form of something seen; **shape** *verb*; **shaped** *adjective*; **shapeless** *adjective*

¹**share** *noun* **1** the part belonging to or done by a person; **2** a part of a company that many people can buy

²**share** *verb* **1** to use, pay, have, take part in, etc, with others or among a group; **2** to divide and give out

shark *noun* a fierce flesh-eating fish that has several rows of sharp teeth, and can be dangerous to people

sharp *adjective* **1** having a thin cutting edge; having a fine point; **2** quick and sensitive in thinking, seeing, hearing, etc: **sharp sighted**; **3** sudden and quick: *a* **sharp** *pain*; **sharply** *adverb*; **sharpen** *verb*

shave *verb* to cut off hair close to the skin with a razor; **shave** *noun*

she *pronoun* (**her, herself**) that female person or animal

141

¹shed *noun* a lightly built hut, used for storing things

²shed *verb* (**sheds, shedding, shed**) to let fall or get rid of naturally, things such as leaves, hair, etc

sheep *noun* (*plural* **sheep**) (*male* **ram**, *female* **ewe**, *young* **lamb**) a grass-eating animal kept for its wool and meat

sheet *noun* 1 a large four-sided piece of cloth used to cover a bed; 2 a piece of paper

a modern cruise ship

shield *noun* a broad piece of metal, wood, or leather once carried by soldiers to protect them from arrows, blows, etc

¹shine *verb* (**shines, shining, shone**) 1 to give off light; to look bright; 2 to direct a lamp, beam of light, etc

²shine *verb* (**shines, shining, shined**) to polish; to make bright by rubbing; **shiny** *adjective*

ship *noun* a large boat

sheikh, sheik (*say* **shake**) *noun* an Arab chief or prince; !! **shake**

shelf *noun* (*plural* **shelves**) a flat usually long and narrow board fixed against a wall or in a frame, for putting things on

shell *noun* the hard covering of an animal, egg, nut, etc: **shellfish**

¹shelter *noun* anything that protects, especially a building

²shelter *verb* to protect from harm; to give shelter to

shepherd (*feminine* **shepherdess**) *noun* a person who takes care of sheep in a field

shirt *noun* a piece of clothing for the upper body, usually of light cloth with a collar and sleeves

shiver *verb* to shake, especially from cold or fear; **shiver** *noun*

shoal *noun* a large group of fish swimming together

¹shock *noun* 1 the strong feeling caused by something unexpected and usually very unpleasant; 2 the sudden violent effect of electricity passing through the body; 3 a violent force, as from a hard blow, crash, explosion etc

²shock *verb* 1 to cause unpleasant or angry surprise to somebody; 2 to give an electric shock to

*15th Century shoes
with long points*

shoe *noun* an outer covering for the foot, usually having a hard sole and a support under the heel

¹**shoot** *verb* (**shoots, shooting, shot**) 1 to fire a weapon at and hit something or somebody; 2 to go fast or suddenly; 3 to kick, throw, etc, a ball in order to score in a game; 4 to make a photograph or film

²**shoot** *noun* a new growth from a plant, especially a young stem and leaves

shooting star *noun* a small meteor from space which burns brightly as it passes through the Earth's air

¹**shop** *noun* 1 a room or building where goods are regularly kept and sold: **shopkeeper**; 2 a place where things are made or repaired

²**shop** *verb* (**shopped**) to buy things; **shopper** *noun*; **shopping** *noun*

shore *noun* the land along the edge of a large stretch of water; !! **sure**

short *adjective* 1 not far from one end to the other; little in distance, length, or height; 2 lasting only a little time; **shortage** *noun*; **shorten** *verb*

shorts *noun* trousers ending above the knees

¹**shot** *noun* 1 an action of shooting a weapon; 2 a kick, throw, etc, of a ball intended to score a point; 3 a sending up of a space vehicle or rocket; 4 a chance to do something; a try

²**shot** *see* SHOOT

should *verb* (**shouldn't**) to have a duty to; ought to

shoulder *noun* 1 the part of the body at each side of the neck where the arms join; 2 either edge of a road outside the travelled part: **hard shoulder**

shout *verb* to speak or say very loudly; **shout** *noun*

shovel *noun* a long-handled tool with a broad blade for lifting and moving loose material such as earth or coal; **shovel** *verb*

¹**show** *verb* (**shows, showing, showed, shown**) 1 to offer for seeing; to allow or cause to be seen; 2 to appear; to be in or come into view; 3 to go with and guide or direct; 4 to explain; to make clear to by words or actions

²**show** *noun* 1 a performance in a theatre, on radio or television, etc; 2 a collection of things for looking at

shower *noun* 1 a short fall of rain or snow; 2 a fall of many small things or drops of liquid; 3 a washing of the body by standing under an opening from which water comes out in many small streams; the thing used for this; **shower** *verb*

S

shrimp *noun* a small sea creature with long legs and a tail shaped like a fan

shrink *verb* **(shrinks, shrinking, shrank, shrunk** or **shrunken)** to make or become smaller, as from the effect of heat or water

shrug *verb* **(shrugged)** to lift and drop your shoulders, especially to show you do not know or do not care; **shrug** *noun*

shut *verb* **(shuts, shutting, shut)** to close; to move into a covered, blocked, or folded-together position

shuttle *noun* **1** a spacecraft that can fly into space and return to Earth: **space shuttle; 2** a plane, train or bus that goes on short journeys from one place to another

shuttlecock *noun* a small light object (see picture on page 14) for hitting across a net in a game of badminton

shy *adjective* **(shyer** or **shier, shyest** or **shiest)** nervous in the company of others; **shyly** *adverb*; **shyness** *noun*

sick *adjective* **1** ill; having a disease; **2** upset in the stomach so that the food comes back out through your mouth; **sickness** *noun*

side *noun* **1** a more or less upright surface of something, not the top, bottom, front, or back; **2** the right or left part of the body, from the shoulder to the top of the leg; **3** an edge; **4** either of the two surfaces of a thin flat object; **5** a sports team

sideways *adverb, adjective* **1** with one side, and not the front or back, forward or up; **2** to or towards one side

sigh *verb* to let out a deep breath slowly and with a sound, usually showing that you are tired, sad, pleased, etc; **sigh** *noun*

sight *noun* **1** the sense of seeing; the power of the eye; **2** something that is seen; **3** something worth seeing, especially a place visited by tourists; !! **site**

¹**sign** *noun* **1** a mark, symbol, or object that is seen and that means something to the person who sees it; **2** a board or other notice giving information, warning, directions, etc: **signpost; 3** also **sign of the zodiac** any of the twelve divisions of the year named after groups of stars

²**sign** *verb* to write your name; **signature** *noun*

signs of the Zodiac

Pisces	Aries
Taurus	Gemini
Cancer	Leo
Virgo	Libra
Aquarius	Sagittarius
Capricorn	Scorpio

¹**signal** *noun* **1** a sound, action, movement, or apparatus meant to warn, command, or give a message; **2** a sound, picture, or message sent by waves, as in radio or television

²**signal** *verb* (**signalled**) to give a signal

silence *noun* the state of not speaking or making a noise: complete quiet; stillness

silent *adjective* **1** not speaking; not using spoken expression; **2** free from noise; quiet; **silently** *adverb*

silk *noun* a fine thread that is produced by a type of caterpillar (**silkworm**) and made into thread for sewing or into cloth; the smooth soft cloth made from this; **silky** *adjective*

silkworm building its cocoon

silly *adjective* not clever or reasonable; foolish; not serious; **silliness** *noun*

silver *noun* **1** a soft whitish precious metal that is used in ornaments and coins; **2** the colour of this metal; **silver** *adjective*; **silvery** *adjective*

similar *adjective* like or alike; of the same kind; partly or almost the same; **similarly** *adverb*; **similarity** *noun*

simple *adjective* **1** easy to understand or do; not difficult; **2** of the ordinary kind; not complicated; plain; **simply** *adverb*

sin *noun* something people think is a very bad act; something your religion teaches you is wrong; **sin** *verb*

since *adverb, preposition, conjunction* at a time between then and now; from then until now: *I haven't seen her* **since** *her illness*

sing *verb* (**sings, singing, sang, sung**) to make music, musical sounds, songs, etc, with the voice; **singer** *noun*

¹**single** *adjective* **1** the only one; not double; **2** not married; **3** for the use of only one person: *a* **single** *room*

²**single** *noun* a CD or tape with only one song on it

¹**sink** *noun* a large basin in a kitchen, for washing dishes, clothes, vegetables, etc, in

²**sink** *verb* (**sinks, sinking, sank, sunk**) to go down below a surface, out of sight, or to the bottom

sip *verb* (**sipped**) to drink, taking only a little at a time into the front of the mouth; **sip** *noun*

sir *noun* a polite way of talking or writing to a man

sister *noun* **1** a girl or woman with the same parents as another girl or woman; **2** a nurse in charge of a hospital ward

sit *verb* (**sits, sitting, sat**) to rest in a position with the upper body upright and your bottom on a chair, the ground, etc: **sitting room**

site *noun* **1** a place where something was or happened; **2** a piece of ground for building on; !! **sight**

S

145

six *adjective, noun* **1** the number 6; **2** a cricket hit that counts as six runs; **sixth** *adjective, adverb*

sixteen *adjective, noun* the number 16; **sixteenth** *adjective, adverb*

sixty *adjective, noun* the number 60; **sixtieth** *adjective, adverb*

size *noun* the bigness or smallness of anything

skate *noun* a special shoe or boot fitted with a metal blade or small wheels: **ice skates, roller skates**; **skate** *verb*; **skater** *noun*

skateboard *noun* a piece of wood or plastic with wheels that you stand on and go along on

skeleton *noun* the bones in a human or animal body

human skeleton

ski (*say* skee) *noun* (*plural* **skis**) a long thin narrow piece of wood, plastic, or metal, curving up in front, that is fastened to a boot for travelling on snow or that you stand on to ski over water (**waterski**); **ski** *verb*; **skier** *noun*; **skiing** *noun*

skill *noun* the ability to do something well; **skilful** *adjective*; **skilfully** *adverb*; **skilled** *adjective*

skin *noun* **1** the natural outer covering of an animal or human body, from which hair may grow; **2** a natural outer covering of some fruits and vegetables; peel

skinny *adjective* thin; without much flesh

skip *verb* (**skipped**) **1** to move in a light dancing way, as with quick steps and jumps; **2** to pass over or leave out something; **3** to jump over a rope that is made to swing over your head and under your feet; **skip** *noun*

skirt *noun* a piece of women's clothing that hangs from the waist

skull *noun* the bones of the head

sky *noun* (*plural* **skies**) the upper air; the space above the Earth where clouds and the sun, moon, and stars appear

slap *verb* (**slapped**) to strike quickly with the flat part of the hand; **slap** *noun*

slave *noun* a person owned by another; a servant without freedom

sledge *noun* a small vehicle made for sliding along snow or ice; **sledge** *verb*

¹sleep *noun* the natural resting state of unconsciousness of the body; the state of not being awake; a period of time of this; **sleepy** *adjective*; **sleepily** *adverb*

S

²**sleep** *verb* **(sleeps, sleeping, slept)** to rest in sleep, as at night

sleeve *noun* a part of a piece of clothing for covering an arm; **sleeveless** *adjective*

slice *noun* a thin flat piece cut from something; **slice** *verb*

¹**slide** *verb* **(slides, sliding, slid)** to go smoothly over a surface

²**slide** *noun* **1** a slipping movement over a surface; **2** an apparatus for sliding down; **3** a square piece of framed film for passing light through to show a picture on a surface; **4** a small piece of glass to put objects on for seeing under a microscope

slight *adjective* small; not important; **slightly** *adverb*

¹**slip** *verb* **(slipped) 1** to slide out of place or fall by sliding; **2** to make a slight mistake

²**slip** *noun* **1** an act of slipping or sliding; **2** a slight mistake; **3** a small piece of paper; **4** a piece of women's underwear

slipper *noun* a soft, light shoe for wearing indoors

slippery *adjective* difficult to hold or to stand, drive, etc, on without slipping

slit *verb* to make a long narrow cut or opening in; **slit** *noun*

slope *noun* a surface that tilts; a piece of ground going up or down; **slope** *verb*

¹**slow** *adjective* **1** not moving or going on quickly; **2** taking a long time or too long; **3** not good or quick in understanding; **4** showing a time that is earlier than the true time; **slowly** *adjective*; **slowness** *noun*

²**slow** *verb* to make or become slower

slug *noun* a small plant-eating creature, like a snail but with no shell, that eats plants and often does damage to gardens

smack *verb* to strike loudly, as with the flat part of the hand; **smack** *noun*

small *adjective* little in size, weight, force, importance, etc; **smallness** *noun*

smart *adjective* **1** neat and stylish in appearance; **2** clever; good or quick in thinking; **smartly** *adverb*

smash *verb* to break or shatter into pieces

¹**smell** *verb* **(smells, smelling, smelled** *or* **smelt) 1** to have or use the sense of the nose; **2** to notice, examine, discover, or recognise by this sense; **3** to have a particular smell

²**smell** *noun* **1** the power of using the nose; **2** something that we discover through the nose

smile *noun* an expression of the face with the mouth turned up at the ends and the eyes bright, that shows amusement, happiness, pleasure, etc; **smile** *verb*

¹**smoke** *noun* gas mixed with very small bits of solid material that can be seen in the air and is usually given off by burning something; **smokeless** *adjective*; **smoky** *adjective*

²**smoke** *verb* **1** to suck or breathe in smoke from cigarettes, cigars, pipes etc; **2** to give off smoke

smooth *adjective* having an even surface without sharply raised or lowered places, points, lumps, etc; not rough; **smooth** *verb*; **smoothly** *adverb*

snail *noun* a small animal with a soft body, no limbs, and a hard spiral-shaped shell on its back

snake *noun* a reptile that has a long body with no limbs, a large mouth, and a fork-shaped tongue, sometimes with a poisonous bite

snatch *verb* to get hold of something quickly

sneeze *verb* to push air and liquid out of your nose and mouth suddenly, making a noise, as when you have a cold; **sneeze** *noun*

sniff *verb* to draw air into the nose with a sound, often to discover a smell in or on something; **sniff** *noun*

snooker *noun* a billiards game played on a table with six pockets, with fifteen red balls and seven balls of other colours

snore *verb* to breathe heavily and noisily through the nose and mouth while asleep

snow *noun* water frozen into small flat flakes that fall like rain in cold weather and may cover the ground thickly: **snowball, snowflake, snowman; snow** *verb*

snowflake

snowboard *noun* a board used for sliding down a snowy hill

¹**so** *adverb* **1** in this way or that way; in the way shown or described; **2** in the same way; also; !! **sew, sow**

²**so** *conjunction* so that; so as to; in order that; therefore; !! **sew, sow**

soak *verb* to remain or leave in a liquid, to become soft or completely wet; **soak** *noun*; **soaked** *adjective*; **soaking** *adjective, adverb*

soap *noun* **1** a substance made from fats or oils, for use with water to wash the body or other things; **2** also **soap opera** a TV programme that goes on for a long time, telling a story about the same group of people; **soapy** *adjective*

society *noun* **1** a group of people with a shared interest or hobby; **2** the people around us

sock *noun* a covering of soft material for the foot and part of the lower leg

socket *noun* an opening, hollow place, or machine part that forms a holder or into which something fits: *an electric light socket*

sofa *noun* a comfortable seat with raised arms and a back and wide enough for usually two or three people

soft *adjective* **1** not hard or stiff; not firm against pressure; giving in to the touch; **2** smooth and pleasant to the touch; **3** quiet; not making much noise; **soften** *verb*; **softly** *adverb*; **softness** *noun*

software *noun* programs that control the way a computer works

soil *noun* the top covering of the ground, in which plants grow

solar *adjective* **1** of the sun; **2** using the power of the sun's light and heat

solar system *noun* the sun together with all the bodies, such as the moon, planets, etc, going round it

some *adjective, pronoun, adverb* **1** a little, few, or small number or amount; **2** used when speaking about people or things without saying exactly which ones: *Come back* **some** *other time*; !! **sum**

somebody also **someone** *pronoun* a person; some but no particular or known person

somehow *adverb* by some means; in some way not yet known

turning somersaults in the air

soldier *noun* a person in an army

¹**sole** *noun* **1** the bottom part of the foot on which you walk or stand; **2** the flat bottom part of a shoe not including the heel; !! **soul**

²**sole** *noun* a flat fish often eaten as food; !! **soul**

solid *adjective* **1** keeping its shape; not liquid or gas; **2** having the inside filled up; not hollow; **3** made of one material all the way through; **solid** *noun*

solve *verb* to find the answer to a puzzle, problem, etc; **solution** *noun*

somersault (*say* summer-solt) *noun* a jump or rolling backward or forward movement in which the feet go over the head before the body returns upright

something *pronoun* a thing which is not known or not named

sometime *adverb* at some time in the past or future

sometimes *adverb* at times; now and then; occasionally

somewhere *adverb* in, at, or to, some place

son *noun* a person's male child; !! **sun**

song *noun* **1** a short piece of music with words for singing; **2** the music-like sound of a bird

soon *adverb* within a short time

soot *noun* a black powder produced by burning, and carried into the air and left on surfaces by smoke; **sooty** *adjective*

soothe *verb* **1** to make less painful; **2** to make less angry, excited, or worried; to comfort or calm; **soothing** *adjective*

sore *adjective* painful or aching from a wound, infection, or hard use; **sore** *noun*; **soreness** *noun*; !! **saw**

sorrow *noun* sadness; a cause of unhappiness

sorry *adjective* used to say you are ashamed or unhappy because of things you have done and wish that you had not done them, or that you are sad because you cannot do what is wanted

¹**sort** *noun* a group of people, things, etc, all having certain qualities; a type; a kind; !! **sought**

²**sort** *verb* to put things in order; to arrange; !! **sought**

soul *noun* the part of a person that is not the body and is thought not to die; !! **sole**

¹**sound** *noun* what is or may be heard; something that causes a sensation in the ear

²**sound** *verb* **1** to make a sound; to produce an effect that can be heard; **2** to seem: *to* **sound** *interesting*

soup *noun* a liquid cooked food often containing small pieces of meat, fish, or vegetables

sour *adjective* having a taste that is not sweet

source *noun* where something comes from; !! **sauce**

south *noun* one of the four main points of the compass; the right of a person facing the rising sun; **south** *adjective, adverb*; **southerly** *adverb*; **southern** *adjective*

southeast *noun* the direction of the point of the compass that is halfway between south and east

southwest *noun* the direction of the point of the compass that is halfway between south and west

¹**sow** (*say* so) *verb* (**sows, sowing, sowed, sown** or **sowed**) to plant or scatter seeds on a piece of ground; **sower** *noun*; !! **sew, so**

²**sow** (*say like* how) *noun* a fully grown female pig

soya *noun* a plant that is grown for food from its seeds (**soya beans**), which are rich in protein

soya beans in a pod

space *noun* **1** what is outside the Earth's air; where stars, planets, moons, and other bodies move: **spacecraft, spaceman/woman, spaceship**; **2** an empty or open place; room; **3** an area or distance between objects

space shuttle *noun* a rocket that can return to Earth

S

spacesuit *noun* a suit for wearing in space, covering the whole body and provided with an air supply

spade *noun* 1 a tool like a shovel for digging earth, with a broad metal blade for pushing with the foot into the ground; 2 a playing card with one or more figures each shaped like a pointed leaf printed on it in black

spaghetti *noun* a food made of pasta in long strings, usually sold in dry form for making soft again in boiling water

spanner *noun* a metal hand tool for turning nuts and bolts

spare *verb* to be able to give or lend something; **spare** *adjective*

spark *noun* 1 a small bit of burning material thrown out by a fire or by the striking together of two hard objects; 2 a passage of electricity across a space that produces light, also used in car engines; **spark** *verb*

sparkle *verb* to shine in small flashes; **sparkle** *noun*

sparrow *noun* a small brownish bird, very common in many parts of the world

speak *verb* (**speaks, speaking, spoke, spoken**) to say things; to use the voice; to talk

speaker *noun* 1 a person making a speech; 2 the part on a sound system, TV, or computer where the sound comes from

spear *noun* a pole with a sharp point at one end used for throwing as a weapon

astronaut in a spacesuit

special *adjective* of a particular kind; not ordinary or usual; **specially** *adverb*

spectacles *noun* glasses that people wear to help them see better

spectacular *adjective* exciting and wonderful to watch

speech *noun* 1 the act or power of speaking; 2 a long set of words spoken for people to listen to

speed *noun* how fast something moves

speed *verb* (**speeds, speeding, sped**) to go fast; **speedy** *adjective*

speedometer *noun* an instrument in a vehicle for telling its speed

¹**spell** *verb* (**spells, spelling, spelt** *or* **spelled**) to name or write the letters of a word in order; **spelling** *noun*

²**spell** *noun* a condition caused by magical power; the magic words producing this condition

S

spend *verb* (**spends, spending, spent**) 1 to give money in payment; 2 to pass or use time

spice *noun* a seed, root, or other part of a plant used to give flavour to food; **spicy** *adjective*

spider *noun* a small eight-legged creature that makes thin threads, which it sometimes makes into nets or webs for catching insects to eat

Australian trap door spider

spill *verb* (**spills, spilling, spilt** *or* **spilled**) to pour out accidentally, as over the edge of a container

spin *verb* (**spins, spinning, spun**) 1 to make thread by twisting cotton, wool, etc; 2 to produce thread, especially in a mass or net; 3 to turn round and round quickly

spinach *noun* a vegetable whose broad green leaves are usually eaten cooked

spine *noun* 1 also **spinal column** the row of bones in the centre of your back; 2 a stiff pointed part of a plant or animal; a prickle

spiral *noun* a curve that winds round and round, such as a spring or the thread of a screw; **spiral** *adjective*

spirit *noun* 1 the part of you that is not body, and that some people think does not die with your body; 2 a being without a body, such as a ghost; 3 a state of mind: *in high **spirits***; 4 a strong alcoholic drink

spit *verb* (**spits, spitting, spat** *or* **spit**) to force liquid from the mouth

spite *noun* 1 not liking and wanting to annoy another person, especially in some small way; 2 **in spite of** even though something else happens; **spiteful** *adjective*; **spitefully** *adverb*

splash *verb* to cause a liquid to fall, strike, or move noisily, in drops, waves, etc; **splash** *noun*

splendid *adjective* very fine; excellent; **splendidly** *adverb*

splint *noun* a flat piece of wood, metal or plastic, used for protecting and keeping a damaged part of the body, especially a bone, in position

splinter *noun* a small needle-like piece broken off something, especially of wood

split *verb* (**splits, splitting, split**) 1 to break from one end to another, especially with force or by a blow or tear; 2 to divide into separate parts; to share; **split** *noun*

spoil *verb* (**spoils, spoiling, spoiled** *or* **spoilt**) 1 to make or become of no use; to ruin; 2 to make a child selfish from having too much attention

¹**spoke** *noun* a bar that connects the outer ring of a wheel to the centre, as on a bicycle

²**spoke** *see* SPEAK

sponge *noun* 1 a sea creature that grows a spreading rubber-like skeleton full of small holes; a piece of this or a substance like it, which is used for washing; 2 *also* **sponge cake** a soft light sweet cake

breadcrumb sponge

sponsor *noun* a person or company that pays for a project or activity to happen

spoon *noun* a tool for mixing, serving, and eating food, consisting of a small bowl with a handle: **spoonful, spoonfuls**

sport *noun* games, competitions, or activities done for pleasure

sportsman (*feminine* **sportswoman**) *noun* a person who plays or enjoys sports

¹**spot** *noun* 1 a part or area different from the main surface, as in colour; a small mark; 2 a particular place; 3 a pimple

²**spot** *verb* (**spotted**) 1 to see; to recognise; 2 to mark with coloured or dirty spots

spout *noun* an opening through which liquid can be poured from a container

spray *verb* to scatter liquid in small drops; **spray** *noun*

¹**spread** *verb* (**spreads, spreading, spread**) 1 to put a thin covering on; 2 to open, reach, or stretch out; to be or make longer, broader, wider, etc; 3 to share or divide over an area, period of time, etc

²**spread** *noun* a substance put on bread: *low-fat* **spread**

spreadsheet *noun* a computer program to work out money or number problems

¹**spring** *noun* 1 a place where water comes up naturally from the ground; 2 the season between winter and summer; 3 a coil of wire, which goes back to its original shape if you pull it, then let go

²**spring** *verb* (**springs, springing, sprang, sprung**) 1 to move quickly as when jumping; 2 **spring a leak** to begin to let liquid through a crack, hole, etc

sprinkle *verb* to scatter in drops or small grains; **sprinkler** *noun*

sprout *verb* 1 to start to grow; 2 to send up new growth, as from a seed or bud; **sprout** *noun*

¹**spy** *noun* a person whose job is to find out secret information, usually from an enemy

²**spy** *verb* 1 to try to get information secretly; 2 to watch secretly

S

square *noun* **1** a shape with four straight equal sides; **2** a piece of material in this shape; **3** an open space surrounded by buildings; **square** *adjective*

¹**squash** *verb* **1** to force or be forced into a flat shape; to press; **2** to push or fit into a small space; to squeeze

²**squash** *noun* **1** an act of squashing; **2** a crowd of people in a small space; **3** a sweet fruit drink; **4** a game played by two or four players, with rackets and a small rubber ball

squeak *verb* to make a high but not loud sound; **squeak** *noun*; **squeaker** *noun*

squeal *verb* to make a long very high sound or cry; **squeal** *noun*

squeeze *verb* to press together from opposite sides; **squeeze** *noun*; **squeezer** *noun*

squirrel *noun* a small four-legged animal with a long furry tail that climbs trees and eats nuts

¹**stable** *noun* a building where animals are kept and fed

²**stable** *adjective* standing firm

stadium *noun* a large open building with rows of seats surrounding a sports field

stag *noun* a fully grown male deer

stage *noun* **1** a time or step in a course of events; **2** the raised floor on which plays are performed in a theatre

stain *verb* to make a mark that cannot be taken away; **stain** *noun*; **stainless** *adjective*

stair *noun* any of the steps in a set of stairs; !! **stare**

stairs *noun* a fixed length of steps connecting floors in a building

stake *noun* a pointed piece of wood, metal, etc, for driving into the ground; **stake** *verb*; !! **steak**

stale *adjective* no longer fresh

¹**stalk** *noun* **1** the main upright part of a plant; **2** a long narrow part of a plant supporting one or more leaves, fruits, or flowers; a stem

²**stalk** *verb* to follow or hunt; **stalker** *noun*

stall *noun* a table or open-fronted shop, especially one in a market

¹**stamp** *verb* **1** to strike downwards with the foot; **2** to stick on a stamp

Olympic stadium, Atlanta, America

²**stamp** *noun* **1** also **postage stamp** a small piece of paper for sticking on mail to be sent to show payment; **2** a tool for printing onto a surface

¹**stand** *verb* (**stands, standing, stood**) **1** to support yourself on the feet upright; **2** to rise or raise to a position of doing this; **3** to be in or take a particular position; **4** to be able to bear; **5 stand for** to mean; **6 stand a chance** to have a chance; **7 stand on your own (two) feet** to be able to do without help from others

²**stand** *noun* **1** a place or act of standing; **2** a piece of furniture for putting something on: **hat stand**; **3** an open building at a sports ground with rows of seats or standing space

¹**standard** *noun* a fixed weight, length, cost, or quality, by which things are measured or judged

²**standard** *adjective* ordinary; of the usual kind

¹**star** *noun* **1** a body, such as the sun or a planet, that appears as a bright point in the sky; **2** a shape with five or more points; **3** a famous or very skilful performer; **starry** *adjective*

²**star** *verb* (**starred**) **1** to mark with one or more stars; **2** to have or appear as a main performer

starboard *noun* the right side of a ship or aircraft as you face forward

starch *noun* **1** a white tasteless substance forming an important part of foods such as grain, rice, beans, and potatoes; **2** a powder used for stiffening clothes; **starchy** *adjective*

stare *verb* to look at something with wide-open eyes, for a long time; **stare** *noun*; !! **stair**

starfish *noun* a flat sea animal with five arms forming a star shape

starling *noun* a common greenish-black bird

start *verb* to begin or commence; **start** *noun*

starve *verb* **1** to die because you do not have enough food to eat; **2** to be very hungry; **starvation** *noun*

¹**state** *noun* **1** a condition in which a person or thing is; **2** the government of a country; **3** a small part of a country: **United States of America**

²**state** *verb* to say or put into words

statement *noun* something that is said

station *noun* **1** a building on a railway or bus line where passengers or goods arrive or leave; **2** a building that is a centre for a particular kind of service: **police station**; **3** a company or machine that broadcasts on the television or radio

stationary *adjective* standing still; not moving; !! **stationery**

stationery *noun* materials for writing such as paper, pens, pencils etc; **stationer** *noun*; !! **stationary**

statue *noun* a human or animal figure, made in some solid material, such as stone

stay *verb* **1** to stop and remain; **2** to continue to be; **3** to live in a place for a while; to be a visitor or guest; **stay** *noun*

S

steady *adjective* **1** firm; not shaking or moving; **2** not changing; regular; **steadily** *adverb*; **steadiness** *noun*

steak *noun* a flat piece of meat or fish; !! **stake**

steal *verb* (**steals, stealing, stole, stolen**) **1** to take something that belongs to someone else without asking for it; **2** to move secretly or quietly; !! **steel**

¹**steam** *noun* the whitish cloudy gas produced by boiling water

²**steam** *adjective* using steam under pressure to produce power or heat: **steamroller, steamship**

the Mallard, a steam locomotive

steel *noun* a hard strong metal made from iron and used for knives, machines, etc; !! **steal**

steel band *noun* a band playing instruments cut from metal drums and tuned to make particular notes

steep *adjective* rising or falling quickly; **steeply** *adverb*

steeple *noun* a church tower with a top part rising to a high sharp point

steer *verb* to direct or guide a ship, car, bicycle, etc

stellar *adjective* of or concerning the stars

stem *noun* the central part of a plant above the ground, or the smaller part which supports a leaf or flower

¹**step** *noun* **1** the act of putting one foot in front of the other in order to move along; the sound this makes; **2** a flat surface, especially in a set of surfaces each higher than the other, for climbing up and down; a stair, rung of a ladder, etc; **3** an act in a set of actions in making or doing something; **4** a type of movement of the feet in dancing; **5 watch your step** to behave or act carefully

²**step** *verb* (**stepped**) to put one foot down usually in front of the other, in order to move along; to walk

stepchild *noun* (*plural* **stepchildren**) the child of somebody's husband or wife by another marriage: **stepbrother, stepdaughter, stepsister, stepson**

stepparent *noun* the person to whom your mother or father has been remarried: **stepfather, stepmother**

stereo *noun* a cassette player, CD, or radio which gives out sound by means of two or more loudspeakers; **stereo** *adjective*

stew *noun* a meal with meat, vegetables, etc, cooked together in liquid; **stew** *verb*

steward (*feminine* **stewardess**) *noun* a person who serves passengers on a ship or plane

¹**stick** *noun* **1** a long thin piece of wood; **2** a long thin piece of any material

²**stick** *verb* (**sticks, sticking, stuck**) **1** to fix or be fixed with a sticky substance such as glue; **2** to push a pointed object into something

sticky *adjective* made of or containing material which can stick to or round anything else

stiff *adjective* **1** not easily bent; **2** painful when moving or moved; **stiffen** *verb*; **stiffly** *adverb*

stile *noun* steps for climbing easily over a fence or wall; !! **style**

¹**still** *adjective* **1** not moving; **2** quiet or silent; **stillness** *noun*

²**still** *adverb* **1** up to and at this or that time: *Does this dress **still** fit you?*; **2** even so

¹**sting** *verb* (**stings, stinging, stung**) **1** to cause sharp pain to, or to feel such a pain; **2** to prick with a sting

²**sting** *noun* **1** a sharp pain, wound, or mark caused by a plant or insect; **2** a sharp organ used as a weapon by some insects; **3** a substance contained in hairs on a plant's surface, which produces pain

stir *verb* (**stirred**) **1** to move round and mix by means of an object such as a spoon; **2** to move a little: *She **stirred** in her sleep*; **stir** *noun*

¹**stitch** *noun* **1** a thread in sewing or knitting made by moving a needle and thread into cloth at one point and out at another in sewing or by a turn of the wool round the needle in knitting; **2** a sharp pain in the side, caused by running

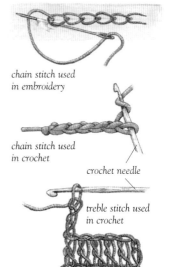

chain stitch used in embroidery

chain stitch used in crochet

crochet needle

treble stitch used in crochet

²**stitch** *verb* to sew; to put stitches in to fasten together or for decoration

stoat *noun* a small brown furry animal

a cow's stomach has four separate parts to help it digest the plants that it eats

stomach *noun* a bag-like organ in the body into which food goes after it has been swallowed

¹**stone** *noun* 1 a piece of rock; 2 a hard substance; rock; 3 a single hard seed inside some fruits, such as the cherry, plum, and peach

²**stone** *noun* a measure of weight equal to 14 pounds or 6.35 kilograms

stool *noun* a seat without a supporting part for the back or arms

¹**stop** *verb* (**stopped**) 1 to finish moving; 2 to prevent something happening, moving, etc; 3 to end; to make an end to; **stopper** *noun*

²**stop** *noun* 1 the act of stopping or state of being stopped; 2 a place on a road where buses or other public vehicles stop for passengers

¹**store** *verb* to put away or keep for future use

²**store** *noun* 1 things kept for future use; 2 a place for keeping things; 3 a large shop

storey *noun* a floor or level in a building !! **story**

storm *noun* very bad weather, with wind, rain, and often lightning; **stormy** *adjective*

story *noun* 1 a tale about something imaginary; 2 a telling of events; !! **storey**

stove *noun* a machine for cooking or heating that works by burning coal, oil, gas, etc, or by electricity

¹**straight** *adjective* 1 not bent or curved; 2 level or upright; 3 tidy; neat; in order; **straighten** *verb*; !! **strait**

²**straight** *adverb* 1 in a straight line; 2 directly: *go straight home*; 3 without waiting: **straightaway**; !! **strait**

strait *noun* a narrow water channel connecting two seas; !! **straight**

strange *adjective* 1 odd or unusual; surprising; 2 not what you are used to; **strangely** *adverb*

stranger *noun* a person you do not know

¹**strap** *noun* 1 a strong narrow band of material, such as leather, used for fastening or holding together; 2 also **shoulder strap** a strap that goes over the shoulder and holds up a piece of clothing, a bag, etc

²**strap** *verb* (**strapped**) to fasten in place with one or more straps

straw *noun* **1** dried stems of grain plants, such as wheat, used for animals to sleep on, for making baskets, mats, etc; **2** a thin tube of paper or plastic for drinking through

strawberry *noun* a red juicy fruit, eaten fresh and in jam; the plant on which this grows

strawberry plant

stream *noun* a natural flow of water, smaller than a river

street *noun* a road with houses or other town buildings on one or both sides

strength *noun* the quality or power of being strong or something that provides this; **strengthen** *verb*

stress *noun* a worried feeling about your life or work

stretch *verb* **1** to make or become wider or longer by pulling; **2** to make as long as possible; **3** to try to reach; **4** to straighten the legs, arms, or body to full length; **stretch** *noun*; **stretchy** *adjective*

strict *adjective* severe, especially in rules of behaviour; **strictly** *adverb*; **strictness** *noun*

¹**strike** *verb* **(strikes, striking, struck)** **1** to hit; **2** to light by hitting against a hard surface: ***strike*** *a match*; **3** to have an effect on; to seem or appear to: *An idea* ***struck*** *me*; **4** to refuse to work

²**strike** *noun* a time when no work is done because of an argument

string *noun* **1** a strong thread or thin rope used especially for tying things up; **2** a thin piece of metal or gut, stretched across a musical instrument to give sound; **stringed** *adjective*

¹**strip** *noun* a long narrow piece of something

²**strip** *verb* **(stripped)** **1** to remove the covering or parts of; **2** to undress or be undressed

stripe *noun* a band of colour, among one or more other colours; **striped** *adjective*

¹**stroke** *verb* to pass the hand gently over something

²**stroke** *noun* **1** a blow; a hit; a movement; **2** a sudden illness in part of the brain

strong *adjective* **1** having power or force; **2** powerful against harm; not easily broken, spoilt, moved, or changed; **strongly** *adverb*

structure *noun* something that has been built, such as a building

struggle *verb* to try very hard to do something; to fight; **struggle** *noun*

stubborn *adjective* not changing your mind or doing what others want; **stubbornly** *adverb*; **stubbornness** *noun*

S

159

student *noun* a person who is studying at a school, college, etc

submarine also **sub** *noun* a ship that can sail under water

mini-sub - a small submarine used to take people on trips to the seabed

studio *noun* **1** a room in which films or radio or television programmes are made; **2** a room where a painter, photographer, etc, works

¹**study** *noun* **1** the act of studying one or more subjects; learning; **2** a room used for studying and work

²**study** *verb* to spend time in learning about one or more subjects

¹**stuff** *noun* material of any sort, of which something is made

²**stuff** *verb* to fill

stump *noun* **1** the base of a tree left after the rest has been cut down; **2** one of the three upright pieces of wood at which the ball is thrown in cricket

stupid *adjective* silly or foolish; not clever; **stupidity** *noun*; **stupidly** *adverb*

style *noun* **1** a way of doing something; **2** fashion, especially in clothes; **3** a type or sort; **stylish** *adjective*; !! **stile**

subject *noun* **1** something studied, as at school, college, etc; **2** something talked or written about; **3** a person who belongs to a country

substance *noun* a sort of material

subtract *verb* to take a part, number, or amount from something larger; **subtraction** *noun*

succeed *verb* to get what you wanted; to do well

success *noun* **1** the act of succeeding in something; **2** a good result; **3** a person or thing that succeeds or has succeeded; **successful** *adjective*; **successfully** *adverb*

such *adjective, pronoun* **1** so large; so much; so good: *Don't be* **such** *a fool!* **2** **such as** of the same kind; like: *flowers* **such as** *roses or daisies*

suck *verb* **1** to draw liquid into the mouth by using the tongue, lips, and muscles at the side of the mouth, with the lips tightened into a small hole; **2** to eat something by holding in the mouth and melting by movements of the tongue; **suck** *noun*

sudden *adjective* happening, done, etc, quickly and unexpectedly; **suddenly** *adverb*

suffer *verb* to experience pain or difficulty; **suffering** *noun*

suffix *noun* letters placed at the end of a word to alter the meaning, such as happi*ness*

sugar *noun* a sweet substance used in food

suggest *verb* to say or write to somebody that something is a good idea; **suggestion** *noun*

¹**suit** (*say like* boot) *noun* **1** a set of clothes that match, usually including a jacket with trousers or skirt; **2** one of the four sets of cards used in games

²**suit** (*say like* boot) *verb* **1** to satisfy or please; to be right for; **2** to match or look right with

suitable *adjective* right for a certain situation

suitcase *noun* a strong hard bag for clothes when you are travelling

suite (*say* sweet) *noun* a set of furniture for a room, especially a sofa and two chairs for a lounge; !! **sweet**

sulk *verb* to be quiet and badtempered; **sulky** *adjective*

Concorde was a supersonic airliner

sultana *noun* a small seedless kind of raisin used in baking

sum *noun* an exercise in using numbers; !! **some**

summer *noun* the season between spring and autumn when the sun is hot and there are many flowers

sun *noun* the very hot bright thing in the sky, which the Earth goes round and from which it receives light and heat: **sunlight, sunshine; sunny** *adjective*; !! **son**

sunbathe *verb* to spend time in strong sunlight, usually sitting or lying; **sunbather** *noun*

Sunday *noun* the first day of the week; the day before Monday

sunrise also **sun-up** *noun* the time when the sun is seen to appear after the night

sunset *noun* the time when the sun is seen to disappear as night begins

super *adjective* wonderful; very nice or exciting

supermarket *noun* a large shop where you serve yourself with food and goods

supersonic *adjective* faster than the speed of sound

supper *noun* the last meal of the day, taken in the evening

¹**supply** *verb* to give or sell what is needed

²**supply** *noun* a store that can be used; an amount

¹**support** *verb* **1** to hold up;
2 to help, especially with
money; **3** to be on the side
of; **supporter** *noun*

²**support** *noun* something that
holds something else up

¹**suppose** *verb* **1** to think; to
guess; **2** to be expected to;
ought to

²**suppose** also **supposing**
conjunction if: *Suppose it rains,
what shall we do?*

sure *adjective* having no doubt;
certain; **surely** *adverb*; !! **shore**

surface *noun* the outside, flat
part, or top of something

surgery *noun* **1** a place where a
doctor, dentist, or vet treats his
or her patients; **2** the skill and
practice of performing medical
operations; **3** the performing
of such operations, usually
including the cutting open of
the skin; **surgeon** *noun*

surname *noun* the name you
share with the other members
of your family; your last name

surprise *noun* an unexpected
event; a feeling caused by this
event; **surprise** *verb*; **surprising**
adjective

surround *verb* to be or go all
round something; **surrounding**
adjective

¹**suspect** (*say* su-*spect*) *verb* to
think that something is true,
though you do not know

²**suspect** (*say* sus-*pect*) *noun* a
person the police think did a
crime

suspend *verb* **1** to hang from
above; **2** to delay or stop

suspense *noun* delay which
frightens or excites people

suspicious *adjective* feeling that
something is wrong; **suspicion**
noun; **suspiciously** *adverb*

¹**swallow** *verb* to move food or
drink down the throat from the
mouth

²**swallow** *noun* a small insect-
eating bird that comes to the
northern countries in summer

swan *noun* (*young* **cygnet**) a
large water bird with white or
black feathers and a long neck,
that lives on rivers and lakes

*a swan and
her cygnets*

swear *verb* (**swears, swearing,
swore, sworn**) **1** to use very
bad language; **2** to promise

sweat *noun* a liquid which comes
out from the body through the
skin to cool it; **sweat** *verb*;
sweaty *adjective*

sweater *noun* a warm piece of
clothing for the top of the body

sweatshirt *noun* a warm piece of
clothing for the upper body,
often worn for sport

sweep *verb* (**sweeps, sweeping,
swept**) **1** to clean by brushing;
2 to move over or cover quickly

¹**sweet** *adjective* **1** tasting like or containing sugar; **2** pleasant or loving; **sweeten** *verb*; **sweetly** *adverb*; **sweetness** *noun*; !! **suite**

²**sweet** *noun* **1** a small sweet thing, such as a toffee or chocolate, eaten for pleasure; **2** a pudding or dessert; !! **suite**

sweet corn *noun* the yellow seeds of the maize plant, eaten as a vegetable

swell *verb* (**swells, swelling, swelled, swollen** *or* **swelled**) to become larger; **swelling** *noun*

swerve *verb* to turn suddenly to one side, when moving; **swerve** *noun*

¹**swift** *adjective* fast, short, or sudden; **swiftly** *adverb*

²**swift** *noun* a small bird with long wings

swim *verb* (**swims, swimming, swam, swum**) to move through water using your arms and legs; **swimmer** *noun*; **swimming** *noun*

swimming pool *noun* a special pool for swimming in

¹**swing** *verb* (**swings, swinging, swung**) to move backwards and forwards, round and round, or in a curve from a fixed point

²**swing** *noun* a seat on which you can swing

swipe *verb* to move a plastic card with electronic information on it through a special machine, usually to pay for something; **swipe card**

¹**switch** *noun* an apparatus for turning electricity on and off

²**switch** *verb* **1** to turn on or off with a switch; **2** to change for another

sword *noun* a weapon with a long blade and a handle

syllable *noun* the divisions in a word which can be heard, caused by the seperation of vowels with consonants

symbol *noun* a sign, shape, or object which stands for something else; !! **cymbal**

sympathy *noun* the feeling of sharing or understanding the pain and joy of others; **sympathetic** *adjective*

synonym *noun* any two or more words that have the same or similar meanings

synopsis *noun* the outline of a story

synthesiser *noun* an electronic musical instrument that can make many different types of sounds

synthesiser

syrup *noun* a thick sweet liquid, especially sugar and water

system *noun* **1** a group of things or ideas working together in one arrangement; **2** a group of computers and the software that runs on them

S

Tt

table *noun* **1** a piece of furniture with a flat top supported by legs: **tablecloth**; **2** a list of information

tadpole *noun* the young of a frog or toad

tail *noun* the movable part growing at the back of an animal's body; **tailless** *adjective*; !! **tale**

Manx cats are tailless

tailor *noun* a person who makes clothes to fit you

take *verb* (**takes, taking, took, taken**) **1** to get hold of something; **2** to borrow or use without asking permission or by mistake; **3** to carry something or go with somebody to another place; **4** to eat, drink, breathe in, etc: **take** *your medicine*; **5** to travel on bus, train, etc; **6** to last: *How long does the flight* **take**?

tale *noun* a story; !! **tail**

¹talk *verb* to use words or make thoughts, ideas, etc, known by means of speech; to speak

²talk *noun* a conversation; a speech

tall *adjective* **1** higher than other people or other things; more than average height; **2** having a particular height: *4 feet* **tall**; **tallish** *adjective*; **tallness** *noun*

¹tame *adjective* gentle and not afraid; not fierce or wild; **tameness** *noun*

²tame *verb* to train an animal to be tame; **tamer** *noun*

tangled *adjective* when two or more things are knotted or caught up together and cannot be undone without difficulty

tank *noun* **1** a large container for storing liquid or gas; **2** a large heavy vehicle with guns on it, that moves on two metal belts

¹tap *noun* something that you turn to control the flow of water, other liquid or gas from a pipe, barrel, etc

²tap *verb* (**tapped**) to strike something lightly; **tap** *noun*

tape *noun* **1** a narrow strip of cloth, paper, etc; **2** a strip of plastic covered with a magnetic material, used for recording sound, pictures, or information

tape recorder *noun* an instrument that can record and play back sound using tape

target *noun* **1** something that is aimed at; **2** an amount you are trying to reach

archery target

¹tart *noun* a piece of pastry with fruit or jam cooked on it

²tart *adjective* a sharp sour taste

¹**taste** *verb* **1** to test the taste of food or drink by taking a little into the mouth; **2** to experience the taste of; **3** to eat or drink a little of; **4** to have a particular taste; **5** to experience: *to* **taste** *freedom*

²**taste** *noun* **1** the sense by which you know one food from another by its sweetness, bitterness, etc; **2** the quality special to any food or drink that makes you able to recognise it when it is in your mouth; **3** the ability to judge whether something is good, bad, beautiful, etc; **tasteless** *adjective*; **tasty** *adjective*

tax *noun* money that is paid to the government

¹**taxi** *noun* a car with its driver, which you pay to take you somewhere

²**taxi** *verb* to go along on a runway before taking off or landing (plane)

tea *noun* **1** a drink made by pouring boiling water onto the dried and cut leaves of the tea bush; these leaves: **teacup, teapot**; **2** a meal eaten in the afternoon or early evening

teach *verb* (**teaches, teaching, taught**) to give knowledge or skill of something to a person; to train or give lessons; **teacher** *noun*

team *noun* a group of people who work together or who play on the same side in a game

¹**tear** (*say like* **here**) *noun* a drop of salty liquid from the eye

²**tear** (*say like* **hair**) *verb* (**tears, tearing, tore, torn**) to pull apart or into pieces

³**tear** (*say like* **hair**) *noun* a torn place in cloth, paper, etc

tease *verb* to make fun of playfully or unkindly

technology *noun* items which work on a scientific or mechanical basis **technical** *adjective*

teenager *noun* a person aged between thirteen and nineteen

telephone *noun* a phone; **telephone** *verb*

telescope *noun* an instrument used for seeing distant objects

the Hubble space telescope orbits the Earth

television also **TV** *noun* **1** the sending and receiving of pictures and programmes with sound by means of electrical waves; the programmes; **2 TV set** a screen in a box, for receiving these programmes

tell *verb* (**tells, telling, told**) **1** to make something known in words to somebody; to give information or advice; **2** to find out; to decide or know

temper *noun* **1** a particular state of mind; the way you feel; **2 lose your temper** to become angry

temperature *noun* the hotness or coldness of a place, object, etc

temple *noun* a place for worship in various religions

temporary *adjective* only lasting for a short time; not permanent; **temporarily** *adverb*

tempt *verb* to try to make somebody do something wrong; **temptation** *noun*

ten *adjective, noun* the number 10; **tenth** *adjective, adverb*

tennis *noun* a game for two people (**singles**) or two pairs of people (**doubles**) who use rackets to hit a ball over a net

¹**tense** *adjective* **1** full of excitement; **2** tightly stretched

²**tense** *noun* the form of a verb that shows when the action of the verb happens: **present tense** *I go,* **past tense** *I went,* **future tense** *I will go*

tent *noun* a movable shelter made of cloth supported by a framework of poles and ropes

mountaineering tent

term *noun* **1** one of the periods of time into which the school, university, etc, year is divided; **2** a fixed period of time; **3 terms** the conditions by which you agree to do something or pay for something

terrible *adjective* very bad or frightening

terribly *adverb* **1** extremely: *terribly exciting;* **2** badly: *terribly injured*

terrific *adjective* excellent; wonderful; **terrifically** *adverb*

terrify *verb* to fill with fear

terror *noun* very great fear

test *noun* a number of questions, things to do, etc, set to measure somebody's ability or knowledge; **test** *verb*

text *noun* any kind of written material

than *conjunction, preposition* used to compare two things or people: *older than you*

thank *verb* to say that you are grateful; **thanks** *noun*

¹**that** *adjective, pronoun* (*plural* **those**) **1** the one described or shown; **2** the one of two or more people or things that is further away; **3** who, whom, or which

²**that** *adverb* so: *I don't like him that much!*

³**that** *conjunction* used for joining two parts of a sentence: *It's true that he's French*

thaw *verb* to warm to above freezing point and so make or become liquid or soft

the 1 used when it is understood who or what is meant; **2** used with a person or thing that is the only one of its kind

theatre *noun* **1** a special building where plays are performed; **2** also **operating theatre** the room where hospital operations are done

theft *noun* stealing

their *adjective* belonging to them; !! **there**

theirs *pronoun* that or those belonging to them

theme *noun* a subject or the focus for a piece of work

then *adverb* **1** at that time; **2** next; afterwards; **3** in that case; if that has happened

there *adverb* **1** to, at, or in that place; **2** used as the first word in a sentence or as the second word in a question with a verb such as be: *There is a man at the door*; !! **their**

therefore *adverb* as a result; for that reason; so

thermometer *noun* an instrument for measuring and showing temperature

digital thermometer

thesaurus *noun* a book that lists different words with similar meanings

they *pronoun* (**them, themselves**) those people, animals, or things; the ones being talked about

thick *adjective* **1** having a large distance between opposite surfaces; wide; not thin; **2** measuring a particular amount from side to side or from top to bottom: *ice 5 centimetres **thick***; **3** not watery or flowing easily: ***thick** soup*; **4** difficult to see through: ***thick** mist*; **5** having many objects set close together; **thicken** *verb*; **thickly** *adverb*; **thickness** *noun*

thief *noun* (*plural* **thieves**) a person who steals

thin *adjective* **1** having little fat on the body; not fat; **2** having a small distance between opposite surfaces; narrow; not thick; **3** watery; flowing easily: thin gravy; **4** not closely packed; **thinly** *adverb*; **thinness** *noun*

thing *noun* **1** any object; anything that can be touched or seen; **2** something that exists; an idea, event, organisation, etc

think *verb* (**thinks, thinking, thought**) **1** to use your mind to imagine, understand, believe, or consider something; **2** to form an opinion or have an idea

third *adjective, adverb, noun, pronoun* **1** the one after the second; 3rd; **2** one of three equal parts into which something is divided

thirst *noun* a feeling of dryness in the mouth caused by wanting or needing to drink; **thirst** *verb*; **thirstily** *adverb*; **thirsty** *adjective*

thirteen *adjective, noun* the number 13; **thirteenth** *adjective, adverb*

thirty *adjective, noun* the number 30; **thirtieth** *adjective, adverb*

this *pronoun, adjective (plural*
these) **1** the one being talked
about or considered; **2** the one
of two or more people or things
that is nearer

*spear
thistle*

thistle *noun* a
wild plant with
prickly leaves
and usually
purple flowers

thorn *noun* a
prickle growing
on a plant

though *adverb, conjunction* in spite
of the fact

¹**thought** *noun* **1** thinking;
2 a result of thinking; an idea,
opinion, etc; **thoughtful**
adjective; **thoughtfully** *adverb*;
thoughtless *adjective*

²**thought** *see* THINK

thousand *adjective, noun* the
number 1000; **thousandth**
adjective, adverb

¹**thread** *noun* **1** a long thin piece
of cotton, nylon, etc, used for
sewing or making cloth; **2** a
raised line that winds round
the outside of a screw

²**thread** *verb* to pass one end of
a thread through the hole in
a needle

three *adjective, noun* the
number 3

throat *noun* **1** the tube inside
the neck that divides into two,
one part taking air to the lungs
and the other taking food to
the stomach; **2** the front of the
neck

through *preposition, adverb*
1 from one side, surface, or
end of something to the other;
2 by means of; **3** as a result of;
because of; **4** among or
between; !! **threw**

¹**throw** *verb* **(throws, throwing,**
threw, thrown) 1 to send
something through the air by a
sudden movement of the arm;
2 to move yourself or part of
your body suddenly and with
force; **3 throw away** to get rid
of something

²**throw** *noun* an act of throwing

thrush *noun* a brownish bird
that sings well

mistle thrush

thumb *noun* the short movable
part of the hand that is set
apart from the fingers

thunder *noun* the usually loud
noise that follows a flash of
lightning; **thunder** *verb*

Thursday *noun* the fifth day of
the week

¹**tick** *noun* **1** the short regularly
repeated sound made by a
clock or watch; **2** a mark (✔)
put against something to show
that it is correct

²**tick** *verb* **1** to make a regularly
repeated tick; **2** to show that
something is correct by
marking with a tick

³**tick** *noun* a small animal that
feeds on the blood of sheep,
cows, etc

ticket *noun* a piece of paper or card that shows that a person has paid for something, such as a journey on a bus

tickle *verb* to touch a person's skin to produce laughter; **tickle** *noun*; **ticklish** *adjective*

tide *noun* the regular rise and fall of the seas

tidy *adjective* neat; neatly arranged; **tidily** *adverb*; **tidiness** *noun*; **tidy** *verb*

¹**tie** *noun* **1** a band of cloth worn round the neck of a shirt **2** an equal score in a competition

²**tie** *verb* (**ties, tying, tied**) **1** to fasten with string, rope, etc; **2** to finish a match or competition with equal points

tiger *noun* (*female* **tigress**, *young* **cub**) a large fierce stripy cat

tight *adjective* **1** closely fastened, held, knotted, etc; **2** fitting too closely; not loose; **tighten** *verb*; **tightly** *adverb*; **tightness** *noun*

tights *noun* a light, very close-fitting piece of clothing that covers the legs

tile *noun* a thin shaped piece of baked clay, plastic, etc, used for covering roofs, floors, etc

¹**till** *noun* a machine in a shop, pub, etc, that adds up the prices of the goods bought

²**till** *preposition, conjunction* until

¹**time** *noun* **1** the passing of the minutes, hours, days, months, or years; **2** a particular point in the day: **bedtime, playtime, teatime**; **3** a period or occasion: *a good time*; **4** a number of minutes, hours, etc, needed for something; **5** the speed, beat, etc, of music

²**time** *verb* to measure the time taken to do something

metronome - used by musicians to measure the beat

times *preposition* multiplied by: *two times two equals four*

timetable *noun* a table of the times at which something happens, such as when buses, trains, etc, arrive and leave or when different lessons begin and end

tin *noun* **1** a soft metal; **2** a small metal box or container: *a tin can*

tiny *adjective* extremely small; minute

¹**tip** *noun* the end point of something

²**tip** *verb* (**tipped**) to lean or cause to lean at an angle; to turn over or cause something to turn over

³**tip** *noun* a place where rubbish is left

⁴**tip** *noun* 1 a small amount of money given for a service; 2 a helpful piece of advice

⁵**tip** *verb* **(tipped)** to give a small amount of money to a taxi driver, waitress, etc

tire *verb* to make somebody feel tired; ‼ **tyre**

tired *adjective* 1 needing rest or sleep; 2 no longer interested; **tiredness** *noun*

tissue (*say* **tish-oo**) *noun* a paper handkerchief

title *noun* 1 the name of a book, film, etc; 2 a word, such as Sir or Dr, used in front of a person's name to show his or her position

to *preposition* 1 in the direction of; towards; 2 as far as; 3 reaching or in the state of: *until the lights change* **to** *green*; 4 in a touching position with; against; 5 until: *from midday* **to** *midnight*; 6 compared with: *5 goals* **to** *3*; ‼ **too, two**

midwife toad - the male carries the eggs on his back

toad *noun* an animal like a large frog that creeps rather than jumps. It usually lives on land, but goes into water for breeding

to and fro *adverb* backwards and forwards; from side to side

¹**toast** *noun* bread made brown by being held in front of heat

²**toast** *verb* to make bread, cheese, etc, brown by holding it close to heat

today *noun, adverb* 1 this day; 2 the present time

toddler *noun* a child who has just learnt to walk

toe *noun* 1 one of the five movable parts at the end of each foot: **toenail**; 2 the part of a sock, shoe, etc, that fits over the toes; ‼ **tow**

together *adverb* 1 in or into one group, body, or place; 2 at the same time

toilet *noun* a lavatory

tolerate *verb* to accept something

tomato *noun* (*plural* **tomatoes**) a red juicy fruit eaten raw or cooked

tomorrow *noun, adverb* 1 the day following today; 2 the future

tongs *noun* a tool consisting of two movable pieces joined at one end, used for holding or lifting things

tongue *noun* the large movable fleshy part in the mouth

tonight *noun, adverb* the night of today

tonne also **metric ton** *noun* a measure of weight equal to 1000 kilograms or 0.98 tons

too *adverb* 1 also; as well; 2 more than enough or is needed or wanted; ‼ **to, two**

tool *noun* an instrument for doing a special job

tooth *noun* (*plural* **teeth**) **1** one of the small hard white bony objects growing in the upper and lower mouth of most animals: **toothache, toothbrush, toothpaste**; **2** one of the narrow pointed parts that stand out from a comb, saw, etc; **toothed** *adjective*; **toothless** *adjective*

¹**top** *noun* **1** the highest part or point; **2** the upper surface; **3** the most important part of anything; **4** a lid; **5** a piece of clothing worn on the upper part of the body; **top** *adjective*

²**top** *noun* a toy that balances on its point and spins

topic *noun* a chosen subject

torch *noun* a small electric light carried in the hand

tortoise *noun* a slow-moving reptile that has a body covered by a hard shell into which the legs, tail, and head can be pulled for protection

¹**total** *adjective* complete; whole; **totally** *adverb*

²**total** *noun* the complete amount; everything added together

¹**touch** *verb* **1** to feel with the hands or fingers or another part of the body; **2** to be on or against something; **3** to have no space separating two things

²**touch** *noun* the sense by which an object is felt and by which it is known to be hard, smooth, rough, etc

tour *noun* **1** a journey during which several places of interest are visited; **2** a short trip to or through a place in order to see it; **tour** *verb*; **tourist** *noun*

tow *verb* to pull a vehicle along by a rope or chain; !! **toe**

towards also **toward** *preposition* **1** in the direction of something or somebody; **2** in a position facing something or somebody; **3** for part payment of: £5 *towards* the present

towel *noun* a piece of cloth or paper used for drying wet skin, dishes, etc

tower *noun* a tall building standing alone or forming part of a castle, church, etc

the Leaning Tower of Pisa, Italy

town *noun* a large group of houses and other buildings where people live and work

toy *noun* an object for children to play with

¹**trace** *verb* **1** to copy a picture, map, etc, by drawing on thin paper over it: **tracing paper**; **2** to find or discover something or somebody, especially by following up clues or signs

²**trace** *noun* a mark or sign left behind by somebody or something

track *noun* **1** a railway line; **2** a rough path; **3** a special path or road for racing; **4** one of the pieces of music on a CD, record or tape; **5** marks left by a moving person, animal, or vehicle

tracksuit *noun* a loose fitting suit of warm material that is usually worn when exercising

tractor *noun* a powerful motor vehicle used for pulling farm machinery or other heavy objects

¹**trade** *verb* **1** to do business with; to buy or sell goods; **2** to give something in exchange for something else

²**trade** *noun* **1** the buying and selling of goods; **2** a job or particular kind of business

tradition *noun* an idea or belief that is handed down from generation to generation

traffic *noun* the cars and other motor vehicles moving along roads

traffic calming *noun* an arrangement of things, such as roundabouts, in a road to stop people going too fast in cars

traffic lights *noun* a set of coloured lights used for controlling and directing traffic

¹**train** *noun* **1** a line of connected railway carriages drawn by an engine; **2** a part of a long dress that spreads on the ground behind the person who is wearing it

²**train** *verb* to make yourself, or somebody or something else ready to do something difficult; **trainer** *noun*; **training** *noun*

trainers *noun* sports shoes for running, jogging, etc

trampoline *noun* a stretchy sheet supported by springs, used for bouncing up and down

transistor *noun* a small part of an electronic circuit for controlling an electric current: **transistor radio**

transparent *adjective* clear; allowing light to pass through so that objects behind can be clearly seen

¹**transport** (*say* tran-*sport*) *verb* to carry goods, people, etc, from one place to another; **transportable** *adjective*

²**transport** (*say* trans-*port*) *noun* **1** the act of transporting goods or people; **2** vehicles, such as cars, lorries, ships, or aircraft, used for transporting goods or people

¹**trap** *noun* **1** a thing for catching and holding an animal; **2** a position in which somebody is caught; a plan for catching a person; **3** a light two-wheeled vehicle pulled by a horse

²**trap** *verb* (**trapped**) to catch in a trap or by a trick

travel *verb* (**travelled**) to go from place to place; to make a journey; **travel** *noun*; **traveller** *noun*

tray *noun* a flat piece of material with raised edges, used for carrying things

treacle *noun* a thick dark sticky liquid made from sugar

treasure *noun* a collection or store of valuable things, such as gold and silver coins

¹**treat** *verb* **1** to act or behave in a particular way towards a person or an animal; **2** to deal with; to handle; **3** to try to cure by giving medicine; **4** to buy or give somebody something special; **treatment** *noun*

²**treat** *noun* something that gives pleasure

¹**treble** *noun* the highest part sung or played in music

²**treble** *adjective, adverb* high in sound

³**treble** *adjective* three times as big, as much, or as many as

tree *noun* a tall plant with a wooden trunk and branches

tremble *verb* to shake without being able to stop, perhaps with fear

triangle *noun* **1** a flat shape with three straight sides and three angles; **2** an instrument made of a piece of metal bent into the shape of a triangle, that is played by being struck with a metal rod; **triangular** *adjective*

tribe *noun* a group of people of the same race, language, habits, etc; **tribal** *adjective*

¹**trick** *noun* **1** an act needing special skill that is done especially to confuse or amuse people; **2** something done to deceive or cheat somebody

²**trick** *verb* to deceive or cheat somebody

trifle *noun* a dish of cake, fruit, and jelly covered with custard and cream

¹**trip** *verb* **(tripped)** to catch your foot and lose your balance

²**trip** *noun* a journey

trombone

trombone *noun* a brass musical instrument with a sliding tube which is pushed out or in to change the note; **trombonist** *noun*

tropical *adjective* to do with or coming from the very hot parts of the world (the **Tropics**) near the Equator

trot *verb* **(trotted)** to move or cause a horse to move at a speed between a walk and a gallop; **trot** *noun*

¹**trouble** *noun* **1** difficulty, worry, or anxiety; **2 in trouble** in the position where you are blamed for doing something wrong or are thought to have done something wrong

²**trouble** *verb* to cause worry, anxiety, pain, etc, to somebody

trousers *noun* a piece of clothing that covers the body from the waist down and divides into two parts, each fitting a leg

truck *noun* **1** a lorry or other motor vehicle for carrying goods; **2** an open cart used on a railway

true *adjective* real; actual; not false; **truly** *adverb*

trumpet *noun* a brass instrument that is played by blowing; **trumpeter** *noun*

173

a tugboat towing a barge full of rubbish

trunk *noun* **1** the main stem of a tree; **2** the human body without the head, arms, and legs; **3** a large box used for carrying clothes when travelling; **4** the long nose of an elephant

trust *verb* to believe in the honesty and goodness of somebody; to have faith in or depend on somebody or something; **trust** *noun*

truth *noun* the true facts; what is true; **truthful** *adjective*; **truthfully** *adverb*; **truthfulness** *noun*

try *verb* **1** to make an effort to do something; **2** to test something; to use, taste, etc, something in order to find out what it is like; **3** to examine a person in a court of law; **try** *noun*

T-shirt *noun* a piece of clothing for the upper part of the body that is made of light material

tub *noun* a large round container

tuba *noun* a large brass instrument that makes a deep sound when blown

tube *noun* **1** a hollow round pipe of metal, glass, plastic, etc; **2** a small soft container for holding toothpaste, paint, etc; **tubular** *adjective*

Tuesday *noun* the third day of the week

¹**tug** *verb* (**tugged**) to pull hard with force or much effort

²**tug** *noun* a sudden strong pull

³**tug** *noun* a small powerful boat used for guiding large ships in and out of a port

tulip *noun* a garden plant that grows from a bulb

tumble *verb* to fall suddenly; **tumble** *noun*

tumble dryer *noun* a machine in which wet clothing is dried

¹**tune** *noun* a series of musical notes that produces a pleasing pattern of sound; **tuneful** *adjective*

²**tune** *verb* to set the strings of a musical instrument so that it produces the correct notes

tunnel *noun* a passage for a road, railway, etc, through or under a hill, river, the sea, etc

turkey *noun* a large farm bird kept for its meat

¹**turn** *verb* **1** to move round; **2** to change direction or position; **3** to become or make something become different: *to turn **brown***

²**turn** *noun* **1** a single movement completely round a fixed point; **2** a change of direction; **3** a place or time in a particular order: *miss a **turn***

turnip *noun* a plant that has a large round root which is eaten as a vegetable

turtle *noun* an animal that lives mainly in water and has a hard shell into which its soft head, legs, and tail can be pulled

green turtle

tusk *noun* a long pointed tooth that grows beyond the mouth in some animals, such as the elephant

TV *noun* television

twelve *adjective, noun* the number 12; **twelfth** *adjective, adverb*

twenty *adjective, noun* the number 20; **twentieth** *adjective, adverb*

twice *adjective, adverb* two times

twig *noun* a thin stem going off from a branch

¹**twin** *noun* **1** either of two children born of the same mother at the same time; **2** either of two things very like each other

²**twin** *verb* **(twinned)** to join a town closely with another town in another country

twist *verb* **1** to wind threads together or round something else; **2** to turn; **3** to hurt a joint or limb by pulling and turning sharply; **twist** *noun*; **twisty** *adjective*

two *adjective, noun* the number 2; !! **to, too**

¹**type** *noun* **1** a particular kind, class, or group; **2** a person or thing that is an example of such a group or class

²**type** *verb* to write something with a typewriter or computer keyboard

typewriter *noun* a machine with a keyboard for printing letters on paper

typical *adjective* having the main signs of a particular kind, group, or class; the same as others of a particular kind; **typically** *adverb*

tyre *noun* a thick rubber tube that fits round the outside edge of a wheel; !! **tire**

mountain bike tyre in cross section

Uu

U *noun, adjective* a film that anyone of any age may see in a cinema

ugly *adjective* unpleasant to look at; not beautiful; **ugliness** *noun*

umbrella *noun* a piece of cloth or plastic stretched over a frame used for keeping the rain off your head

unable *adjective* not able to do something

uncle *noun* the brother of your father or mother or the husband of your aunt

uncomfortable *adjective* not comfortable; **uncomfortably** *adverb*

unconscious *adjective* not conscious; not knowing what is going on around you and not feeling anything; **unconsciousness** *noun*

under *preposition, adverb* 1 in or to a lower place than; directly below; 2 less than; 3 lower in position than; serving or obeying; 4 beneath the surface of: **underground**; 5 during; in

underneath *preposition, adverb* under; below

understand *verb* (**understands, understanding, understood**) 1 to know or get the meaning of something; 2 to know or feel closely the nature of a person, feelings, etc; **understandable** *adjective*; **understandably** *adverb*

underwear *also* **underclothes, underclothing** *noun* the clothes worn next to the body under other clothes: **underpants**

undo *verb* (**undoes, undoing, undid, undone**) to unfasten or untie

undress *verb* to take your clothes off

unexpected *adjective* not expected; **unexpectedly** *adverb*

unfasten *verb* to stop being fastened; to undo

unhappy *adjective* not happy; **unhappily** *adverb*; **unhappiness** *noun*

unicorn *noun* an imaginary creature like a horse, with one horn

unicorn

uniform *noun* clothing that all members of an army, etc, wear

uninteresting *adjective* not interesting

unit *noun* 1 a single piece or portion of a whole piece; 2 a single-digit number

unite *verb* to join together

universal *adjective* for all people or every purpose

universe *noun* all space and all the stars, planets, etc, that are in it

university *noun* a place of education at the highest level

unkind *adjective* not kind; cruel or thoughtless; **unkindly** *adverb*; **unkindness** *noun*

u

unless *conjunction* if... not; except in the case that

unlikely *adjective* not likely to happen or be true; not expected

unlock *verb* to unfasten the lock of

unlucky *adjective* not having or giving good luck

unnecessary *adjective* not necessary; **unnecessarily** *adverb*

unpack *verb* to remove things from boxes, suitcases, etc, where they have been stored

unpleasant *adjective* not nice or pleasant; **unpleasantly** *adverb*

unsteady *adjective* not safe or sure; **unsteadily** *adverb*

untidy *adjective* not tidy; **untidily** *adverb*; **untidiness** *noun*

untie *verb* to undo string, a knot, etc

until also **till** *preposition, conjunction* up to the time that

unusual *adjective* 1 not usual; strange; 2 interesting because different from others; **unusually** *adverb*

up *adverb, adjective, preposition* 1 to, at, or in a higher place or position; above; 2 at an end; so as to be completely finished; **upwards** *adverb*

upon *preposition* on

upper *adjective* in a higher position; further up

upright *adjective* straight up and down

upset *verb* (**upsets, upsetting, upset**) 1 to knock over; 2 to cause to worry, be unhappy, etc; 3 to make ill, usually in the stomach; **upset** *noun, adjective*

upside down *adverb* with the top turned to the bottom

upstairs *adverb, adjective* at, on, or to the upper floor or floors of a building; **upstairs** *noun*

Uranus *noun* the planet seventh in order from the sun

the planet Uranus

urgent *adjective* needing immediate attention; showing that something important must be done quickly; **urgently** *adverb*; **urgency** *noun*

urn *noun* 1 a large metal container in which large quantities of tea or coffee may be made; 2 a large vase in which the ashes of a dead body are kept; !! **earn**

¹**use** (*say* yuze) *verb* 1 to do something with; 2 to have a purpose for; 3 **use up** to finish: *All the paper has been* **used up**; 4 **used to** to have done regularly or often: *We* **used to** *go there every year*

²**use** (*say* yuse) *noun* 1 using; being used; 2 the purpose or reason for using something; **useful** *adjective*; **usefully** *adverb*; **useless** *adjective*; **uselessly** *adverb*

user-friendly *adjective* easy to use: *a* **user-friendly** *computer program*

usual *adjective* done or happening regularly; normal; **usually** *adverb*

u

Vv

vacuum *noun* a space that is completely empty of all air or gas

vacuum cleaner *noun* a tool for cleaning floors and floor coverings by sucking up the dirt

vain *adjective* too proud of yourself, especially of what you look like; !! **vane, vein**

valley *noun* **1** the land lying between two lines of hills or mountains; **2** the land through which a river flows

value *noun* what something is worth; **valuable** *adjective*

van *noun* a covered vehicle for carrying goods and sometimes people

vane *noun* **1** one of the blades of a windmill, propeller, etc; **2** also **weather vane** a movable metal apparatus which shows wind direction; !! **vain, vein**

vanish *verb* to go out of sight; to disappear

variety *noun* a lot of different things

various *adjective* several different

vase *noun* a container used either for flowers or as an ornament

VDU also **visual display unit** *noun* the screen of a computer

visual display unit (VDU)

vegan *noun* someone who does not eat food that comes from animals **vegan** *adjective*

vegetable *noun* a plant that is grown for food

vegetarian *noun* someone who will not eat meat; **vegetarian** *adjective*

vehicle *noun* something in or on which people or goods are carried from one place to another; a car, lorry, train, etc

vein *noun* a tube that carries blood from any part of the body to the heart; !! **vain, vane**

velvet *noun* a fine silky cloth having a short soft thick raised surface of cut threads on one side only; **velvety** *adjective*

Venus *noun* the planet second in order from the sun, and next to the Earth

verb *noun* a word (or words) that tells you what somebody or something does or is: *be, go, carry* are *verbs*

verse *noun* a set of lines that forms one part of a poem or song, and usually has a pattern that is repeated in the other parts

vertical *adjective* a line or object that stands upright, not sideways

very *adverb* especially; most

vest *noun* a short piece of underwear for the upper part of the body

vet also **veterinary surgeon** *noun* an animal doctor

viable *adjective* **1** able to live; **2** able to be done; possible *a virus viewed through an electron microscope*

video *noun* **1** film for showing on your TV; **2** also **video recorder, VCR** a machine for recording programmes or playing videos

view *noun* **1** something you see, especially pleasant countryside; **2** a picture of a piece of scenery, a building, etc; **3** an opinion, idea, etc

village *noun* a small collection of houses and other buildings, smaller than a town

vine also **grapevine** *noun* a type of climbing plant that produces grapes

vinegar *noun* a very sour liquid used for flavouring food

viola *noun* a stringed musical instrument like a violin, but a little larger

violent *adjective* having great force or strength; hurting people; **violence** *noun*; **violently** *adverb*

violet *noun* **1** a small plant with purplish-blue flowers; **2** a purplish-blue colour; **violet** *adjective*

violin *noun* a four-stringed wooden musical instrument, supported between the left shoulder and the chin and played by drawing a bow across the strings; **violinist** *noun*

virus *noun* **1** something that causes an illness; **2** instructions put into a computer secretly, that stops the computer working properly

visit *verb* to go and spend some time in a place or somebody's house; **visit** *noun*; **visitor** *noun*

vitamins *noun* chemicals that we must have in our diet to keep healhy

vixen *noun* a female fox

vocabulary *noun* the number of words that a person knows

voice *noun* the sound or sounds you produce when speaking and singing

volcano *noun* (*plural* **volcanoes** *or* **volcanos**) a mountain with a large opening (**crater**) at the top through which lava, steam, etc, escape from time to time

volt *noun* a measurement of electricity

volume *noun* **1** the amount of sound something makes; **2** the space inside or filled by something; **3** a large book; one of a set of books of the same kind

vowel *noun* any of the five letters a, e, i, o, u, or their sounds – compare CONSONANT

Ww

wag *verb* **(wagged)** to shake to and fro; **wag** *noun*

wage *noun* money given to us for the work we do

wail *verb* to make a long cry showing sadness or pain; **wail** *noun*; !! **whale**

waist *noun* the narrow part of the human body just above the hips; !! **waste**

wait *verb* to stay somewhere until somebody comes or something happens; **wait** *noun*; !! **weight**

waiter (feminine **waitress**) *noun* a person who serves food at the tables in a restaurant

wake *verb* **(wakes, waking, woke** *or* **waked, woken)** to stop or make somebody stop sleeping

¹**walk** *verb* **1** to move along on your feet at a normal speed without running; **2** to take for a walk; **walker** *noun*

²**walk** *noun* a journey on foot

wall *noun* **1** an upright dividing surface, especially of stone or brick, that goes round a house, town, field, etc; **2** the side of a room

walrus *noun* a large animal like a seal, with two long tusks

wander *verb* to move about in no particular direction; **wander** *noun*

want *verb* **1** to wish to have something; **2** to need; **want** *noun*

war *noun* fighting between people, countries, etc

ward *noun* a room of a hospital with beds for patients

warden *noun* a person who looks after a place and people

wardrobe *noun* a room or cupboard in which you hang up clothes

warm *adjective* **1** fairly hot; **2** able to keep in heat: *warm clothes*; **warm** *verb*; **warmly** *adverb*; **warmth** *noun*

warn *verb* to tell of something bad that may happen, or of how to prevent something bad; !! **worn**

the Great Wall of China

w

¹**wash** *verb* 1 to make clean with water; 2 to flow over or against continually; **washing** *noun*

²**wash** *noun* 1 washing or being washed; 2 things to be washed

washing machine *noun* a machine for washing clothes

wasp *noun* a flying stinging insect related to the bee, usually yellow and black

¹**waste** *verb* to use wrongly, not use, or use too much of; !! **waist**

²**waste** *noun* 1 an act of wasting; 2 things that are used, damaged, or not wanted: **wastepipe**; !! **waist**

¹**watch** *verb* 1 to look at; 2 to take care of

²**watch** *noun* 1 a small clock worn on the wrist or carried in a pocket; 2 one or more people ordered to watch; 3 act of watching

in the 16th century, naval officers used a pocket sundial like this as a watch to tell the time

¹**water** *noun* the most common liquid, without colour, taste, or smell, which falls from the sky as rain, forms rivers, lakes, and seas, and is drunk by people and animals; **watery** *adjective*

²**water** *verb* 1 to pour water on, especially onto land or plants: **watering can**; 2 to supply with water

waterfall *noun* water falling straight down over rocks

waterproof *adjective* not allowing water to go through

watt *noun* a measurement of electrical power

¹**wave** *noun* 1 a raised curving line of water on the surface, especially of the sea; 2 an evenly curved part of the hair; 3 a form in which some forms of energy move: **radio waves**; **wavy** *adjective*

²**wave** *verb* to move in the air, backwards and forwards, up and down, or from side to side; **wave** *noun*

wavelength *noun* 1 a radio signal sent out on radio waves a particular distance apart; 2 the distance between one energy wave and another

wax *noun* a solid material of fats or oils that melts when heated and is used for making candles, polish, crayons, etc

way *noun* 1 a road or path; 2 the right direction to follow; 3 the distance to be travelled to reach a place; 4 how a thing is done or works; !! **weigh**

we *pronoun* (**us, ourselves**) the people speaking or doing

weak *adjective* 1 not strong in body; not strong in character; 2 containing a lot of water: **weak soup**; **weaken** *verb*; **weakly** *adverb*; **weakness** *noun*; !! **week**

wealthy *adjective* rich

w

weapon *noun* a tool for injuring or killing

wear *verb* (**wears, wearing, wore, worn**) 1 to have or carry on the body; 2 to change by continued use; 3 to last; !! **where**

weasel *noun* a small thin furry animal with a pointed face

weather *noun* the condition of wind, rain, sunshine, snow, etc, at a certain time; !! **whether**

weave *verb* (**weaves, weaving, wove, woven**) 1 to form threads into material by drawing one thread at a time under and over a set of longer threads on a special machine (**loom**); 2 to make something by doing this !! **we've**

web *noun* 1 a net of threads spun by spiders and some insects; 2 the skin between the toes of swimming birds and animals; 3 a computer system that allows people all round the world to share information on their computer screens; **webbed** *adjective*

duck's webbed foot

w

website *noun* a place on the internet where people can prepare pages on a particular subject, to be read by anyone else

wedding *noun* a marriage ceremony and celebration

Wednesday *noun* the fourth day of the week

weed *noun* a wild plant that grows where it is not wanted

week *noun* 1 a period of seven days and nights, especially from Sunday to Saturday; 2 the period of time during which you work, go to school, etc; **weekly** *adverb*; !! **weak**

weekday *noun* any day except Saturday or Sunday

weekend *noun* Saturday and Sunday

weep *verb* (**weeps, weeping, wept**) to let tears fall from the eyes; to cry

weigh *verb* 1 to find the weight of something, especially by a machine; 2 to have a certain weight; !! **way**

weight *noun* 1 the heaviness of anything; 2 a heavy object for holding something down: **paperweight**; !! **wait**

¹**welcome** *verb* to greet somebody with pleasure

²**welcome** *adjective* wanted; happily accepted

³**welcome** *noun* a greeting when somebody arrives

¹**well** *adjective* in good health; not ill

²**well** *adverb* (**better, best**)
  1 in a good or satisfactory
  way; **2** completely;
  3 much; quite; **4** as well
  also; **5** very

³**well** *noun* a place where water
  or oil comes from underground

oil well

west *noun* one of the four main
  points of the compass; the
  direction in which the sun sets;
  west *adjective, adverb*; **westerly**
  adverb; **western** *adjective*

wet *adjective* (**wetter**) **1** covered
  in liquid or not dry; **2** rainy;
  wet *verb*; **wetness** *noun*

whale *noun* a very large animal
  that lives in the sea. Whales
  look like fish, but are mammals.
  They breathe air and feed their
  young with milk; !! **wail**

¹**what** *adjective, pronoun* **1** which
  thing or person? **2** which?
  3 that which; a/the thing that:
  I believed **what** *he told me*

²**what** *adverb* to what degree?

whatever *adjective, pronoun* **1**
  anything at all that; no
  matter what; **2** what?

wheat *noun* a grass plant with
  grain seeds that are made into
  flour

wheel *noun* **1** a circular object
  with an outer frame which
  turns round an inner part
  (**hub**) to which it is joined,
  used for turning machines,
  making vehicles move, etc;
  2 the steering wheel of a car
  or ship; **wheeled** *adjective*

when *adverb, conjunction*
  1 at what time? **2** at the time
  at which

whenever *adverb, conjunction*
  1 at any time at all that; every
  time; **2** when?

where *adverb, conjunction*
  1 at or to what place? **2** at, in,
  or to which; !! **wear**

wherever *adverb, conjunction*
  1 at or to any place at all that;
  2 where?

whether *conjunction* **1** if... or not;
  2 no matter if...;
  !! **weather**

which *adjective, pronoun* **1** what
  thing or person? **2** being the
  one or ones that; **3** which is
  which? what is the difference
  between the two? !! **witch**

whichever *adjective, pronoun*
  1 any one that; **2** no matter
  which; **3** which?

while *also* **whilst** *conjunction*
  during the time that; all the
  time that

whine *verb* **1** to make a high
  sad sound; **2** to complain
  unnecessarily; **whine** *noun*;
  !! **wine**

w

¹whip *noun* **1** a long piece of rope or leather fastened to a handle used for punishing somebody, driving an animal, or spinning a top; **2** a sweet food made of beaten eggs and other foods

²whip *verb* **(whipped) 1** to beat with a whip; **2** to beat eggs, cream, etc, until stiff

whirl *verb* to move or make something move round and round very fast; **whirl** *noun*

whisker *noun* **1** one of the long stiff hairs near the mouth of a cat, rat, etc; **2 whiskers** hair allowed to grow on the sides of a man's face

rat's whiskers

¹whisper *verb* to speak quietly with noisy breath

²whisper *noun* **1** whispered words; **2** a soft windy sound

whistle *noun* **1** a simple musical instrument that makes a high sound when you blow it; **2** the high sound made by passing air or steam through an instrument, your lips, etc; **whistle** *verb*

white *noun* **1** the colour of snow; **2** the white part of the eye; **3** the white part of an egg ; **white** *adjective*; **whiteness** *noun*; **whitish** *adjective*

who *pronoun* **1** what person or people? **2** that one person; those ones

whoever *pronoun* **1** any person that; **2** no matter who; **3** who?

¹whole *adjective* complete; total; the entire thing; not spoilt or divided; !! **hole**

²whole *noun* the complete amount, thing etc; !! **hole**

whom *pronoun* used instead of who after words such as to, with, or from: *the man to* **whom** *he talked*

whose *adjective, pronoun* **1** of who or whom? **2** belonging to who or whom

why *adverb, conjunction* **1** for what reason? **2** the reason for which something happens

wicked *adjective* very bad; evil; **wickedly** *adverb*; **wickedness** *noun*

¹wide *adjective* **1** large from side to side; **2** fully or completely open; **widely** *adverb*

²wide *adverb* completely

width *noun* the distance from one side of something to the other; the breadth of something; how wide something is

wife *noun* (*plural* **wives**) the woman to whom a man is married

wiggle *verb* to move from side to side, or up and down

wild *adjective* **1** living in natural conditions and having natural qualities not produced by human beings; not tame; **2** having strong feelings; **3** great; wonderful; terrific; **wildly** *adverb*

¹will *verb* (**would; won't; wouldn't**) **1** used to say something about the future: *I will come*; **2** used to ask someone to do something: *Will you come?*; **3** used to show what is possible: *Oil will float on water*

²will *noun* **1** the power in the mind to choose what you do; **2** what we want to do; **3** a piece of paper on which a person says who will have his or her property after his or her death

willing *adjective* eager; ready; **willingly** *adverb*; **willingness** *noun*

willow *noun* a tree which often grows near water; the wood of this tree

win *verb* (**wins, winning, won**) **1** to be the best or first in a fight, competition, race, etc; **2** to get as the result of success in a competition, race, or game of chance: *He won a prize*; **winner** *noun*

¹wind (*say* wind) *noun* air moving quickly; **windy** *adjective*

²wind (*say* wynd) *verb* (**winds, winding, wound**) **1** to turn round and round; **2** to bend and turn; **3** to make into a ball or twist round something; **4** to tighten the working parts of by turning: *to wind a clock*

windmill *noun* **1** a building containing a machine that crushes grain into flour, pumps water, etc, driven by large sails turned round by the wind; **2** a toy consisting of a stick with four small curved pieces at the end that spin when blown

window *noun* **1** an opening in the wall of a building to let in light and air, usually with glass in it; **2** a space on a computer screen to look at another program or piece of information

wine *noun* drink made from grapes or other fruit, plants, etc; !! **whine**

wing *noun* **1** one of the two limbs of a bird or insect with which it flies; **2** one of the parts of a plane that support it in flight; **3** any part which stands out from the side: *the west wing of the house*

wink *verb* to close and open one eye quickly; **wink** *noun*

winter *noun* the cold season between autumn and spring; **wintery, wintry** *adjective*

wipe *verb* **1** to pass a cloth over something to remove dirt, liquid, etc; **2** to get rid of; **wipe** *noun*

wire *noun* a thin metal thread

wise *adjective* sensible, clever, and able to understand; **wisdom** *noun*; **wisely** *adverb*

these wind turbines are modern windmills

¹**wish** *verb* **1** to want something to happen or to have somthing; **2** to try to cause a particular thing by magic; **3** to want something or somebody to be or to have: We **wish** you a merry Christmas; **4** to want: Do you **wish** to buy these shoes?

²**wish** *noun* **1** a feeling of wanting; **2** an attempt to make a particular thing happen by magic; **3** what is wished for

witch *noun* a woman who has magic powers; !! **which**

with *preposition* **1** in the company of; beside, near, among, or including; **2** having; **3** using; **4** because of

within *adverb, preposition* in; inside; not beyond or more than

without *adverb, preposition* not having

wizard *noun* a man who has magic powers

wobble *verb* to move or make something move unsteadily; **wobble** *noun*; **wobbly** *adjective*

wolf *noun* (*plural* **wolves**) (*young* **cub**) a wild animal of the dog family, which hunts in a pack

wolf

woman *noun* (*plural* **women**) a fully grown human female

¹**wonder** *noun* **1** a feeling of surprise and admiration; **2** somebody or something causing this feeling

²**wonder** *verb* **1** to be surprised; **2** to wish to know

wonderful *adjective* unusually good; **wonderfully** *adverb*

wood *noun* **1** the material of which trunks and branches of trees are made; **2** a place where trees grow, smaller than a forest; !! **would**

wooden *adjective* made of wood

carved wooden throne from Tutankhamen's tomb in Egypt

wool *noun* **1** the soft thick hair of sheep and some goats and rabbits; **2** thread or cloth made from this; **woollen** *adjective*; **woolly** *adjective*

word *noun* **1** a letter or letters, a sound or sounds that together make something we can understand; **2** news; a message; **3** a promise

word processor *noun* a computer you use for writing letters, etc, on which you can change the words and the style of the letters on the screen before printing

¹**work** *noun* **1** activity which uses effort, especially with a special purpose, not for amusement; **2** a job or business; **3** what is produced by work

²**work** *verb* **1** to do an activity that uses effort, especially as employment; **2** to be active; to move or go properly; **3** to make somebody or something work; **worker** *noun*

workman *noun* (*plural* **workmen**) a man who works with his hands

world *noun* **1** the Earth; **2** a planet or star system; **3** all human beings thought of together

worm *noun* a small thin creature with a soft body without bones or legs: **earthworm**

¹**worry** *verb* to make or be anxious; **worried** *adjective*

²**worry** *noun* **1** a feeling of anxiety; **2** a person or thing that makes you worried

worship *verb* (**worshipped**) to pray and show great respect, admiration, etc; **worship** *noun*

¹**worst** *see* BAD, ILL

²**worst** *noun* the most bad thing or part

¹**worth** *preposition* of the value of

²**worth** *noun* value; **worthless** *adjective*; **worthy** *adjective*

¹**wound** (*say* **woond**) *noun* an injury to the body caused by violent means, or an injury to your feelings; **wound** *verb*

²**wound** (*say* **wownd**) *see* WIND

wrap *verb* (**wrapped**) to cover; to fold round; **wrapping** *noun*

¹**wreck** *noun* a ship, car, building, etc, that has been partly destroyed; **wreckage** *noun*

²**wreck** *verb* to destroy or cause to destroy

wren *noun* a very small song bird

wrestle *verb* to fight by holding and throwing a person to the ground; **wrestler** *noun*; **wrestling** *noun*

wriggle *verb* to twist from side to side; **wriggle** *noun*

wring *verb* (**wrings, wringing, wrung**) to twist; to remove water by twisting and pressing; **wring** *noun*; !! **ring**

wrinkle *noun* a line in something that is folded or squashed, especially on the skin; **wrinkle** *verb*; **wrinkly** *adjective*

wrist *noun* the joint between the hand and the lower arm

write *verb* (**writes, writing, wrote, written**) **1** to make letters or words, especially with a pen or pencil on paper; **2** to produce and send a letter; **writer** *noun*; !! **right, rite**

¹**wrong** *adjective* **1** not correct; **2** evil; not good; **3** not suitable; **wrongly** *adverb*

²**wrong** *noun* what is bad

w

Xx

x-ray *verb* (**x-rays, x-raying, x-rayed**) to photograph, examine, or treat by X-rays

X-ray of a hand

X-ray *noun* (*plural* **X-rays**)
1 a powerful invisible beam of light that can pass through substances which are not transparent, and that is used for photographing conditions inside the body, for treating certain diseases, and for various purposes in industry; **2** a photograph taken using this

xylophone *noun* a musical instrument made of flat bars that produce musical notes when struck with small hammers

xylophone

Yy

yacht (*say* **yot**) *noun* a sailing boat; **yachting** *noun*

¹**yard** *noun* a measure of length equal to 3 feet or 0.91 metres

²**yard** *noun* **1** a piece of ground next to a building, with a wall or fence round it; **2** a piece of ground used for a special purpose: **coalyard, shipyard**

yawn *verb* to open the mouth wide and breathe deeply as when tired or bored; **yawn** *noun*

year *noun* a measure of time equal to 365 $\frac{1}{4}$ days, 52 weeks, or 12 months; the time it takes the Earth to travel round the sun; **yearly** *adverb*

yell *verb* to shout loudly; to cry out; **yell** *noun*

yellow *noun* the colour of butter, gold, or the yolk of an egg; **yellow** *adjective*; **yellowish** *adjective*

yes *adverb* a word used to answer a question, to show agreement

yesterday *adverb, noun* the day before this one

yet *adverb* at this moment; then; so far; up to now

yogurt or **yoghourt, yoghurt** *noun* a dessert made from milk treated in a special way to make it thick and a bit sour, often with fruit in it

yolk (*say* **yoke**) *noun* the yellow central part of an egg surrounded by the white

you *pronoun* (**yourself, yourselves**) **1** the person or people being spoken to; **2** one; anyone

¹**young** *adjective* not having lived very long; not old; **youngish** *adjective*; **youngster** *noun*

²**young** *noun* young people or animals

your *adjective* belonging to you; !! **you're**

you're shortened form of you are; !! **your**

yours *pronoun* **1** that or those belonging to you; **2** written at the end of a letter: *yours sincerely*

youth *noun* **1** the time when you are young; **2** a young man; **3** young people as a group; **youthful** *adjective*

yo-yo *noun* a toy made of a round piece of wood, plastic, etc, that can be made to run up and down a string tied to it

Zz

zebra *noun* a wild animal like a horse, that has black or dark brown and white stripes

zebra

zebra crossing *noun* a street crossing marked by black and white lines

zero *noun* (*plural* **zeros** or **zeroes**) the figure 0; a nought; nothing

zigzag *noun* a line shaped like a row of Zs

¹**zip** *noun* **1** also **zip fastener** a fastener that is often used on clothes, and has two sets of teeth which can be joined together; **2** a zipping sound

²**zip** *verb* (**zipped**) **1** to open or fasten with a zip, especially trousers; **2** to make the sound of something moving quickly through the air

zodiac *noun* an imaginary area in space along which the sun and planets appear to travel, divided into twelve signs each named after a special group of stars (see page 144)

zoo *noun* a collection of wild animals kept in a park for people to look at or for conservation purposes

zoom *verb* to go or rise quickly

y
z

Metric
Measurements

Weight

mg 1000 milligrams = 1 gram
g 1000 grams = 1 kilogram
kg 1000 kilograms = 1 tonne

Length

mm 10 millimetres = 1 centimetre
cm 100 centimetres = 1 metre
m 1000 metres = 1 kilometre

Area

1 hectare= 10, 000 m^2 or 2.471 acres
1 acre = 4047 metres^2 or 4840 yards^2

Capacity

ml 10 millilitres = 1 centilitre
cl 100 centilitres = 1 litre
l 1000 litres = 1 kilolitre